Nathaniel Caine

History of the Royal Rock Beagle Hunt

Nathaniel Caine

History of the Royal Rock Beagle Hunt

ISBN/EAN: 9783743324978

Manufactured in Europe, USA, Canada, Australia, Japa

Cover: Foto ©ninafisch / pixelio.de

Manufactured and distributed by brebook publishing software (www.brebook.com)

Nathaniel Caine

History of the Royal Rock Beagle Hunt

History

of the

Royal Rock Beagle Hunt.

BY

NATHANIEL CAINE.

Issued by Subscription.
IN THE YEAR OF JUBILEE OF THE HUNT.
1895.

> "I think this lady to be my child Cordelia."
> *King Lear, act iv, scene 7.*
>
> "Your old kind father, whose frank heart gave you all."
> *King Lear, act iii, scene 4.*

Dedication

TO

MISS CATHERINE E. KING,

ONLY DAUGHTER OF THE LATE COLONEL KING,
POINT OF AYR, OXTON.

To whom can any treatise on the Royal Rock Beagles be more appropriately dedicated than to her, who, during the later years of the Mastership of Vincent Ashfield King (who was not only her father, but also the "father of the Hunt"), was his constant companion in the field, and in his summer tramps among the Swiss mountains?

By her kind permission, this volume is respectfully dedicated to Miss King, as an acknowledgment of the indebtedness of the Royal Rock Beagle Hunt to her family in the past, and to herself in the present for her unflagging interest in all that concerns the prosperity of the Hunt.

May she long remain the kind friend and indulgent "landlord" of the Royal Rock Beagles!

NATHANIEL CAINE.

INTRODUCTION.

"No leveli'd malice infects one comma in the course I hold."
Timon of Athens, act i, scene 1.

HE near approach of the Jubilee Year of the Royal Rock Beagles inspired the writer with the ambitious design of formulating a record of the origin and progress of this famous pack of hounds. The extraordinary interest evinced by all past and present members of the club in anything relating to the Royal Rock Beagles, must be the author's apology for venturing to present this volume to their notice. He feels that, like himself, there must be many enthusiastic beaglers who will be glad to have an account of the doings and traditions of the Hunt in a convenient form.

The materials available for the compilation are somewhat meagre, consisting of the Minute Book and Sport Book for the first ten years of the existence of the Hunt, some letters and accounts preserved by Mr. C. Rawson, and the traditions retained in the memories of the few original members now living. For the information contained in the Minute and Sport Books, we are mainly indebted to the industry of the late Henry Walford, the indefatigable Secretary to the club, and to V. A. King, the Chairman and Master, who, during that time, took the pains to record anything connected with the R.R.B. which seemed to them as being of interest or worth registration. It is matter for regret that since then, and up to the present, no one has taken the trouble to systematically record the sport with the R.R.B. It would certainly be the privilege of the Master to perform this service (though it cannot be said to be his duty), and he alone is competent, as every circumstance of importance necessarily comes to his knowledge; while his constant presence in the field, and management of the hounds during the sport, clearly point to him as the one best qualified to keep a record of the sport with the hounds.

Some years ago, William Joynson, who took great interest in the R.R.B., contributed accounts of specially notable runs to the *Field*, under the *nom de plume* of "Little Jelly Dog"; and he was followed in a similar manner by C. Tempest Dixon, who wrote, and still writes, under the name of "Storm." These spasmodic efforts are only of temporary interest, demanding really brilliant runs to justify communication to the public press; and, not being preserved in the annals of the Hunt, are not available for perusal by successive generations of beaglers, who would be charmed to study the systematic records of the most ordinary days' sport, when invested with the dignity of by-gone years.

The author has had the pleasant privilege of personal interviews with several of the surviving originators of the

INTRODUCTION.

R.R.B., and he here desires to acknowledge his indebtedness especially to Mr. C. Rawson, who still retains a deep interest in the pack, and who, although it is now more than forty years since he left the neighbourhood, has preserved interesting letters, newspaper cuttings, songs, photographs, and various memoranda relating to the Royal Rock Beagles, all of which he freely placed at the disposal of the compiler of this volume.

Christopher Rawson stands alone, so far as the writer has been able to discover, in having kept any written or printed memoranda of the early days of the R.R.B.; and although Tinley Barton and D. O. Bateson have reminiscences, which they are willing to impart to the ready listener, yet the great lapse of time has caused the exact details to fade from their memories, and they are unable to furnish much information about the hounds and the sport of their epoch, suitable for the purposes of this record.

The author joined the Royal Rock Beagles in 1876, and thus has had the experience of nearly twenty seasons. He yields to none in his affection for the members of the Hunt, and in his intense enjoyment of the sport and the exercise to be obtained therefrom.

The remarks on hare-hunting and on hounds in the following pages, are culled from the best available authorities; and if there is nothing new in them, it is because there is nothing new to be said. Somerville and Beckford were such thorough masters of the science of hare-hunting, that all subsequent writers have freely availed themselves of their works; and it is only because there are many beaglers of the present day who have not read, and evidently do not read, books on sport, that the writer has ventured to incorporate some of the well-known axioms of the above-mentioned authors, in the hope that their interest in the R.R.B. will induce these beaglers to peruse this book, and lay the lessons to heart.

CONTENTS.

"O, like a book of sport thou'lt read me o'er."
Troilus and Cressida, act iv, s. en. 5.

	PAGE
DEDICATION	v
INTRODUCTION	vii
LIST OF ILLUSTRATIONS	xii

CHAP.		
I.	INAUGURATION OF THE ROYAL ROCK BEAGLES	1
II.	THE FORMATION OF THE PACK	8
III.	SECURING COUNTRY	13
IV.	FINANCE	19
V.	CRISES IN THE HISTORY OF THE HUNT	22
VI.	THE MASTERS	31
	TINLEY BARTON	35
	CHRISTOPHER RAWSON	37
	DITTO AS VOLUNTEER	43
	VINCENT ASHFIELD KING	46
	DITTO AS BEAGLER	49
	DITTO AS VOLUNTEER	55
	DITTO AS CITIZEN	61
	LOUIS RUDD STEVENSON	66
	JOHN WILLIAM MACFIE	68
	J. GOULD SMYTH	70
VII.	THE HUNTSMEN	72
	THOMAS KAY	72
	HUMPHREY JONES	74
	JOHN DAVIES	76
	JOHN VAUGHAN	76
	CHARLES WILLIAMS	76
	JONATHAN COLL	78
	FRANK JAMES DAVIES	80
VIII.	THE MEMBERS	81
	CHRONOLOGICAL LIST OF MEMBERS	83
	CELEBRITIES OF THE HUNT—ANCIENT	86
	DITTO MEDIÆVAL	99
	DITTO MODERN	104
	MEMBERS, 1894-5	111

CHAP.		PAGE.
IX.	Notable Runs	112
X.	Lunches	125
XI.	The Country	127
	Increase of Population	129
	Topography of Wirral	131
XII.	The Landlords	134
XIII.	The Farmers	146
	Barbed Wire	152
XIV.	Shooting Men	157
XV.	The Hounds	159
	Formation of a Pack	160
	Breeding of Hounds	163
	Hounds in Kennel	170
	R.R.B. Hounds at Work	174
	The Lurcher	177
XVI.	Hares, and Hare-Hunting	179
	Scent	190
	Distribution of Hares	194
	Cruelty of Hunting	196
XVII.	R.R.B. Visits to other Countries	198
XVIII.	Neighbouring Packs	203
	The Cheshire Beagles	203
	The Wirral Harriers	206
	The Llangollen Harriers	207
	The Malpas Beagles	209

ILLUSTRATIONS.

	TO FACE PAGE
Portrait of Tinley Barton	35
Ditto C. Rawson	39
Ditto V. A. King	52
R.R. Beaglers at Beeston	86
Ditto at Whitby	101
Ditto at Raby	111
Cheshire Beaglers at Crewe	205
Malpas Beaglers: A Kill	210

. It is to be regretted that the reproduction of the picture of Ancient Beaglers at Beeston has not come out well; but the daguerreotype was very old and faded. However, the lithographer has done the best he could with it.

CHAPTER I.

INAUGURATION OF THE ROYAL ROCK BEAGLES.

> "I see you stand like greyhounds in the slips,
> Straining upon the start. The game's afoot;
> Follow your spirit."
>
> *King Henry V., act iii, scene 2.*

HALF-A-CENTURY ago, on the 28th March, 1845, a few gentlemen interested in sport met in Rock Ferry, at the house of Mr. Christopher Rawson, Junior, to inaugurate the now well-known pack of hounds—The Royal Rock Beagles.

A month or two earlier, Mr. Tinley Barton had received as a present from Mr. George Atherton, of New Brighton, three couple of small hounds. These were probably rabbit beagles, as C. Rawson says they were only thirteen-inch hounds; and with these, Mr. Barton, accompanied by Mr. John Okell, both on horseback, hunted hares over a few Wirral farms. They had taken no steps to secure a country, but merely asked permission from such of the farmers as they knew to allow them to hunt on their land.

At this time the only organized pack of hounds in Wirral was Sir William Massey Stanley's foxhounds, kept at Hooton Hall. The country was then so well wooded and strictly preserved, as to boast of a sufficient number of foxcovers to provide sport for this pack two days per week during the season.

Messrs. Barton and Okell experiencing great enjoyment from their sport, occasionally invited one or two friends to join them; and, talking matters over with one another, they came to the conclusion that it would be desirable to form a club, for the purpose of hunting hares over the Hundred of Wirral.

A number of young men were readily found to enter heartily into the scheme, and some fifty or sixty names were registered as the first subscribers. All these gentlemen were engaged in business in Liverpool, at least half being resident in Rock Ferry, the others in Birkenhead and Liverpool.

Rock Ferry being the residence of the majority of the first subscribers, a convenient centre for the proposed country, and possessing a suitable building for the kennels in the immediate vicinity, gave rise to the title of the hunt—The Royal Rock Beagles. The origin of the prefix "Royal" is somewhat obscure. Rock Ferry is said to derive its title to be called a royal ferry, from the fact that the Duke of Clarence (afterwards William IV) once availed himself of this route from Liverpool to the south. Sailing boats then brought passengers from Liverpool, landing them on the rock which still shows itself at the north side of the present slip, whence they could pass up a dry sandy shore (far different to the soft mud slope now visible) to the coaches waiting to take them to London and elsewhere. Mr. Tom Johnson, of Malpas, is responsible for the suggestion that the Rock Beagles were called *Royal* because they belonged to old *King*.

The first question for decision was whether the hounds should be harriers or beagles. The fact that the Hooton foxhounds were in possession of the country, and that farmers could not be expected to tolerate the followers of two packs riding over their land, and also that most of the subscribers were young men engaged in business, not desirous of plunging into the expensive sport of hunting on horseback, decidedly turned the scale in favour of beagles. It was not the fashion of the time for the junior votaries of commerce to give up one or two days a week to sport, but Saturday afternoons were available, and Mr. Rawson claims that his efforts in inducing the merchants of Liverpool to allow their young men to go out hunting on these afternoons were largely conducive to the now well-established Saturday half-holiday.

As above stated, a preliminary meeting of the subscribers was held in Rock Ferry, on the 28th March, 1845, at the house of C. Rawson, Junior, who took the chair, the other gentlemen present being

Henry Barton,   J. T. Raynes,
Tinley Barton,   W. F. Foster,
W. W. Perry,   R. Hemingway,
A. L. Edgar,   W. Parkinson.

They discussed and passed two resolutions, viz. :—1st, That Messrs. Rawson and Raynes should call on the Rev. R. M. Feilden, of Bebington, and on Mr. George King, of Higher Bebington Hall, to solicit permission to sport over their respective estates. 2nd, That a general meeting of the subscribers be convened for 5th April, 1845, at Rock Ferry Hotel, at 8 p.m., to agree upon rules and regulations for the management of the Hunt.

The above-named landowners cordially granted the desired permission, and Mr Rawson and others busied themselves in procuring the same privilege in various other quarters.

EXTRACT FROM THE FIRST MINUTE BOOK OF THE HUNT.

On the morning of the 29th March, 1845, we, the undersigned, waited upon George King, Esq., at Bebington Hall, when he was not at home. On the evening of the same day we again called upon him, and were most kindly received. He at once granted permission for the members of the Hunt to sport over his estate with their beagles.

In answer to a question, "whether or not it will be necessary for Rector King, of Woodchurch, also to be seen on the same subject?" he replied in the negative, his permission being sufficient. We proposed to make him an honorary member, to which he assented.
C. RAWSON, JUNR.
J. T. RAYNES.

Mr. Joseph Hegan most kindly granted permission for the Hunt to sport over his estates to Mr. Rawson. This was done in a railway carriage between Liverpool and Manchester.

Pending the arrangements for securing a good hunting country, the subscribers busied themselves in framing rules for the club, and forming an efficient executive for the management of the Hunt. If we look at the list of members, we can see readily enough, among the names of the first sixty subscribers, plenty of good material from which to select a capital committee of management; sportsmen whose names still live with us, and whose deeds are recorded in the annals of the Hunt.

The general meeting called for the 5th April, 1845, was duly held, and the following subscribers were present:—

G. J. Wainwright (in the chair),

H. Barton,	W. Robinson,	Thomas Clint,
W. W. Perry,	J. B. Amey,	E. Mengens,
J. T. Raynes,	J. C. Kemp,	W. Comer,
W. Parkinson,	H. Jenkins,	G. Comer.

The meeting formulated the following rules (which were revised 24th April, 1863, and again revised 7th October, 1889), and appointed a committee of ten members, to hold office till the general meeting, in August, 1846, viz.:—

C. Rawson, Junior, Chairman (and Head of the Hunt),

W. W. Perry,	G. Comer,	R. Hemingway,
J. B. Amey,	S. Vertue,	A. L. Edgar,
G. J. Wainwright,	J. Higginson,	

J. T. Raynes, Secretary and Treasurer.

Original Rules of the R.R.B.

1. That the pack be called the "Royal Rock Beagles."
2. That the subscription be two guineas per annum, to be paid in advance before the first day of May in each year.
3. That a Committee of ten members be annually elected to arrange the times and places of meet, and to conduct all affairs necessary to the management of the Hunt, the Master of the Hounds being *ex officio* a member of the Committee. The Chairman to have a casting vote, and three to form a quorum.
4. That each member shall be furnished by the Secretary, on or before every Saturday during the season, with a notice of the meets for the following week.
5. That a Master of the Hounds be annually appointed by the Committee, who shall have the exclusive management and direction of the dogs *(sic)* on the field.
6. That any member interfering with the hounds on the field shall be subject to a fine of half-a-crown; and on a repetition of such offence, five shillings. All instances of such interference to be laid before and decided by the Committee.
7. That no member be allowed on horseback on the field, excepting the Master and the Whipper-in, and they only with the consent of the Committee.
8. That no new member be admitted without having been balloted for; two black balls in ten to exclude.
9. That all candidates for admission into the Hunt shall have their names entered into the candidates' book, with the names of their proposer and seconder, at least a week previous to their being balloted for; the boxes to be open from two to six o'clock in the afternoon.
10. That the Hunt shall have the power of excluding any member at a special general meeting, to be called for the purpose on a requisition being presented to the Secretary signed by at least seven members, the question to be decided by ballot, seven black balls in ten to exclude.
11. That a hunt costume be chosen by the Committee, and all members are expected to provide themselves with it; and that the Committee in particular are expected to appear in such costume as often as possible.
12. That the annual meeting of the Hunt be held at the Rock Ferry Hotel on the first Monday in August of each year, or at such other place as the Committee may appoint.

Present Rules, as revised 7th October, 1889.

1. That the title of the Hunt shall be the "Royal Rock Beagle Hunt."
2. That the number of members be limited to sixty.
3. That an annual general meeting of the Hunt be held as early as possible in October of each year, at such place and time as the Committee may appoint.
4. That the management of the affairs of the Hunt be entrusted to the officers of the Hunt, and a Committee.
5. That the officers of the Hunt shall be elected at each annual meeting, and shall be *ex officio* members of the Committee.
6. That the Committee shall consist of ten members, to be elected at the annual meeting, of whom two members shall retire annually by rotation, and shall be ineligible for re-election for twelve months. The Chairman to have a casting vote, and five to form a quorum. The Committee to have power to fill up vacancies.
7. Notice shall be sent to each member at least fourteen days before the annual meeting, that such meeting shall be held on a given date, and intimating

the names of the retiring members of Committee. It shall then be competent for any member to nominate by note (to be sent to the Secretary) any member or members as candidate or candidates for the vacancy. Such nominations shall be duly seconded, in writing, and election shall take place at the annual meeting.

8. The two members to retire during the first five years after the election of the Committee shall, unless the members of the Committee agree among themselves, be determined by ballot. In every subsequent year the two who have been longest in office shall retire. The members of the Hunt may, from time to time in general meeting, increase or reduce the number of the Committee, and may also determine in what rotation such increased or reduced number is to retire.

9. Any member of the Committee who shall continuously absent himself from the meetings of the Committee may be requested to retire by vote of eight members of the Committee.

10. That the subscription be four guineas per annum, to be paid in advance on the first day of October in each year, and that one guinea per annum from each member's subscription be placed to a special entertainment fund, which shall be applicable for any contribution or subscription for the benefit of the farmers, as well as for entertainment purposes.

11. It shall be a condition of membership of the Hunt that the annual subscription shall be a debt from the member to the Honorary Treasurer for the time being.

12. That the election of members of the Hunt shall be as follows, viz.:— The names of all the candidates for admission, with those of their respective proposers and seconders, shall be forwarded to the Secretary. These shall be read out at a general meeting, and if approved shall be submitted to the Committee for election.

13. That any member wishing to leave the Hunt must send notice of his intention to the Secretary, on or before the first of October, or he will be held liable for his subscription for the following season.

14. That any member may be excluded from the Hunt at a special general meeting to be called for the purpose, on a requisition being presented to the Secretary, signed by at least seven members.

15. That no member or other person be allowed on horseback in the field.

16. That each member shall be furnished by the Secretary with a notice of the meets during the season.

17. That all members are expected to appear in the field in the hunt costume.

18. The Master or his deputy shall have exclusive management of the hounds in the field, and any member interfering shall be reported to the Committee.

19. That no members of the Hunt shall carry whips in the field, except such as shall be appointed by the members at the annual meeting, subject to the approval of the Master. If any whip shall resign during the season, the Committee shall have power to fill the vacancy.

20. The Secretary shall, at the request of the Master, or upon the written requisition of ten members of the Hunt, call a special general meeting. Such meeting to be convened by notice, specifying the business to be laid before the meeting, to each member at least seven days before date of such meeting.

21. The Committee to have power to elect honorary members at their discretion.

22. The Secretary shall furnish each member on election with a copy of these rules.

A few remarks on Rules 10 and 17 will be taken in good part by those members who may be conscious of not giving them the attention they deserve.

The late Colonel King always made a point of being the first member to pay his subscription; he invariably handed it to the treasurer at the annual meeting. This is an example for all Royal Rock Beaglers to follow at a respectful distance.

Various reasons make it important that members should wear the uniform on all occasions when out with their own hounds, but particularly so in their own country. The farmers in Wirral, especially at the northern extremity, are annoyed by frequent transits of runners over their farms, and through and over their fences. There are numerous so-called harrier clubs and paper chasers from Birkenhead and Liverpool, who may be said to infest this country; and although we should not grudge to these young men the enjoyment of their healthy exercise, yet we should take care that our sport is not mistaken for a game of "hare and hounds." Our green coats and white breeches can be identified at a great distance, and our worthy friends the farmers have their minds set at rest when they see us approaching.

On a recent occasion Mr. Webster, of Upton, complained to our Master, that his grounds had been invaded by a lot of fellows who said they were the R.R.B., but as none of them wore the uniform, he was uncertain whether they were the drag hounds or a hare and hounds lot. This was one of the Wednesday meets, at which members have got into the habit of appearing in *mufti*, although the Master sets a good example by always himself wearing the uniform, but on this day he was not present.

List of First Season Members.

J. Higginson, Rock Ferry.	H. Wilson, Rock Ferry.	H. Barton, Rock Ferry.
R. Hemingway, „	J. Budd, „	T. Clint, „
G. J. Wainwright, „	W. Pike, Birkenhead.	J. Herd, Liverpool.
W. Robinson, „	H. Aspinall, „	T. Barton, Barnston.
J. Okell, „	J. Aspinall, „	M. Richardson, Rock Ferry.
G. Comer, „	S. Willoughby. „	D. Cannon, „
J. Stephenson, „	H. Watson, „	W. Comer, „
J. B. Amey, „	W. Cole, „	G. A. Brown, „
W. W. Perry, „	F. Kulenkamp, „	J. Black, „
C. Hemery, „	H. Williams, „	C. Higginson, „
R. Christie, Junr., Bootle.	J. Carter, Tranmere.	A. Turneur, „
J. Thompson, „	R. Barton, Manchester.	F. Clarke.
J. W. Harden, Rock Ferry.	A. Barton, „	A. Aikin, Rock Ferry.
W. Stockley, „	R. J. Hardman, Rock Ferry.	W. S. Baldwin, Birkenhead.
W. F. Foster, Liverpool.	T. A. Bushby, „	B. Kinnear, Liverpool.
T. B. Sands, „	A. Walford, „	— Morewood, Rock Ferry.
A. L. Edgar, Rock Ferry.	W. Watson, „	J. M. Woolley, „
F. Lyon, „	W. Whittaker, „	J. Scott, Liverpool.
H. Walford, „	B. Parkinson, „	V. A. King, Bebington.
C. Rawson, Junr., „	— Jamieson, „	H. Royds, Liverpool.

INAUGURATION.

R. J. Tinley, Liverpool.	T. Lutwyche, Rock Ferry.	— Martigny, Liverpool.
R. G. Ramsden, ,,	T. Sleddell, Liverpool.	D. O. Bateson, ,,
G. A. Tinley, ,	J. Matthie, ,,	W. Brancker, Rock Ferry.
T. H. Irwin, ,,	H. Molyneux, ,,	A. Lyon, ,,
Capt. Barton, Rock Ferry.	B. Southern, ,,	E. Matthias, ,,
S. Vertue, Bromborough.	D. Bellhouse, ,,	J. F. Williams, Landigan.
W. Parkinson, Rock Ferry.	B. Littledale, ,,	— Lowe, Liverpool.
E. Mengens, ,,	F. Duncan, ,,	J. A. Scott, ,,
J. T. Raynes, ,,	C. H. Steele, Rock Ferry.	H. Hassall, ,,
H. Jenkins, ,,	E. Lane, ,,	J. Dixon, Birkenhead.

The above list of ninety members comprises all those gentlemen who joined the club before and during the first season, and not one of them was elected by ballot, but by subscribing became, as it were, a kind of syndicate to start the Hunt. Many of them only joined in order to give the club a fair start, and at the end of the first season thirty-two of them resigned.

In looking over this list of members, it is interesting to note the manifest influence of Mr. Rawson. He resided at Rock Ferry, and from his neighbours and friends came the largest number of recruits to the new club. More than half of the original members hailed from Rock Ferry and neighbourhood.

   48 from Rock Ferry and New Ferry
   24 from Liverpool and Bootle
   2 from Manchester
   11 from Birkenhead and Tranmere
   5 from elsewhere
   —
   90

During the course of time this preponderance has left Rock Ferry, and now we have not a single member from that quarter, our late worthy master, J. W. Macfie, having gone to reside at Waverton a year or two ago. Although the pack has always been called the Royal Rock Beagles, many people here and there still speak of them as the Rock Ferry Beagles. The late Colonel King, after the departure of Mr. Rawson, attained to a paramount influence in the club. He resided at Oxton, and to this day the majority of the members are from Oxton and Claughton, notwithstanding the spasmodic efforts made to spread the interest by inviting candidates for admission from outlying parts of the country.

Having now got the club well established, the next few chapters must be devoted to a description of the steps taken to provide a good pack of hounds and a hunting country, and of the rise and progress of the Hunt.

CHAPTER II.

THE FORMATION OF THE PACK.

> "My hounds are bred out of the Spartan kind,
> So flew'd, so sanded; and their heads are hung
> With ears that sweep away the morning dew;
> Crook-kneed, and dew-lapp'd like Thessalian bulls;
> Slow in pursuit, but match'd in mouth like bells,
> Each under each. A cry more tunable
> Was never halloo'd to, nor cheered with horn,
> In Crete, in Sparta, nor in Thessaly.
> Judge when you hear."
> *Midsummer Night's Dream*, act iv, scene 1.

The same evening (5th April, 1845) on which the rules were framed, the Committee held their first meeting, and appointed Tinley Barton to be the first Master of the Hounds.

At this time the hounds in the possession of the club must have been the three couple previously alluded to as having been presented to T. Barton by Mr. Atherton, and there can be no doubt that some of the members had been amusing themselves by hunting so late in the season as April, and getting into trouble with Mr. Ralph Brocklebank by trespassing in Prenton Wood.

EXTRACT FROM THE MINUTE BOOK.

It having been intimated to the Committee that Mr. Ralph Brocklebank was much annoyed at the dogs having entered Prenton Mount Wood, C. Rawson and J. T. Raynes waited upon him at his office in Liverpool on the morning of the 7th April, 1845, in order to make an apology and also to solicit for permission to hunt over his manors. Mr. Brocklebank was in Cheltenham, but Mr. Fisher was seen, who is joint tenant with Mr. Brocklebank for the manors of Tranmere and Prenton; he accepted the apology, and would consult Mr. Brocklebank relative to granting permission for the Royal Rock Beagle Hunt to sport over Tranmere.

These few hounds were found too small to make their way easily through or over the strong and close fences of Wirral, so Messrs. Rawson and Barton cast about to find a pack of hounds which they could purchase for the club. As good luck would have it, Captain J. Anstruther Thomson, of Exeter, was disposing of his beagles, which mainly consisted of a lot he had got from the famous Parson Honeywood, of Essex. On the 11th April, 1845, Captain Thomson submitted the following list of twelve couple of hounds:—

NAME.		AGE.	PEDIGREE. SIRE. DAM.	SOURCE.	DESCRIPTION.
Brilliant	Bitch	Aged	Trojan—Beauty	Mr. Honeywood, Essex.	Black and white, first-rate hunter, good feeder.
Baronet	Dog	,,	,, ,,	,,	Do., short tail, shy feeder.
Driver	,,	,,	Bred in Kent	,,	White, grey face, fair hunter, long tail, sulky and timid, greedy feeder.
Ringwood	,,	,,	Bred in Cambridge	,,	
Trusty	Bitch	,,	Manful—Cruel	,,	White, almost worn out but best breed in England.
Gaiety	,,	2 years	Radical—Gay Lass	,,	White, yellow ears, very good.
Beeswing	,,	,,	Wanderer—Brilliant	,,	Black, white, and tan, one eye white, perfect.
Wanton	,,	1 year	Blamer—Woodbine	,,	White, large head, crooked legs, good.
Beauty	,,	2 years	Radical—Dainty	,,	Yellow and white, very handsome, good, but noisy.
Darling	,,	Aged	Bred in Devonshire	Mr. Radford	White and yellow, very good.
Boisterous	Dog	,,	,, ,,	,,	Do., large, bad tempered and shy.
Rosamond	Bitch	,,	,, Yorkshire	Mr. Marjoribanks	Black, white, and tan, good, but noisy.
Chantress	,,	1 year	,, Devonshire	Mr. Clarke	Black and tan, not proved.
Margaret	,,	,,	,, Wiltshire	Mr. Long	Grey, white, and tan, strong, fast, noisy.
Milkmaid	,,	,,	,, ,,	,,	White and yellow, wall eye, very good.
Rallywood	Dog	,,	,, Hampshire	Mr. Smith	Blue, large, very good.
Chumney	,,	2 years	,, ,,	,,	Do., immense head, first-rate.
Rector	,,	1 year	By a dog of Lord Andover's, out of Gipsey.	Not entered.	Large, a few blue spots.
Royal	,,	,,			White, large black spot on side.
Regent	,,	,,			Do., black ears.
Ganymede	,,	,,	Blueman—Gaiety	....	Do., spotted like Royal, hunts well.
Champion	,,	2 years	Bred in Devonshire	Mr. Poole	Black, short ears, capital hound.
Gipsey	Bitch	Aged	,, Wiltshire	....	Short ears, like a terrier, not thoroughbred.
Bluebell	,,	1 year	Ringwood—Blossom	....	Very small, not hunted.

Mr. Rawson succeeded in purchasing this lot of twelve couple of good hounds at a cost of £25 2s. 6d., or one guinea each hound, which must be said to be decidedly cheap and a great bargain, considering that they were well known and justly celebrated. Most of them were pedigree hounds, and their strain remains in our kennels to this day. When Macfie took charge of the hounds, as Deputy Master, he found that the kennel books had not been kept up for some years, but with the assistance of W. E. Hall and Williams the huntsman, he was enabled to fill up the blanks, and so keep the record complete.

This pack arrived at Rock Ferry early in April, 1845, the railway carriage costing £7 3s. The kennels apparently had not been got ready, as R. Hemingway wrote to C. Rawson—"The dogs had better be sent to my "stable. They can be put in the coach-house until we can make some "further arrangement. I will send over some ship's biscuit for them. I am "glad you have acted so promptly."

Thus was formed the nucleus of a tidy little pack of hounds, and the authorities of the Hunt proceeded to beat up all England for further supplies. During the summer of 1845, Kay the huntsman was sent to several places to look at those offered, with a fair result.

6	Hounds	coming	from	Rev. J. Beecroft, of Worcester.
3	,,	,,	,,	Rev. C. Everett.
8	,,	,,	,,	London.
7	,,	,,	,,	Lancaster.
5	,,	,,	,,	Oldham.
5	,,	,,	,,	Warrington.
3	,,	,,	,,	Lord Sefton.
4	,,	,,	,,	T. Beal, of Weymouth.
6	,,	,,	,,	Cumberland.
6	,,	,,	,,	Mr. Royds.

26½ couples.

The goal aimed at by C. Rawson was to get an even musical pack, about 14½ inches in height. The occurrence of the lamentable Irish famine in 1846 enabled him to achieve this design, as several small packs of beagles were offered to the Royal Rock Beagle Hunt merely for the cost of carriage. These packs were given up by the sporting gentry of Ireland, who nobly did their duty by their unfortunate tenantry. They remitted the rents, and, in consequence, were obliged to economize in every possible way. Hunting was abandoned in many districts of Ireland for several years, and, as regards beagles, has not since been freely resumed, only two packs of Irish beagles being mentioned in *Badminton*. It is melancholy to consider that this most disastrous famine, which necessitated a grant of £10,000,000 sterling from the British Government for the relief of the starving peasantry, should have been instrumental in forming our pack of hounds.

In the first season 1845-6, the Royal Rock Beagles had somewhere about thirty-three couple in their kennels, from which they drafted ten couple as being either too large or too small for their standard. In those days beaglers seemed to like to have out a large number of hounds, as they used to take out seventeen or eighteen couple each time of hunting; at the present day, ten to twelve couple are thought to be amply sufficient for beagling.

The first lot of hounds arrived in April, 1845, with no kennels ready, and no huntsman to look after them, and the committee had plenty to do for a month or two to get these matters comfortably arranged. A cottage was found at Woodhey, near Rock Ferry, with sufficient spare space for kennels, yards, &c., at a rental of £14 per annum, and £68 was expended in building the kennels, paving the yards, &c.

These kennels were occupied by the Royal Rock Beagles till the year 1883, when the hounds were removed to their present kennels at Higher Bebington, on account of complaints by neighbours of their noise

FORMATION OF THE PACK.

at night, &c. In 1845 the kennels were almost isolated in the country, but during the last twenty years quite a hamlet has sprung up at Woodhey, and the kennels were entirely out of place in the locality. Our old huntsman, Charles Williams, kept the old kennels for his business as cowkeeper when the removal was made to the new kennels; and on his retiring from the post of huntsman, he took up his residence in the old cottage, where he is still to be found, well and hearty as ever.

In preparation for the first season, the Committee of ten divided themselves into five couples, to undertake the duty, month by month in rotation, of visiting the kennels and superintending the general management, but so as not to interfere with the duties of the Master. This arrangement must surely have led to confusion and divided counsels, unless some one or two took the lead; and we cannot find in the records of the Hunt that it lasted over the first season.

At the end of the season 1846-7, the character of the pack was entered in the Sport Book as follows:—

Dogs.

Finder .... Once as good a hound as ever ran; now old, slow, and jealous.
Regent .... Hard-working, steady hound.
Bachelor ...... Excellent, very steady, always to be relied on.
Testy .... True and steady.
Comely .... Very good and true, never tired.
Handy .... Very steady and to be relied on, hard working.
Hero .... As good as Handy, but not as strong or fast.
Bellman .... True, hard working, but delicate in wet weather.
Watchful ...... Good and true.
Slasher .... Good, but never very prominent.
Wanderer ...... Too old; true, but very noisy.
Trumpeter...... Excellent, steady, true, and indefatigable.
Rallywood...... Hardly tried.
Ringwood ...... Do.
Ganymede...... Do.

Bitches.

Duchess......... Very good and true, but soft in wet weather.
Blossom .... Will not hunt, nearly blind, very handsome.
Dimple .... Excellent, very steady and true.
Mischief......... Quite a pup, but wonderfully true, active, and steady.
Barmaid......... Good and true, but free.
Governess ...... Excellent, remarkably active and steady.
Wishful .... Very good and steady.
Chantress ...... Very slow and noisy.
Riotous .... Hardly tried.
Rhapsody ...... Do.

Bluebelle ...... Too noisy, but active and true.
Bounty .... The leading hound. Most excellent, true, steady and active.
Ruin .... An excellent bit of stuff, never tired, very true and steady.
Wisdom......... Very steady, but too slow and rather noisy.
Frantic .... Hard working, true and steady.
Beauty .... Excellent, active, true and steady.
Frolic............ Very true, good road hound. Old and rather slow.
Milkmaid ...... A terrible babbler.
Merry............ Excellent, very active, true and steady.
Gipsey .... Old, but very good, steady and true.

Of these, Rallywood, Ringwood, Regent, Ganymede, Beauty, Chantress, Milkmaid, Gipsey, and Bluebelle had come with the first pack from Captain Anstruther Thomson.

CHAPTER III.

SECURING COUNTRY.

> " Wilt thou hunt?
> Thy hounds shall make the welkin answer them,
> And fetch shrill echoes from the hollow earth."
> *Taming of the Shrew, Induction, scene 2.*

The cordiality with which the landowners and farmers of Wirral received the application of the Royal Rock Beagle Hunt to sport over their estates and land, is worthy of our highest admiration, and we cannot but feel proud that this permission, granted fifty years ago, has in only one instance ever been withdrawn by either the original grantors or their successors. This withdrawal, the first painful incident in the history of the Hunt, will be referred to more explicitly on a subsequent page.

With one exception, all the landowners approached by the members readily granted permission to hunt over their estates, subject to the hounds not being allowed to interfere with the sport of the foxhounds, or to enter the fox covers. The exception was Mr. Mainwaring, of Bromborough Hall, who could not be persuaded, though persistently entreated, to place his nice little estate at the disposal of the Hunt.

Time has overcome that particular difficulty, and now there is no part of Wirral, suitable for hunting, where beagles are not welcome, save and except that choice bit of country, belonging to Sir Thomas Brocklebank, lying around Storeton. This bit of country, extending from Landican to Prenton, Higher Bebington, Brimstage, and Barnston, covers some four square miles of lovely hunting country, and we live in hope that some day we may be permitted to run on this land, at any rate to the extent of following a hare put up outside the forbidden ground; for many a good run has been spoiled by having to "whip off" if hounds run on Storeton."

It is, perhaps, not an unmixed evil that this paradise is barred to us, as being strictly preserved it acts as a nursery for hares, from which surrounding districts are supplied, should they from any cause become depleted. When in 1887 the R.R.B., in conjunction with the Wirral Harriers, put down eighty-five imported hares, there was no need to place any around Storeton.

There is one other estate which is now forbidden to us. Mr. Haigh, of Ledsham, will not allow the beagles to go on his land, and unfortunately any hare found on the Ledsham side of Hadlow Road, is practically sure sooner or later to run on Mr. Haigh's land. When this occurs, the field remain standing in the lane, while the huntsman alone follows his hounds and makes good the ring, which nearly always brings the hare back to our own ground. Surely if Mr. Haigh could witness the pathetic sight of twenty or thirty eager beaglers fuming in the lane, and dreading lest the hare should go boldly forward over the railway line, so throwing them hopelessly out of the run, he would relent and withdraw his interdict!

The farmers of Wirral have always been noted for their love of sport, and they one and all gave a most cordial welcome to the beagles.

ENTRY IN THE MINUTE BOOK, 24TH JANUARY, 1846.

As we were returning from hunting we met a farmer in a cart, who told us his name was ——, and he should be very glad to see us with the dogs at Oldfield, near Thurstaston, and would always find us a hare.

The friendly feeling thus initiated between the farmers and beaglers has continued without interruption to the present time, and there is little reason to fear that our successors will ever have the favour of the farmers withdrawn from the Hunt.

Some of the letters from the principal landowners have been preserved by Mr. Rawson, who was the prime mover in the formation of the R.R.B.; and it will, no doubt, be of interest to many that a selection of these letters should be recorded. Mr. Rawson's letter to Sir W. M. Stanley is a fair specimen of the manner in which the appeal was made to the landlords, either personally or by letter.

Rock Ferry, 14th April, 1845.
To Sir William Massey Stanley, Bart., Hooton.

Sir,—I have had the honour of being deputed, as Chairman of the "Royal Rock Beagles," to request from you the favour of being allowed to hunt over your property in this Hundred.

Our object in forming the pack has been for the sake of the excellent exercise it will afford us, and the amusement it will cause to many.

One of the standing rules of the Hunt is that horses are strictly forbidden. We purpose hunting entirely on foot.

We would at all times strictly avoid any of your covers, and on any closely preserved country the hares would be far too plentiful for our sport. We should therefore never willingly trespass on such.

It was our intention that a deputation should have formally waited on you for the purpose of asking your kind permission, but in your absence from Hooton this is impracticable, and I have therefore been deputed to write you on the subject.

To all similar requests already made to the principal landowners in our immediate neighbourhood, I am proud to say we have hitherto received their willing assent, and knowing how anxious you have ever been to promote "sport" in this district of Cheshire, we have every hope that you will, with your usual liberality, accede to the request we have made.

I have the honour to be, Sir, your obedient humble servant.

C. RAWSON, JUN.

The answer to this letter is not now forthcoming, but it is to be presumed that it was favourable, as there is an entry in the minute book of the Hunt, dated 22nd January, 1846, signed by Tinley Barton:

I saw Sir William Stanley out hunting, he enquired after the beagles, and said he should have great pleasure in seeing them hunt over his unpreserved grounds. He wished a fixture to be appointed at Raby, and notice to be sent to his keeper there. He expressed the best possible feeling towards the hounds, but hoped they would always be stopped from going into his fox covers, and the same when they came on to preserved grounds where there were too many hares.

COPIES OF LETTERS FROM LANDLORDS TO C. RAWSON.

From John Shaw Leigh, Esq.

September 29th, 1845.

Dear Sir,—I can have no possible objection that the Royal pack of Beagles may traverse my small property in Cheshire, provided it will not molest Sir Wm. Stanley's movements with the more elevated class of animals employed in this rational amusement.

From J. B. Glegg, Esq.

Thurstaston Hall, November 24th, 1845.

Sir,—In reply to your application as Chairman of the Committee of the Royal pack of Beagles, I beg you will assure the gentlemen comprising that body, they are at perfect liberty to hunt over my property in the Hundred of Wirral, on the terms stated, with the sole exception of my fox cover, which has always been reserved for my friend, Sir W. M. Stanley.

From William Latham, Esq.

Gayton, 3rd December, 1845.

Sir,—I have to acknowledge the receipt of your letter of 1st instant, and premising to you that I own no land in Wirral; yet as I have the right of the game over Gayton and Pensby, I have not the least objection to your hunting the beagles over both occasionally, provided the farmers do not cry out against it, and that it does not interfere with Sir Wm. Stanley's hounds, both of which you can no doubt guard against.

From J. R. Shaw, Esq.

Arrow Hall, December 9th, 1845.

My dear Rawson,—Many thanks for your kindness in sending Neilson and myself the letters on the cultivation of wheat. I feel extremely gratified that the gentlemen of the Royal Rock Beagles were pleased with my reception of them, and with their day's sport. I should feel obliged by the dogs being drawn off in future if the hare enters the park, or any of the young plantations round the Hall, within the wall, and on the other side from Mr. Neilson's upper farm down to the keeper's house. This is the only restriction I wish to put upon the Royal Rock Beagles. I feel, also, that this will not interfere with your sport, as the hares are too numerous.

From John Wilson Patten, Esq., M.P., Lord of the Manor of Woodchurch.

To J. N. Wright, February 16th, 1846.

Dear Sir,—In reply to your letter of 13th, I have no objection at all to your young friends, whom you mention as having established a pack of beagles for the purpose of hunting on foot, going over my property in Wirral, but I have divested myself of the right of giving them permission. One of my tenants there has the preservation of the game, and they should apply to him. I rather think that Mr. Williams, of Landican, who has recently succeeded Mr. Ball, who previously had the shooting, has also succeeded him as the preserver of the game. I should much enjoy a run with the beagles myself just now.

From R. W. Barton, Esq.

(Extract.) 18th February, 1846.

To W. Robinson,—I have no objection whatever to the beagles meeting on Caldy Common.

From Ralph Brocklebank, Esq.

To C. Rawson, Rumford Street, Liverpool, October 20th, 1845.

Dear Sir,—I am sorry to say that I have had a strong complaint from Mr. Lewis of Tranmere, one of Mr. Orred's farmers, of the damage done to his fences and wheat especially, by the hunters with the beagles, who, I am told, ran upon his farm in great numbers. He requests me to put a stop to it, and as the holder of the deputation of the Manor of Tranmere from Mr. Orred, I feel constrained to withdraw the privilege, granted to yourself and Mr. Wainwright, to run the beagles upon any portion of the Manor of Tranmere.

From the conversation I had with you, I only expected that the number of hunters would have been so limited as to have prevented any complaint, and I regret the course that I feel compelled to take.

This was the first rebuff for the Royal Rock Beagles, and was specially unfortunate, as it was so early in their first season. The cause of complaint must have arisen on their fourth fixture, that for October 13th, at the kennels. This serious difficulty was ably met by the Committee, who decided that—

Mr. Hemingway and the Master (Mr. Tinley Barton) having kindly promised to see the tenants on Tranmere and Prenton, it is resolved that, when consent is got from them, Mr. Wainwright and Mr. Rawson be desired to call on Mr. Brocklebank, and try to change his determination of refusing the R.R.B. permission to hunt on Tranmere.

These gentlemen appear to have been successful, and Mr. Brocklebank generously withdrew the veto. A minute, dated 21st Nov., 1845, reads as follows :—

G. J. Wainwright and C. Rawson called on R. Brocklebank, Esq., to beg him to rescind his refusal, as conveyed in his letter of Oct. 20th last. After much pressing, Mr. Brocklebank consented to grant us the same permission he formerly did over part of Tranmere, if we could gain the permission of the tenants thereon. He also granted us full permission to hunt over Oxton. We pledged ourselves not to trespass on Prenton, or the part of Tranmere near the house.

Letter from the Rev. James Mainwaring.

To C. Rawson. Bromborough Hall, November 24th, 1845.

Dear Sir,—In reply to your note, forwarded thro' our friend Mr. Vertue, I regret that it is not in my power to accede to the request contained in that note of sporting over my property in Brembro' with the Royal Rock Beagles.

After having so long surrendered my coverts to the Hooton Hunt, I could not think it consistent to permit any interference with Sir Wm. Stanley's amusements, or of those who usually attend that Hunt. And in addition to this, I must study the convenience of my tenantry, who would suffer damage in their fences by the pedestrians who are assembled on such occasions.

Had I a property outlying from Bromboro', I should have been glad to have granted the permission, but I cannot consent to have the privacy of my little estate interfered with.

From the same.

December 2nd, 1845.

Dear Sir.—I was favoured with yours last morning, and in reply beg to observe, that whatever the law allows in the pursuit of game, I must, it is presumed, of necessity submit to, but more than that I cannot concede in the way of sporting over my property in Bromboro'.

I have the honour to remain, yours obediently,

JAMES MAINWARING.

No record has been preserved of the letter written by C. Rawson to Mr. Mainwaring, in reply to the above letter of 24th November, 1845, but it is evident that Mr. Rawson pointed out that although Mr. Mainwaring refused permission to the R.R.B. to draw on his land, yet in accordance with the etiquette of sport, they claimed the privilege of following the hare on to the forbidden ground. As a matter of fact the R.R.B. never attempted to fix any meet from which it was likely that a hare would run on to Mr. Mainwaring's land, until in 1851 they began to meet at Spital station. Bromborough Hall was at this time occupied by Mr. Rankin, and he appears to have allowed the beagles to hunt over the land between Spital and Bromborough, but there is an entry in the Sport Book of the Hunt—

Monday, 14th March, 1853. Spital Station. A desperate wet day; however, Mr. Macfie showed up and worked on to Bromborough, and had the pleasure of being warned off by Mr. Rankin's keeper, and did nothing.

At the first annual general meeting of the subscribers to the Royal Rock Beagles, held at the Royal Rock Ferry Hotel, on the 29th August, 1846 :—

Present.

Mr. C. Rawson, Junior, in the chair.

T. A. Bushby,	E. Morgan,	W. Pyke,
H. Walford,	J. Hasleden,	E. Matthias,
A. Walford,	T. Sleddell,	G. Johnston.
J. Scott,	J. B. Amey,	

The following report was read by the Chairman :—

Your Committee have called you together in accordance with Rule No. 12, though circumstances prevented this meeting being held on the first Monday in August as therein ordered.

The accounts for the fourteen months ending May, 1846, are prepared, and on the table for your inspection.

Your Committee have had to meet many heavy extra expenses during the first fourteen months, in purchasing hounds, preparing kennels, &c., &c., which will not again occur.

Your Committee have recommended a donation of one pound from each member to defray the above extra expenses, and they have no doubt that the subscription for the current year will amply cover the outlay, the greatest economy in every department being strictly adhered to.

Your Committee have the pleasure to announce that there are now 95 subscribers to the Hunt, and that they have succeeded in collecting a pack of beagles which have been universally admired, and from which they anticipate excellent sport for the ensuing season.

Your Committee have selected Humphrey Jones as their new huntsman, in place of Thomas Kay, who met with so melancholy an end on the Rock Ferry pier, whilst in performance of his duty.

Your Committee have to acknowledge the great civility and kindness they have received from the landowners and farmers of this part of Wirral. It has been their object to cultivate their goodwill in every way, and they have heard very general satisfaction expressed at the conduct of all the members. They have to congratulate the Hunt on the large tract of country over which they have permission to hunt, and they trust that it will continue to be the aim of each member to do all in his power to retain the good opinion in which the Hunt is now held.

CHAPTER IV.

FINANCES OF THE CLUB.

"Before the game's afoot, thou still let'st slip."
King Henry IV, part I, act i, scene 3.

In the beginning, the subscription to the Royal Rock Beagles was fixed at two guineas, and during the first year ninety-one members joined, producing an income of £191 2s. 0d. The Committee had made a careful estimate of the cost of keeping up a pack of fifty beagles, as follows :—

ESTIMATE.

	£	s.	d.
Feeding, straw, coals, &c.	50	0	0
Huntsman's wages, clothes, licence	60	18	10
Whipper-in, at 2/6 per week and clothes	7	10	0
Rent of kennels	14	0	0
Duty on twelve couple of hounds	16	16	0
Sundries, medicine, &c.; tips to keepers	10	0	0
Extra expenses, walks for pups, &c.	27	0	0
Total	£186	4	10

The actual expenses, as per account presented at the first annual general meeting, 29th August, 1846, were—

	£	s.	d.
Feeding, straw, coals, &c.	41	0	3
Huntsman, wages and clothes	33	2	9
Whipper-in, ditto	6	10	6
Rent of kennels	14	0	0
Duty on twelve couple of hounds	16	16	0
Sundries, medicine, &c.; tips to keepers	8	5	6
Extra expenses, walks for pups, &c.	4	13	5
Purchase of hounds	67	0	9
First expenditure on kennels, and repairs	70	18	4
Total	£262	7	6

This statement of accounts left the club in debt to C. Rawson, who generously financed the matter, to the amount of over £70, and the Committee explained the deficit, by having been obliged to meet many extra heavy expenses during the first fourteen months, in purchasing hounds, and preparing the kennels for their reception, which expenses were not likely to recur.

The Committee recommended a donation of one pound from each member, and had no doubt that the subscription for the current year would amply cover the outlay, and they further promised the strictest economy in every department.

The next annual statement shows that, with unpaid subscriptions, £40, Rawson was still £60 out of pocket, notwithstanding that the income account shows that the call of £1 was freely responded to by the members. The number of members then enrolled being 85, it was resolved, that in future each new member should be charged an entrance fee of £1. Among the first batch of members to pay entrance fee were P. F. Currie, the coroner, W. Chambres, and W. T. Hall.

Notwithstanding these efforts at "raising the wind," and the economy practised by the Committee, the debit balance still continued over the next two years, and in 1850 it was only reduced by £10. At the general meeting of members it was resolved to abolish the entrance fee and raise the subscription to three guineas. The result of this, during the following year, was to reduce the debt to £40, but the number of members had fallen to seventy. In 1852 the debt was £45, and the number of members only fifty-five.

In 1853, when C. Rawson resigned the mastership, the debt had again increased to £88, of which £63 was due to H. Walford and £25 to C. Rawson. It was resolved that the new Master, V. A. King, and D. O. Bateson should "interest themselves with all connected with the Hunt to obtain "donations towards liquidating the balance due to the secretary."

The efforts of these gentlemen, if seriously made, did not appear to meet with much success, as the following year found the club in much the same plight, £50 still due to the secretary, and the members were earnestly requested each to make a donation of £1. The next account showed a debit of only £15, and this balance was wiped out in 1856, since when the club has never again been badly in debt until 1892, when there appeared a balance due to the treasurer of £55, which was immediately liquidated.

In 1869 the subscription was raised to four guineas for each ordinary member, and two guineas for young gentlemen "not in business on their own "account." This latter provision was cancelled in 1889, at which time the number of members was limited to sixty, with a subscription of four guineas, and out of each subscription one guinea per annum was to be placed to the credit of a "special entertainment fund," to be used for subscriptions to farmers' societies, and to accumulate for providing a ball or other entertainment for the farmers and their families.

Financially, the club is now on a sound basis, as it has, in the main, always been, except during the few early years of its existence, when special calls had to be made on the members to wipe out debit balances. It is clear that the originators of the Hunt tried to work on too small a subscription. Two guineas was too meagre, even had they been able to maintain their numbers at 100. Since limiting the numbers to sixty, the club has always kept full, and usually there are candidates waiting for admission to vacancies. The subscription of four guineas is considered sufficient to pay the expenses of the hounds, and leave a handsome surplus for the farmers' entertainment fund. This surplus varies, as the table given below will show.

COMPARISON OF ACCOUNTS FOR VARIOUS YEARS.

	1845-6.			1846-7.			1886-7.			1890-1.			1891-2.			1892-3.			1893-4.		
	£	s.	d.	£	s.	d.	£	s.	d.	£	s.	d.	£	s.	d.	£	s.	d.	£	s.	d.
Feeding, straw, coals....	41	0	3	64	10	0	53	13	1	63	19	4	96	13	3	57	11	8	71	2	1
Wages, clothes	39	13	3	49	17	3	71	17	0	67	7	6	59	5	0	67	14	6	74	1	6
Rent of kennels	14	0	0	14	0	0	20	16	9	24	15	0	23	15	0	23	13	11	23	13	4
Duty on hounds	10	16	0	22	16	0	11	5	0	14	5	2	15	11	11	15	15	2	18	10	5
Purchase of hounds	67	0	9	5	7	6	15	0	0	16	14	0	9	0	0	..	..		..	..	
Medicine, tips to keepers	8	5	6	11	1	4	8	0	5	2	17	6	2	3	6	12	2	3	6	15	4
Repairs, &c., to kennels .	70	13	4	3	18	5	26	1	11	11	15	0	3	2	6	5	9	5	3	11	4
Extra expenses—Walking, pups, excursion, &c.	4	13	5	35	0	10	41	1	0	20	12		46	7	9	16	5	2	34	16	9
	262	7	6	203	11	4	253	15	2	227	6		255	18	11	198	12	1	232	10	9

The expenses of the Cheshire Beagles for 1893-4, for the same items as are included in above table, were:—

	£	s.	d.
Feeding, straw, and coals	105	2	11
Wages and clothes	57	7	6
Rent and taxes	14	6	9
Duty on hounds	13	1	0
Purchase of hounds............(Cr.)		...	
Medicine, &c............................	8	18	6
Repairs to kennels	23	5	3
Extra expenses, van, &c............	45	12	6
	£267	14	5

The Cheshire Beagles usually have a greater number of hounds in kennel than are kept by the Royal Rock Beagles.

CHAPTER V.

CRISES IN THE HISTORY OF THE HUNT.

> "In food, in sport, and life-preserving rest
> To be disturb'd, would mad or man, or beast."
> *Comedy of Errors*, act v, scene 1.

The Royal Rock Beagle Hunt having fairly started, in favour with both landlords and farmers, and having a good hunting country, went smoothly on for some years, enjoying the sport, and well satisfied with each other and with their surroundings. The even tenor of their way was only chequered by the inevitable variations in the list of members, changes in the executive, and the loss of their valued master, C. Rawson, who left Liverpool to reside in the south of England in the year 1852. The Hunt was carried on in perfect accord with the Master of the Hooton Foxhounds, Sir William M. Stanley, who never gave the Committee of the R.R.B. the slightest trouble on any count; and they, on the other hand, did their utmost to keep in his good graces, by fixing their meets so as not to clash with those of the foxhounds, by taking special care not to disturb fox covers, and by general attention to the rules of sport.

The first event from outside, which had any bearing on the interests of the Hunt, was the inauguration of the Chester Beagles in 1854. There is no record in the annals of either pack of any arrangement having been settled as to the limitation of the country. Up to that time the R.R.B. had found amply sufficient hunting ground at the northern end of the Wirral peninsula, and it was probably a matter of little moment, at the time, that another pack was being formed at the southern extremity of their country. In the light of later events, and of the changes which have taken place in Wirral, we can now clearly see that the Committee of the R.R.B. ought to have anticipated our future needs, and secured to their successors a country only limited on the south by the canal between Chester and Ellesmere Port. At this period the only effect of the formation of the Chester Beagle Hunt upon the fortunes of the Royal Rock Beagles, was the cessation of the annual visits to Beeston for two or three days' hunting. On December 3rd, 1846, the R.R.B. for the first time went to Beeston, at the invitation of Mr. Bird. The record of the run they enjoyed thus winds up in the Sport Book :—

Altogether a most glorious day's sport, and much are we indebted to Mr. Bird's kindness in opening this new country to us, and bidding us welcome whenever we choose to come.

From this time to 1853 inclusive, the R.R.B. went every season to Beeston, and sometimes twice in the season, for two days' hunting, which they always wound up by a dinner to the principal farmers at the Tollemache Arms. The final occasion of their visit was in 1853, December 10th, and the last day they could not hunt, as the ground was covered deep in snow. Since then Beeston has formed part of the country hunted by the Chester Beagles, and for the last two or three years has proved a very valuable bit of country for them.

The Royal Rock Beagles have always been on cordial and friendly terms with the Chester Beagles; so much so, that, at a critical period in the history of the latter, the R.R.B. were confidently appealed to for support. In 1888, on Mr. J. T. Pownall's retirement from the mastership of the Chester Beagles, a great many of the members and subscribers took that opportunity to sever their connection with the Hunt. The new Master, Mr. C. W. Smith, made strenuous efforts to fill up the gaps in his subscription list, and among others appealed to the R.R.B. for support. This was readily accorded, and many of the members of the R.R.B. became either members of or subscribers to the Chester Beagles. At the present time twelve members of the R.R.B. figure on the subscription list of the Chester Beagles.

Inauguration of the Wirral Harriers.

"Let us score their backs,
And snatch 'em up, as we take hares, behind.
'Tis sport to maul a runner."
Antony and Cleopatra, act iv, scene 7.

The first serious crisis in the history of the Royal Rock Beagles was the starting of the Wirral Harriers in 1868, when the Royal Rock Beagles had existed for twenty-three years, and V. A. King had been master for fifteen years.

After Sir William Massey Stanley had left the neighbourhood, and dispersed his pack of foxhounds, some of the gentlemen who had habitually hunted with the Hooton hounds, looked with longing eyes on the pack of beagles, and wished to hunt them on horseback. It is to be feared that a few of the beaglers were not averse to this proposal, but, be this as it may, the plan did not meet with "ould King's" approval. He strongly resented the manner in which the promoters of the Wirral Harriers set about the formation of their club.

Much as the beaglers of the present day desire to revere and approve of all their beloved old master's sayings and doings as a beagler, we must admit, although we cannot now be aware of all the circumstances, that his usual tact was not displayed on this occasion.

There can be no doubt that at the time, and even up to the present, there was plenty of room in the country for both packs to hunt without unduly interfering with one another; but the signs are rapidly accumulating that the country will not long endure the two packs of hounds, and the making of the new Wirral Railway through Burton, Neston, Heswall, Prenton, Upton, and Bidston, along with the extensive use of wire in the fences, will eventually make it not worth the while of the Wirral Harriers to hunt the country.

The following correspondence between the masters of the respective packs is deeply interesting and instructive. While our master displayed his well-known ability as a letter-writer, we cannot but regret that he did not adopt a more conciliatory tone, and treat the matter with fuller resignation to the inevitable. On the other hand, it is clear that the somewhat sarcastic and patronizing tone of the harrier master's remarks was ill calculated to conciliate an autocrat like King, who had grown to love his beagles, and to regard them as his own peculiar, sacred property. If the contentions of the harrier master were propounded anew at the present day, there would be little cause for surprise if a similar storm of resentment were raised among existing beaglers. We should certainly treat with well-merited scorn the pretension that harriers were superior to beagles, simply because they were hunted on horseback!

Correspondence between Beagles and Harriers.

*"Where you shall see
How hardly I was drawn into this war;
How calm and gentle I proceeded still
In all my writings."*
Antony and Cleopatra, act v, scene 1.

Circular from V. A. King to the Members of the R.R.B.

11th December, 1868.

Dear Sir,—I take the liberty of sending to you copies of a correspondence which has passed between Mr. Court and myself upon the subject of a Harrier Club, who are now hunting upon the country which the Beagle Hunt have possessed for the last twenty-five years, and which land, I think, in a sporting sense, this club has not any right to hunt upon.

My reason for circulating this correspondence is chiefly because I believe great misapprehension prevails in the district regarding the Beagle Hunt, which I am anxious, if possible, to remove.

This Harrier Club made all their arrangements without even consulting with, or informing the Beagle Hunt of what they proposed to do; and it was only at the end of September that they waited upon me, and even then did not say they intended to hunt upon the beagle country.

The beagles have hunted the lower end of the Hundred of Wirral for a quarter of a century. I hope always in a gentlemanly manner. During the whole of this period, there has been the best and kindest feeling between the farmers and the members of the Hunt, and not a single farmer has ever made any serious complaint of damage being done.

It is perfectly clear to me that in this lower end of the Hundred there is neither sufficient land nor sufficient hares for two packs of hounds. In fact, there is barely enough for one pack, and I think it is my duty as Master of the Beagles to protect as far as I can the sport which is enjoyed, not only by the members of the Beagle Hunt, but by a great number of other gentlemen also, and which sport will be entirely ruined if the harriers hunt the country.

With reference to the question of "right" to the country, which I consider the Beagle Hunt have, and which I contend the Harrier Club have not, I am quite aware that this right simply means a privilege granted by the kindness of the landowners and the farmers, and I would most respectfully ask these gentlemen for their favourable consideration of this question, which I have now the honour to lay before them.   Your faithful servant,

V. A. KING.

Park Road West. Birkenhead, 24th Nov., 1868.

Dear Col. King.—You would oblige me and the members of the Wirral Harrier Club generally if you would kindly furnish me with your fixtures for the next month. We are most anxious to avoid clashing with your arrangements or interfering with your sport in any way, and it is solely with a view to this object that I wish, and am instructed to make, what I trust will not be deemed an unwarrantable request.   Believe me, yours sincerely,

J. R. COURT.

Lieut.-Col. King.

Oxton, Birkenhead, 25th Nov., 1868.

Dear Sir,—I have to thank you for your note of yesterday, asking me, on behalf of the Wirral Harrier Club, for the Beagle fixtures, to avoid clashing with our arrangements or interfering with our sport.

I beg to express my obligations for this kind feeling on the part of your club; but, permit me to say, that I have always understood, since I had the pleasure of seeing your deputation, that your club proposed to hunt upon the country near to Chester, and not at all upon our country at the lower end of the Hundred, and of course if you do this it is useless to give you our fixtures, as you cannot by any possibility interfere with our sport, and, therefore, I confess I cannot quite understand the object of your note.

If, however, the request contained in it means that your club propose to hunt upon the country which the Beagles have hunted over for a quarter of a century, then I can only reply to you now as I did when the deputation above referred to did me the honour to wait upon me, that I believe there is a law, which may be called a law of that high courtesy which governs all the relations of gentlemen between each other, and which plainly says, that under no circumstances whatever shall any pack of hounds interfere with the country hunted by an older pack.

If your club violate this law, then it will be with feelings of deep pain that I shall most reluctantly be obliged to decline to acknowledge them as sportsmen.

May I be allowed to take this opportunity of saying, that for some months past many of the members of your club have stated to landowners, to farmers, and to others, something to the following effect, viz. :—That both I and the Beagle Hunt were favourable, or at all events not unfavourable, to the establishment of a pack of harriers ; that the beagles were to be given up, &c., &c.

Now, with reference to these statements, I can only express my sorrow that such misrepresentations should have been made, and that my name should have been used in such an unauthorised manner.

Believe me, yours faithfully,

John R. Court, Esq.   V. A. King.

Park Road West, Birkenhead, 27th Nov., 1868.

Dear Sir.—I, on behalf of the Wirral Harrier Club, have to express my regret you should labour under a mistake, that the deputation to which you allude ever acquiesced in or suggested the proposal of confining the Harriers to the country round Chester, that is to say to an area of a few miles, leaving untouched, as sacred ground, the north end of the Hundred, which as you are aware, comprises by far the largest portion of the district ; in fact, such a proposition would be tantamount to the extinction of the Harriers altogether.

We are most anxious to work in harmony with the members of the Royal Rock Beagles, nor do I see any reason why, by acting in mutual concert, we should ever interfere with each other's sport. But, with a view to effect this object, it is essential we should be previously acquainted with your fixtures, in which case you may confidently rely on our not meeting in your neighbourhood ; but, short of this, I see no other way of hunting the district compatible with our existence as a hunting club. I think, therefore, you will see that if there should be any " violation of the laws of courtesy," the blame will not rest with us. We have exhausted every means of conciliation ; but we, while respecting the rights of others, cannot relinquish our own.

Believe me, yours faithfully,

Lieut.-Col. King.   J. R. Court.

Oxton, Birkenhead, 30th November, 1868.

Dear Sir,—I have to thank you for your note of the 27th, and to apologise for not having answered it on the day of its receipt.

I am not aware I ever said that your deputation either suggested or acquiesced in any proposal to confine the Harriers to the country round Chester. Immediately after I had seen the deputation, Mr. * * * * informed me that you had told him that the Harrier Club did not intend to hunt upon any part of the Hundred which was hunted upon by the Beagles. In consequence of this information I declined to fix any meets at Sutton, and I can only express my sorrow that my forbearance has not been appreciated by your club.

That portion of the Hundred of Wirral hunted by the Beagles does not comprise more than one-half of it. In fact, I much doubt if it is one-half, but as you are, perhaps, much better acquainted with the Hundred than I am, I forbear discussing the question of acreage with you.

I certainly claim, on behalf of the Beaglers, as " sacred ground," if such a word is at all applicable to the subject, the land upon which they have hunted for a quarter of a century. I claim this land upon precisely the same grounds as the Cheshire Foxhounds claim their country. I am not aware that any sportsman would think of disputing this claim.

I observe that you say, that while respecting the rights of others you cannot relinquish your own.

Now I quite fail to perceive that your club propose to respect the rights of the Beaglers. On the contrary, if they intend to hunt upon our country, it is to my mind a clear proof that they do not respect them.

I am also sorry to say that I am quite unable to perceive what the rights of your club are.

I may, perchance, be allowed to remark that not only in the above sentence, but also from the whole tenor of your letter, you appear to assume the principle that the Harrier Club have an abstract right to hunt upon any country which they please to do; or, supposing, for instance, they were a pack of foxhounds, would have a right to go into the upper part of the county, and hunt the country now hunted by the Cheshire Foxhounds. Now I would observe, with the greatest respect, that I hold a strong opinion the direct reverse of this; therefore as our opinions upon the principle at issue are so utterly irreconcilable, it appears to me idle to discuss the question.

I observe you say you have exhausted every means of conciliation. Now, without wishing to say one unkind word, I am not aware of any attempt at conciliation being made. For months past the members of your club have been misrepresenting the opinions of the Beagle Hunt, and freely using my name in a most unauthorised manner. If this be conciliation, then I am sorry to say I have again the misfortune to differ from you in opinion.

It appears to me that the tone of your note is something of this nature: that the Harrier Club are in the right and the Beagle Hunt in the wrong. In fact, I think, that anyone who had to judge of the merits of the case from your letter alone would come to the conclusion that the Harrier Club had held possession of the country for twenty-five years, and that the Beagle Hunt were now invading it. Such is my impression, but of course I may be mistaken.

I have answered your letter simply because I should be sorry to be thought wanting in respect or in courtesy, but you will perhaps allow me to remark, that I cannot see any advantage in the continuance of the correspondence.

I remain, dear Sir, your faithful servant,

John R. Court, Esq.   V. A. KING.

                          Claughton Park, Birkenhead, 14th December, 1868.

Dear Sir,—I, on behalf of the subscribers to the Wirral Harriers, cannot have the remotest objection to the publication of our correspondence, though I cannot see that the differences between them and the Beagle subscribers are fit to become historical; and I certainly have no wish that you should appear in the unamiable position of attempting to interfere with the sport of others, in matters which cannot possibly detract from your own. If we act in concert, as indeed all reasonable men ought, in what earthly manner can we interfere with each other's sport or diminish our mutual enjoyment? The Harriers only meet twice a week, and may, on an average, kill a brace of hares. Can it be even pretended that so vast a destruction, in a district comprising some 140 square miles, could deprive you of even a single run in a quarter of a century? If anyone ought to complain it really should be the shooting gentlemen; but they, with the generous impulses of sportsmen, have chosen rather to subject themselves to this inconvenience, than to deprive their fellow sportsmen of the pleasure of hunting the district.

You really treat the Wirral Hundred as if it only contained a few acres of cabbage garden, in which beagles and harriers could not possibly meet without running their heads against each other. But, surely, the Wirral Hundred is large enough for both of us. This extraordinary pretension of the Beagle Club, to engross all the capabilities of a large tract of country, not more than a small portion of which they can enjoy, only affords another illustration of the celebrated Æsopian fable we are usually taught in the nursery, which, doubtless, the experience of the world has not destroyed, but only confirmed in your recollection.

I regret to hear you challenge our rights, which certainly appear, even in a sporting, conventional sense, as substantial as yours; with two exceptions, we have the consent of everybody who has a shadow of an interest in the soil, from the proprietor of the land down to the gentlemen who merely have the right of shooting over it. The farmers are with us, almost to a man. If any gentlemen should claim a right, in the sporting code, to hunt the Wirral Hundred, it surely ought to be the residents of Birkenhead and its vicinity. Now, there is not a man in the Wirral Harrier Club who does not reside in what may be called the Wirral district: while, I believe, a large proportion of the subscribers to the Beagles reside in Lancashire. Our rights are, therefore, the rights of gentlemen to hunt their own county, as against strangers, who can only allege in their favour the claims of not a very venerable antiquity. In the sporting calendar, it will not be denied, that beagles are as much inferior to harriers as harriers are to foxhounds; and, therefore, I cannot understand how you can claim for your description of hunting those high privileges and prerogatives which alone appertain to the higher; and were, even, our rights less substantial than they are, and one of us was called on to give way, I contend that the superiority of the one class of hunting to the other ought alone to decide in our favour. But there is, fortunately, not this desperate alternative before us. We have only to act in harmony, and we can each enjoy fully our peculiar rights and privileges, without interfering any more with each other's movements than if the one hunted in Lancashire and the other in the Isle of Man.

In favour of this harmonious concert I could cite numerous examples, but I will not go further than our own doors. The Chester Beagles hunt, in common with the harriers kept by Captain P. Yates, the district of Backford and Wyrven. There is room enough for both, and green-eyed jealousy (as I hope may be so in our case) has not succeeded in destroying an atom of their friendship for each other.

I cannot conclude without expressing my regret you should deny not only that we had exhausted every means of conciliation, but even that we had made the slightest effort to meet you in a conciliatory spirit. Why, the members of our Hunt, before the harriers were started, sought permission to hunt the beagles on horseback, in preference to starting a rival club, which, had you assented to, the harriers would never have been heard of. Was not this conciliation? Even when your refusal drove them to other measures, instead of setting up a rival club, did they not invite you to merge your beagles into a hunting club? Was not this conciliation? Even when, by your rejection of this overture, they were driven to the establishment of the harriers, did they not invite you to accept of the mastership? I suppose this was not conciliation. Even after these efforts to propitiate you, did they not commission a deputation to wait upon you, with a view to effect an amicable arrangement, and have I not twice written to solicit your fixtures, for the same purpose? This, of course, was not conciliation. Why, every step we have taken has been marked by the most anxious desire on our part to act in concert as sporting brethren; and even in the closing sentence of this letter, our last act is to offer you the hand of good fellowship, and give you an opportunity, by its acceptance, of preventing another quarrel from being added to the feuds of the sporting world.

As this letter is a reply to yours of the 30th ultimo, which I did not answer, as you then wished the correspondence to be closed; but, as yours of the 9th instant informs me you are going to publish the correspondence, I must view any publication of these letters as garbled in which this is not included.

I remain, yours faithfully,

Lieut.-Col. V. A. King.   J. R. COURT.

Oxton, Birkenhead, 16th December, 1868.

Dear Sir,— I have to thank you for your letter of the 14th instant, which I received yesterday evening.

I waited for an answer to my note of the 9th instant until the 11th instant before publishing the correspondence between us. As you say you will consider this correspondence garbled if your letter above referred to does not appear in it, the Beagle Hunt will have great pleasure in publishing it also.

Almost the only portion of your letter which it appears needful for me to refer to is that part in which you speak of overtures being made for the purpose of allowing gentlemen to ride to the beagles—about converting the beagles into harriers, &c., &c. I confess I am inclined to think this must be a good deal in your own imagination, for I do not know anything about it.

However, I certainly should have objected to convert the beagles into harriers, because I would not accept the responsibilities of the Master of a pack of harriers, as I am certain they must do very serious damage to the farmers.

The Beagle Hunt complain, and I think with reason, that the Harrier Club, in making their arrangements, and in their application to the landowners, not only entirely ignored them, but misrepresented their opinions.

It may be well here that I should very plainly state—That I consider the first time I, as Master of the Beagles, knew anything officially about the Harrier Club was when the deputation waited upon me the end of September, at which time they made me the offer of the mastership of the pack. Now, as, according to common report, all their arrangements had been made, and you chosen as Master months before, I confess I did not see any compliment in this offer.

The only other time when you spoke to me upon the subject was one Sunday afternoon last May, at Mr. * * * *'s house, and, considering our slight acquaintance, you will, perhaps, pardon me for saying I did not think the remarks you made upon that occasion respecting the beagles in very good taste.

You, perhaps, will hardly expect me to admit that beagles are inferior in any way to harriers, or to allow the superiority of the members of the Harrier Club over those of the Beagle Hunt implied in your letter.

I have looked in vain in your long letter for any explanation of the misrepresentations and unauthorised use of my name by the members of your club.

I must also confess with pain that my search has also been in vain, not only in the closing sentence of your letter, but in every sentence of it for any evidence of a conciliatory feeling.

Believe me, yours faithfully,

John R. Court, Esq.   V. A. KING.

The intrusion of the Wirral Harriers into our country was a serious menace to the continuity of the Royal Rock Beagles, as, had there been any marked defection of horse-owning members, it is quite probable that the Hunt would have been broken up. The members, however, proved loyal, and the crisis was safely passed. Both Hunts have been carried on ever since without friction, and of late years some show of friendliness has been fostered between them. "Ould King," however, never forgave the harriers during his lifetime, and took it almost as a personal affront if any of his beaglers joined the harriers also.

The only other crisis in the history of the Royal Rock Beagles arose on the death of the master, V. A. King, in 1882. He had been master for so many years, that the club had become identified with him, and to some of the older members it appeared impossible and undesirable to carry on the Hunt any longer; but the younger members being in the majority succeeded in overruling this counsel. A fuller reference to this crisis will be found under the heading of "L. R. Stephenson, Master."

Since then, and up to the present year of jubilee, the Royal Rock Beagle Hunt has flourished exceedingly, and has been carried on with all the ancient interest intensified. The enthusiasm of the members is inexhaustible, and the club is respected far and near.

CHAPTER VI.

THE MASTERS.

> "You have that in your countenance, which I would fain call master."
> "What's that?"
> "Authority."
>
> *King Lear, act i, scene 4.*

A Master of Hounds occupies a high and honourable place in the sporting world. and one that demands various important qualifications for its successful fulfilment, in those who attain to the eminent position of "Head of the Hunt." He must be able to exercise authority over the hounds, the Hunt servants, the members of the Hunt, and the varied followers in the field; and, withal, to maintain the dignity of his high office in the respect of all with whom he comes in contact. His tact must be conspicuous in dealing with offenders against the canons of sport or the etiquette of hunting, complaints from farmers, difficulties with shooting men, and the rare instances of grumbling about trespass. He must be quick in decision when any emergency arises, and steadfast in carrying out his purposes. Vacillation should never be exhibited by a Master of Hounds. It may almost be said that it is better for a Master to continue on a doubtful course till it is proved wrong, than to hesitate and waver in the presence of his field. The Master must be courteous to all, punctual in his appointments, of healthy physique, and, to sum all, he must be a gentleman. It is his place to be first in everything, and, as regards the members of the R.R.B. on hunting days, his rule begins so soon as they assemble at the meet.

The privileges of the Master of the R.R.B. are numerous. He presides at all meetings of the club, and takes the head of the table at all club dinners. If we are invited as beaglers to any social function, the Master, whether young or old, married or single, is the principal guest. In the field or in the kennels, his sway is supreme, and he is entitled to willing obedience and loyal service from all persons out with his pack. He gives up a great portion of his leisure for the sport of others, and they in return cannot pay him too many of those little attentions which go to make up the courtesies of beagling, and serve to maintain the importance of the honourable position of a Master of Hounds.

Members who bring a friend out with the hounds, should take an opportunity of presenting their guest to the Master. This formality is too frequently omitted. It should be strictly adhered to, as not only is it the correct thing, but it serves to distinguish the invited guest from those who may have joined the sport without any invitation.

The Saturday meets of the R.R.B. are usually attended by a sufficiently large field of members, and a numerous addition of unauthorised strangers is always objectionable and detrimental to the sport. There is an instance in the early records of the Hunt.

21st October, 1848. Poulton-cum-Seacombe. Beat the whole parish well, and could not see a vestige of a hare. On coming to Ripley gorse-cover we must have had a mob of near a hundred men and boys. By way of shaking the whole off, and giving the real dealers in the sport a run, we put on the steam and made for Morton, crossing the Marsh and Fender, when we had a select field of a dozen.

It is the duty of the Master to be present at all the fixtures, or to appoint a deputy to represent him. He should also be punctual, and not throw off before the appointed hour, though he may give as much law as he likes after, to enable late comers to arrive. No one may grumble if he throws off punctually to time. Once, in 1892, the fixture was Ness, by omnibus from Woodside, at 11-45 a.m. The 'bus was expected to arrive at Ness by 1 p.m., but the roads being heavy, we did not reach it till 1-15 p.m., and found the Master had thrown off by himself at 1 sharp. Now if he had found immediately and got clean away, we should have had a distinct grievance. It is of course possible for the Master to be prevented from turning up at the meet, in which case, if he has not appointed some one to act as his deputy, at least half an hour's law should be given him before any steps are taken towards hunting ; and the question arises : who is to take charge for the day and give orders to the huntsman ? If the member usually deputed by the Master to represent him is to the fore, the duty naturally devolves upon him ; but if not, a leader must be sought from the ranks of the whips or Committee, whom failing, the senior member present takes the lead.

After a steady frost it is quite a common occurrence, on the first hunting day, for the weather to be of such a doubtful character that very few turn up at the meet. The huntsman should take the hounds home if no members are present. If the Master alone appears, of course he acts as pleases him best, or as he considers for the benefit of the hounds. If one member only turns up, although he has the right to have the hounds thrown off for his edification, yet, as the responsibility is great in judging whether the land is really fit for hunting or not, and accidents might happen with sheep, trains, &c., it is better for the individual to waive his right, and send the hounds home. If two or more members attend the meet, they are quite justified in hunting, if the majority consider it fit to do so.

Hunting for precedents for the above criticism, we find several in the early records of the R.R.B.

25th November, 1846. Met at Tranmere Church. Had some very pretty hunting among the gardens at the roadside, &c., &c. Mr. Dean was very civil, and made not the smallest objection to our knocking about his garden; on the contrary, appeared much to enjoy the sport. V. A. King was the only member out, in consequence of the rain.

8th December, 1847. Oxton Bridge. Tried over Oxton in vain. At last found on Noctorum, and after some good rings and excellent hunting, lost in a lane near Upton, where some sheep had destroyed the scent. One member. (A. Walford.)

When Jones was huntsman, some instances are on record of his hunting the hounds without any members or any one else being present, and once when only two strangers attended.

18th November, 1848. New Hall. A wet afternoon. Most of the members having had so heavy a day on Thursday, no one went to the meet. Jones made nothing of it.

28th March, 1853. Moreton. No member turning up, Jones walked off, and was met by Mr. Macfie, so he threw off on the Upton side, but made nothing of it.

24th January, 1853. Thingwall Mill. Found just under the mill. Scent very bad; however, after knocking her about for near an hour, she went into Arrow. There being only two strangers present, Jones went home after the first run.

Here is an instance of a liberty taken with a fixture by the Master, probably at the instigation of Henry Walford :—

10th February, 1849. Arrow Hall. Mr. Rawson (the Master) being down (at that time he was very seldom in the neighbourhood), we met early on Noctorum, but did not find till near one, when, after a short spin, we had to trot off to Arrow to lunch at 2 p.m., and join the party in the 'bus. We found a capital lunch prepared, to which ample justice was done. Mr. Shaw being from home, had desired the keeper to get a "bagged" hare turned out, which gave us a sharp quarter of an hour. We then made for Irby, and chopped a hare in a stubble. We soon found another, which took us as straight as a fox to Caldy, where we lost her on the hills. We did no more good afterwards.

Now this fixture was for a Saturday afternoon's 'bus meet at Arrow Hall, two p.m., and it certainly strikes us as not at all a fair thing for some of the members to waylay the hounds on their way to the meet, and, because the Master happened to be present that day, hunt the hounds beforehand in another stretch of country. Suppose they had found a straight-going hare, which might have taken them to Leasowe or Hoylake, they could not have been back with the hounds at Arrow till after three p.m., when they would have gone in to lunch, turning out afterwards for a half-hearted draw, with failing scent and waning light. What would have been the state of mind of enthusiastic beaglers, coming out with the 'bus in the hope and expectation of a good afternoon's sport, and finding no hounds awaiting them at the meet?

Among the duties of the Master is to send cards of the fixtures to various farmers over whose land we expect to hunt; so that they may, if necessary, prepare for the advent of the hounds, by bringing up ewes, or young colts, &c., which might be injured by running about in their excitement; and it is every beagler's business to report to the Master any complaint from farmers which reaches his ears, as it is the Master's province to judge whether the case demands immediate attention.

The Royal Rock Beagles have ever been fortunate in the selection of their Masters. The right man has always turned up whenever they have been in the predicament of having to choose another Master, and each has been a distinct success, well suited to his period. From the inauguration of the Royal Rock Beagles in 1845 to this year of jubilee, there have been six Masters:—

Tinley Barton	from 1845 to 1848, for	3 seasons.
Christopher Rawson	„ 1848 „ 1853, „	5 „
Vincent Ashfield King	„ 1853 „ 1882, „	29 „
Louis Rudd Stevenson	„ 1882 „ 1889, „	7 „
John William Macfie	„ 1889 „ 1890, „	1 „
J. Gould-Smyth	„ 1890 „ 1895, „	5 „
		50 seasons

In the first days of the Royal Rock Beagles, the Master was not, as now is the case, the head and forefront of the club, but was elected annually by the committee, in accordance with Rule 5, as Master of the hounds in the field, being, *ex officio*, a member of the committee. According to the rules and practice of the club, the committee were the real rulers, and the chairman, having a casting vote, was the supreme head, occupying the chair at all meetings and dinners, and taking the lead on all occasions.

With the exception of Colonel King, all the gentlemen who have been Masters of the R. R. B. are still living, and the last three remain valued members of the Hunt.

The following accounts of the individual Masters will be of interest to all past and present beaglers, and no apology need be offered for the extreme length of the record of the late Colonel King, as any scrap of information about him will be cherished by all members of the R. R. B. who enjoyed the charm of his acquaintance.

TINLEY BARTON.

Thomas Tinley Barton.

> "And you may then resolve what tales I have told you."
> *Cymbeline, act iii, scene 3.*

Tinley Barton was the originator of the Royal Rock Beagles, and to him must be ascribed the honour and glory of having founded this famous pack. As described in the account of the formation of the club, he had been hunting hares in Wirral with three couple of hounds, and so aroused the interest of his friends, C. Rawson, J. Okell, and others, in the sport. With his experience he was selected as the first Master of the Hounds, and he held that position during the first three seasons, after which he left Wirral to reside in Scotland.

T. Barton was born August 26th, 1813, at Mount St. John's, near Thirsk, where his father, Captain Henry Barton, then resided. Captain Barton hunted the Hamilton Foxhounds for many years, so that his son Tinley was imbued with a fondness for sport at an early age ; in fact it must have been during his boyhood, for at the age of thirteen he entered the old East India Company's service, and remained at sea till he was twenty. On his return to England his father was residing at the Grange, Rock Ferry, and Tinley Barton took up his abode with him for a few years, pursuing the occupation of farming. Shortly after starting the Royal Rock Beagles, Tinley Barton went to reside and farm at Barnston, at which time he was also agent for R. W. Barton, Esq., of Caldy Manor, who was always a friend to the R.R.B.

At the dinner given to Sir William M. Stanley in 1846 (a full account of which will be found elsewhere), Tinley Barton responded to the toast of "the farmers." His speech is reported as follows :—

Mr. T. Barton returned thanks. He was sure that the farmers felt it an honour to have such a landlord as Sir William Stanley ride across their land (applause). They were delighted to see him on all occasions, and Mr. John Stanley as well (applause). He had also to return thanks to Sir William for allowing the Rock Beagles to run over his unpreserved lands (loud applause).

In 1848 Tinley Barton resigned his membership of the R.R.B., and went to Scotland for four years, returning to England in 1852, when he took up his quarters at King's Gap, Hoylake, residing there for eighteen years, in 1870 removing to his present residence, Avondale, Llangollen. Here, only a few years ago, in 1888, this veteran sportsman, notwithstanding his having exceeded his "three-score years and ten," assisted Mr. Sam. Jagger and Captain Hughes Parry (Mr. Barton's son-in-law) to found the Llangollen

Beagles, and he is to this day one of the keenest supporters and advisers of the Hunt, keeping the beaglers well amused with stories of his early sporting reminiscences.

Mr. Barton was appointed Master of the Hounds by the Committee of the R.R.B. on the 5th April, 1845, and the first season found him strictly attentive to his duties. He hunted the hounds on horseback, for the reason that Sir William Stanley, in giving his assent to the beagles hunting the country, had stipulated that the hounds should be at once stopped on approaching any fox cover. At the close of this first season T. Barton wished to resign his position as Master of the Hounds, but the committee were able to prevail upon him to remain Master for a year or two longer. The reason why he was so seldom at the meets, was probably because he preferred riding with the foxhounds. Whenever the beagle meets were fixed at Barnston, T. Barton hospitably entertained the beaglers at lunch, and found them a hare on his farm. On one of these occasions the Sport Book records :—

We were greatly grieved during this run, at the conduct of one of our members, and record the circumstance as a warning to him and to others. Just as we viewed the hare for the last time, completely done, we were electrified by hearing this excited member shout to the Master, who was close to the hare, " Kill her, Tinley ; d—n her, kill her ! " Comment is needless. Surely, surely such a scene will never again occur with the Royal Rock Beagles.

Mr. Barton still remembers this incident, but has forgotten the name of the culprit, and it is quite as well that it should rest in oblivion. Though the originator of the club, Tinley Barton was only enrolled as the sixty-third member.

Mr. Barton was recently asked for an explanation of the inference, which may be drawn from the records of the sport from 1845 to 1847, that the majority of the beaglers of that period were fine-weather sportsmen. There are numerous entries to this effect :—" Heavy rain ; no one at the " meet "—" Heavy rain ; only three members present." And this sometimes after a long stop by frost, when beaglers might be expected to be keen to go out to make up for lost time. His answer to this question was, " That " many of the members did not care to pay for driving to the meet on a wet " day, unless there was a prospect of a lunch afterwards." In the early days of the R.R.B. a good lunch was a frequent institution, which must have been detrimental to sport.

Mr. Barton is one of the few original members of the R.R.B. now living, and still takes great interest in all that concerns his old pack. As beaglers, let us one and all wish health and long life to this good old friend to sport.

Christopher Rawson.

> "This was the noblest Roman of them all.
> His life was gentle; and the elements
> So mix'd in him, that Nature might stand up,
> And say to all the world, 'This was a man!'"
> *Julius Cæsar, act v, scene 5.*

This fine old sportsman and English gentleman was quite a young man when, in conjunction with T. Barton, he originated the Royal Rock Beagles. Although not the first Master of the Hounds, he was the leading spirit of the club in its earlier years, and was first Chairman of Committee. This post in those days, as has been previously explained, was one of superiority to the Master of the Hounds, and carried the responsibility and leadership in everything, except the management of the hounds in the kennel and in the field. C. Rawson took the chair at all meetings at which he was present, and presided over the annual dinners, &c. C. Rawson was mainly instrumental in forming the pack, and in obtaining the permission of the landowners and farmers to hunt the country. Many letters which have been preserved show the high opinion in which he was held by the magnates of the county.

One of the objects C. Rawson had in view when starting the R. R. B., to quote his own words, "was to afford to the young men and clerks of "Liverpool an opportunity of exercising their limbs, in fresh country air, at "a cheap cost. They had no winter games, and I am sure the running with "the beagles did them good, and was very inexpensive to them. By asking "some of the leading merchants to allow them to leave their offices at noon "on Saturdays, I believe I greatly helped in establishing the now universal "Saturday half-holiday."

C. Rawson was under thirty years of age when he accepted the responsible position of Chairman of the Royal Rock Beagle Hunt, and he felt his great responsibility so keenly that he decided to have a Chaplain to the Hunt. He therefore invited the Rev. W. Bannister, Chaplain to the Liverpool Workhouse, who was fond of sport, to accept that post. In the early days Mr. Bannister often went out with the hounds, and also attended the annual dinners to the farmers, and so good was his influence with the members, that he was able to assure Mr. Rawson "that he never heard "a single word uttered in his presence which he could regret as a clergyman." This influence is still manifest in the R. R. B., for on Mr. Bannister's resignation in 1852 it was not found necessary to continue the office, and no successor has been appointed to this day. Bad language is unknown with the R. R. B., except the moderate use of strong words allowed, on occasion, by custom and etiquette to a Master of Hounds.

If Mr. Rawson had occasion to rebuke any of the members for any act contrary to sport, or for the common fault of "hallooing to fresh hares," he always waited for an opportunity of talking to the offender in private and convincing him of his guilt. By these means he soon got his field into good order, and inculcated a set of unwritten rules for the conduct of members in the field, the good influence of which has been handed down to our own times. It is almost unheard of with the R. R. B. for the Master to have occasion to rebuke a member for unsportsmanlike conduct in the field: of course the minor offences of leaving gates open, breaking fences, or running over springing wheat in wet seasons, are dealt with by the more experienced members, who witness the transgression.

Among other accomplishments, C. Rawson was a bit of a poet, and he composed several hunting songs which he either sang or recited at the Hunt dinners. A place will be found for one or two of these effusions elsewhere.

Mr. Rawson was in the habit of inviting one or other of his business friends from Manchester to have a run with his beagles. He relates how on one occasion a German gentleman was invited, who came with alacrity. On his way from the train he called at Rawson's office, where, as it so happened, he saw one of the hounds which had been lost a day or two before, and had been brought to his office that morning. The German at once jumped to the conclusion that each sportsman took a hound out with him, and apologised for not having brought a dog. He also went on to say, that having a bad cold he feared he would be of no use, as he had *lost his scent!* Another gentleman, a Frenchman, said, after they had enjoyed a good run and a kill, "when the hare was first found it passed quite near me, "and if I'd had a gun I could have shot it and saved all that trouble!"

As head of the Hunt, C. Rawson gave great satisfaction to his fellow members. At the second annual meeting of the club a vote of thanks, in the following flattering terms, was proposed by T. A. Bushby, seconded by W. Robinson, and carried unanimously—"That the best thanks of all the "members are due to C. Rawson, for his constant attention to all connected "with the Hunt, without which we never should have reached the perfection "we are now in."

It is worthy of note that, although the rule for the election of Master provided for election by the committee, when Mr. Rawson was elected in 1848 it was by resolution of the club at the annual meeting, and he was then styled "Master of the Hunt"; whereas T. Barton was always mentioned as "Master of the Hounds." No chairman was appointed that year, but in the following year V. A. King was made Chairman, and C. Rawson Master of the Hounds.

At the beginning of the season 1851-52 C. Rawson expressed a wish to resign, as he was leaving Liverpool and could not be much with the hounds,

C. RAWSON AND HUNTSMAN (JONES).

but he was persuaded by the club to retain the mastership till the return of V. A. King, then absent in Bombay.

At the eighth annual general meeting, held August 18th, 1853, C. Rawson "regretted that the time had come that he was obliged to resign the office of Master. Now that he had left Liverpool, he was seldom able to visit these parts, and he was sure it was more for the good of the Hunt to have a Master not only resident but well known in the neighbourhood. He had great pleasure in proposing Mr. V. A. King as a gentleman suited in every respect to the honourable office of Master to the R.R.B. Hunt." This being seconded by H. Walford, was carried unanimously. V. A. King was kind enough to accept the office, and took the chair.

C. Rawson was born at Halifax, Yorkshire, November 26th, 1816, and at the age of seventeen went out to China, where he remained for five years. Soon after his return from abroad (in 1839), he came to Liverpool to engage in business. He was married in 1840, and came to reside in Rock Ferry in 1842. He was always fond of sport, and before starting the R.R.B. used to hunt with the Cheshire foxhounds, and also with the Hooton pack.

Being the moving spirit in the institution of the R. R. B. he was made the first Chairman, and on the retirement of T. Barton, became Master of the Hounds in 1848, which position he retained for five seasons. In 1852 he left Liverpool for the South of England, where he resides to this day, still keeping an unflagging interest in all that concerns his dear old pack.

It would appear that C. Rawson had given indications of leaving Liverpool for a year or two before he finally did so, as in 1848 the beaglers and a few others of his intimate friends had a beautiful picture of himself, the huntsman and hounds, painted by a celebrated artist, which picture was presented to him at a public dinner. The following account of this dinner is taken from the *Liverpool Mail*, and Mr. Rawson has kindly furnished a photograph of the picture, which he still values as one of his most cherished possessions.

The re-production of the photograph on the opposite page will be of intense interest to present-day beaglers, as it is practically a representation of the first pack of hounds formed by the R. R. B. The picture was painted by Herr Trautschaw, the scene being laid at Thurstaston, and the hounds each standing for its likeness. The pack ran about $14\frac{1}{2}$ inches.

Mr. Rawson appears on the left of the picture, with his curved horn and baldric well in view : the other figure is that of the famous huntsman, Jones, with his leaping pole. The hound leaping up at Rawson's hand is Charity, and that on the extreme left is Trumpeter. The three hounds in the foreground are Forester (left), Dairymaid (centre), and Bounty, and the hound on the right, looking at them, is the noted Finder. The hound sitting above Forester's back is Beauty, with Hero just in front of her, but indistinct, while Blossom's head covers Hero and his stern touches Rawson's coat.

The white-breasted hound under Jones' right elbow is Handy, and the two above Finder are Daisy and Governess, the latter looking up at Jones. The hound in the extreme right background is Merry, stooping to Tearboy, whose head just appears in the picture.

> "Howsl have thought of this, and of these times,
> I shall recount hereafter; for this present,
> I would not, so with love I might entreat you,
> Be any further moved."
>
> *Julius Cæsar*, act i, scene 2.

Extract from "*Liverpool Mail*," *Saturday, May 6th, 1848.*

On Friday evening a public dinner, given by the friends of Christopher Rawson, Esq., took place at the Royal Rock Hotel, Rock Ferry, as a testimonial of respect to Mr. Rawson, prior to his leaving the neighbourhood.

About eighty gentlemen were present, and at the request of the committee, the Rev. T. Redhead took the chair, the vice chairs being occupied by T. Littledale, Esq., and Robert Christie, Junr., Esq. Among the company were the Rev. Mr. Hassall, of St. John the Baptist's, Toxteth Park;

Mr. J. W. Wright,	Mr. C. Woodward,	Captain Richardson,
,, R. J. Tinley,	,, W. Bowman,	Mr. T. Shaw (Arrow Hall),
,, James Tyrer,	,, W. Hayes,	,, F. Peel,
,, W. Tobin,	,, H. Jenkins,	,, W. Todd-Naylor,
,, T. A. Bushby,	,, Jos. Haselden,	,, J. De Winton,
,, J. W. Harden,	,, Henry Aspinall,	,, W. Harrison,
,, Alfred Walford,	,, S. Kearsley,	,, W. G. Barton,
,, Henry Walford,	,, W. H. Tobin,	,, Robert Alexander, &c.

After the cloth had been withdrawn, and the "Non nobis Domine" sung, the Chairman proposed the usual loyal toasts of the period:—The Queen, Prince Albert, The Dowager Queen Adelaide, &c.

The Rev. Mr. Hassall, of Toxteth Park, responded to the toast of The Bishop and Clergy of the diocese. After a few preliminary observations, he said that it was quite unnecessary for him to refer to the former Bishop of the diocese, and perhaps the excellent gentleman who had so lately come amongst them, and who now so worthily adorned the episcopate, was not at present so well known to the people of this neighbourhood, still he (Mr. Hassall) could assure them that his Lordship was a man remarkable for piety and virtue. (Applause.) With reference to the clergy, he could state that it was always their aim to stand well with their brethren of the laity. This, indeed, ought to be the wish of the clergy after the handsome manner in which the laity had come forward in support of the Church; for he saw around him a goodly band of athletic sons of the Church, who to his (Mr. Hassall's) certain knowledge had come forward in support of the Church, and in her defence would fight manfully for her, if the clergy were not unmindful of her faithful sons. (Applause.) Besides these, and Mr. Littledale, the Vice-chairman, no one was more zealous in her support than his friend, Mr. Rawson, on his left. (Loud applause.) The gentleman who had to propose the toast of the evening would excuse him if he (Mr. Hassall) said that the name Rawson was well known on the other side of the water, in Toxteth Park, as well as on that, the Cheshire side of the Mersey. Both father and son were as well known on one side as on the other, for they were remarkable for their unostentatious charity, and the old-fashioned sort of hospitality, which brought around them a numerous band of friends in that neighbourhood. (Loud applause.) All present were imbued with a feeling of deep regret at their leaving the neighbourhood, in which he (Mr. Hassall) could well sympathize, for although on the Liverpool side the son had succeeded the father, they had not yet found the place of that son had been filled up. (Loud applause.)

Mr. Henry Walford acknowledged the toast on behalf of the navy.

The Chairman then said:—Gentlemen, I rise with mingled feelings of emotion, to discharge a duty now devolving upon me, which ought to have been entrusted to abler and better hands. If I possessed the fluency and eloquence of an orator, I could not hope to do more than justice to him whose name I am about to introduce to your notice. But, gentlemen, I do possess one qualification in which I will yield to no man present, and that is the extent to which I carry my respect for him whom we honour to-night. Gentlemen, if I were to adopt the language of fulsome or exaggerated praise, our guest would be the first to be offended at its introduction; but I may say, and the assertion will meet with the approval of all, that in his removal to another locality, we are sustaining a public, I had almost said an irreparable, loss. Gentlemen, were I to make any distinction among his many claims to our respect, I should hardly know where to begin—whether to speak of his social qualifications, or of those public duties he has discharged in so admirable a manner; but, gentlemen, I shall strike a chord which will vibrate in every heart, when I thank him earnestly, thank him on your and my own behalf, for his able and energetic services in promoting such manly English amusements and pursuits, which, while they brace and improve the physical, never degrade the moral man. Gentlemen, I am in an assembly of British merchants, men whose words are deeds, and whose deeds are unimpeachable; yet I may say that it has seldom fallen to the lot of many to occupy the position of our guest. Malvolio says, " Some men are born to greatness, some achieve greatness, some have greatness thrust upon them." It rarely happens that the same individual is the possessor of these three contingent possibilities. But nature has made our friend one of her own true gentlemen; his birthright, his own active, energetic perseverance has placed him in the foremost rank of competitors for commercial renown; and you have shown him to-night that there are proud epochs in a man's history, when the true greatness of universal respect is thrust upon him. Gentlemen, we know our friend not only as our valued neighbour of Rock Ferry, but as the unwearied advocate of a measure for carrying the "cup which cheers but not inebriates" into our streets and alleys at minimum cost. We know him, not only as the leader of his musical pack, following them through brake and brier, flood and field, but also as the merchant of Liverpool and of London; as a man whose name is known, and not only known but respected in two hemispheres. Gentlemen, I repeat, his departure is a loss, all but irreparable. We shall feel daily the absence of one who, never taking from business that time which it requires, nor ever giving to pleasure that which ought to be devoted to duty, has taught our youth that moderate recreation, simple pleasures, and honourable gratification are quite compatible with attaining to an enviable position and reputation in business, and also to have cheerful domestic retirement from its bustle and anxieties. But I will not, at this hour, detain you further than to ask you, in drinking this toast, to do him every honour, and let him see that he departs from us with every mark of esteem and affection in our power to bestow. Gentlemen, I beg to propose the health, long life, and happiness of our guest, Christopher Rawson.

After the applause had subsided, Mr. Rawson rose and said:—Gentlemen, the most kind and eulogistic manner in which the Chairman has proposed my health, and the warm and enthusiastic reception you have given it, have touched a chord in my heart which renders me even more inefficient than usual in expressing my deep sense of your kindness. But, gentlemen, be assured of this, that though unable adequately to convey to you my gratitude, the feeling is there, and so long as this heart is allowed to beat, so long will the remembrance of this day be indelibly stamped upon it. Gentlemen, I must candidly and openly confess (and it is no mock humility which induces me to say so), that I feel a sort of shame in receiving the high and distinguished honour you now confer upon me. I have done so little to merit it at your hands, that it seems as if I were appropriating a compliment which ought never to belong to me. I cannot boast of any great or public acts to win your approbation. Beyond the immediate circle of my friends my name even is unknown, and I can but feel that this great and undeserved compliment is owing, not to my own merit, but to the warmth of your own hearts. You must have known and felt how gratifying so public a demonstration of your kindly feelings would be; what a lasting subject of delightful and proud recollection it would ever afford; and without weighing the merits of the receiver, your kind hearts dictated the compliment. This idea, gentlemen, only renders it more gratifying, for I read in the events of this evening, and above all in the right hearty greeting with which you received my health, I read it, I say, with pride and pleasure, that though I cannot boast of public services, I have so conducted myself in private life as to win your good opinion and esteem, an esteem which though I have done little to merit, at least I have done nothing to forfeit. Gentlemen, it is now hardly eight years since I came to Liverpool, unknown to all, and without one friend in this great Metropolis of the North. Could I dream that I should so soon be able to boast of seeing myself surrounded by so many warm and valued ones as I behold on this occasion? Gentlemen, be assured that no time, no distance, and no circumstances, prosperous or adverse, can efface the remembrance of your kindness this evening. There is not one present of whom I shall not have some agreeable moments to remind me. With some I have engaged in public, with others in the whirl of private business. With many I have shared the healthful sports of the field, or the still more pleasing delight of social intimacy; and I say to all, that the distinguished honour you have conferred upon me will but make me more anxious so to conduct myself in future years, as never to give you cause for being ashamed of having this evening given me so public a mark of your regard and esteem. It needed not this compliment to ensure the remembrance of such friends, and deeply do I regret being obliged to leave those I esteem so highly. Gentlemen, most warmly and heartily I thank you. May every blessing, this and a future world can give, be yours; and believe, that one of my greatest pleasures will be to hear and know that you, my kind and valued friends, are happy. May God bless you all.

After the toasts of the Chairman and the Ladies, the Landlords of Wirral was the next toast, given by the Vice-Chairman, Mr. Thomas Littledale, and responded to by John R. Shaw, Esq., of Arrowe Hall, who concluded by proposing, "Continued success to the Royal Rock Beagles," and assured the members of the Hunt whom he saw around him that he, as one of the landowners of Wirral, would always feel great pleasure to see them cross his land. This toast having been received with great cheering, was replied to by Mr. Alfred Walford, on behalf of the members of the Hunt.

Robert Christie, Jun., then rose and presented Mr. Rawson with a splendid picture in testimony of the high opinion entertained of that gentleman by his friends. In the course of the discharge of that duty he said, My dear Rawson, the pleasing duty has been most kindly assigned me of presenting to you on this occasion, in the name of those assembled, and of many other friends unable to be with us this evening, a testimonial of regard at parting. I am not sufficient connoisseur to point out its merits or defects. It is before you for judgment, and whatever the verdict I feel assured that you will take the will for the deed. Perhaps as years roll on, a peep at that bright sky, Old Finder, Trumpeter, Tearbox, or other special favourites, coupled with thoughts of "Auld lang syne," may chase dull care away, and cause you to rejoice that such a souvenir of happy days is near you, and will continue to your family as a pleasing proof of the high estimation in which we hold you. We know you as a zealous Mason and a friendly brother, but remember that ours is the R.R.B. or grand central lodge, and that nowhere will you find more true fraternity than with us. I have more cause to regret your departure than many, but, trusting it is to your advantage, will not selfishly regret, but say most heartily with all around us, God bless you. (Applause.)

Mr. Rawson rose to reply, and said:—Mr. Christie and gentlemen of the Royal Rock Beagles, the great and highly appreciated compliment you pay me, in presenting me with the picture of our little pack, would in any case be a most flattering testimonial, but when presented to me in this public manner, and with such kind expressions as I have just heard, it is painfully gratifying—painful, as being a farewell gift preceding my departure from among you, but deeply gratifying, as giving proof of the warm and friendly feelings entertained towards me. Gentlemen, the testimonial, with which you have just honoured me, will long, very long, I hope, be an heirloom in my family. To that picture I can point, and show my sons, and, I trust, my sons' sons, that their father received that proof of the esteem and regard of his Liverpool friends; and teach them the valuable lesson, that the strong and earnest wish to do right will enable the most humble individuals to obtain the good opinion of their fellow-townsmen. Gentlemen, however I may have failed in practice, this has been my earnest endeavour, and that you appreciate that intention I have a sufficient proof this day. For this flattering token of your esteem, I am most grateful. It will often remind me of the happy days and much innocent and healthful amusement, but, above all, it will remind me of the kind and excellent friends who enjoyed those pleasures with me. If, gentlemen, I have been instrumental in establishing in this neighbourhood a sport which has created so much enjoyment and good fellowship, believe me, I have been amply and fully repaid, for I have to thank the Rock Ferry Hunt, not only for many days of pleasure, but I am also indebted to it for many friends now around me, with whom, without such a rallying point, I might never have become acquainted. Gentlemen, with most cordial and heart-felt gratitude, I thank you. May the Hunt long continue prosperous and flourishing, and as creative of good and friendly feeling as it has ever been. I shall never look upon that flattering testimony of your good opinion without remembering you whose gift it is, and whose friendship I trust through life to retain. (Loud applause.)

The next toast was Mrs. Rawson; and after some other toasts, the proceedings terminated.

C. Rawson as Volunteer.

"That in the captain's but a choleric word
Which in the soldier is flat blasphemy."
Measure for Measure, act ii, scene 2.

Though not able to claim the distinction of being the promoter of the Volunteer force as it at present exists, C. Rawson may lay claim to being one of the originators of the movement, as a few years before the formation of the force he and others had brought the subject before the notice of the

Government of the day. The following is an extract from the *Liverpool Daily Post*, of 22nd April, 1881:—

OUR VOLUNTEERS: THEIR ORIGIN AND DEVELOPMENT.

The meeting of Volunteers at Brighton, and the smaller gathering at Aintree during this holiday season, naturally call for reference in this city, where, we are proud to say, the Volunteer instinct had its first developments as an active principle. . . . . . In years more recent, however, what the vitality of the nation means in making conscription unnecessary, was shown prior to the organization of the Volunteer force. The second epoch, as it may be termed, began so long ago as 1848, and what it was may be best stated in the words of one who had much to do with it. Christopher Rawson, whose name will bring to recollection old memories of Liverpool, but who still lives (and whose son,* by the way, is Captain of H.M.S. "Minotaur"), has written, under date of March 30th, to this effect:—

"I have hunted up my Volunteer reminiscences, and have sent you herewith a copy of the circular relating to the meeting at my office in 1848. The offer of raising the corps, entirely at our own expense, arms and everything, was sent by me as Chairman, through the Mayor of Liverpool; and the reply, refusing our services, came through the same channel. I, unfortunately, have no copy of this correspondence, but I have no doubt it could be found among the archives of the Liverpool Town Hall, as well as at Whitehall. Four years later, Walpole refused a similar offer from Surrey, on the ground of its injuring his Militia Bill, as you will see by the letter I have copied, and of which I have the original. I am certain our Cook Street meeting was the first that was held on the subject, and that ours was the first offer made. We all shut up after the Government refused, and very properly, I think. The origin of our offer was the unprotected state of Liverpool, at the time of the Chartist scare, when you and other friends formed my company of special constables, and drilled under Captain Richardson." Winding up, this grand old Liverpool man says, "Does not this recall some glorious old days?" The reminiscences are certainly exhilarating.

Liverpool has been the birthplace and the nursery of what we call the volunteer movement; but, as we have indicated, it is necessary to remember that we have men among us who were volunteers when such men as Colonel Bousfield were boys. The Colonel of the 1st L.R.V. and his brother-in-law (Colonel Steble) are dear to all volunteers, but before them there were in the field equally good men, and men who have remained active volunteers. Among these we would mention Colonel Tilney, who has perhaps done more in Liverpool for the cause than any other man, in his own quiet way. But in this relationship personal references would be invidious, and we close with the reference to the Cook Street meeting of 1848, to which we have referred. It is as follows:—

"At a meeting held at Mr. Rawson's office, 10, Cook Street, on Monday, the 13th March, 1848, the following gentlemen were appointed as a preliminary committee of the proposed Liverpool Volunteer Rifle Corps:

T. B. Lloyd,	J. Campbell,	H. Perkins,	A. Shand,
R. Neilson,	B. E. Melhuish,	R. Harvey,	J. Higson,
C. Rawson,	Henry Royds,	W. Foster,	R. J. Tinley (now
B. Littledale,	H. Molyneux,	W. Tobin,	Lieut.-Col. Tilney,
T. A. Bushby,	H. Scott,	W. Lyon,	5th L.R.V.),
T. B. Hughes,	J. Pownall,	C. R. Cameron,	J. E. Naylor,

* Now Admiral Rawson.

The next meeting will be held on Monday next, the 20th instant, at 2 o'clock, at the above office. Signed, C. RAWSON, Chairman."

The History of the Volunteer Movement and its Promoters, by Sir Duncan Macdougall, page 60, says:—

Since the publication of the first edition, I have been placed in possession of the following information, by which it appears that Mr. C. Rawson was a prominent promoter of the Volunteer movement. On the 13th March, 1848, a meeting was held at the office of Mr. Rawson in Liverpool, when it was proposed to form a Volunteer Rifle Corps, and Messrs. Lloyd, Littledale, Neilson, Campbell, and Rawson, together with twenty other influential gentlemen of the city, formed themselves into a committee for the purpose of carrying it out, but, unfortunately the Government of that day gave no encouragement to the proposition.

In 1852 Mr. Rawson most zealously exerted himself in endeavouring to get up a Surrey Volunteer Rifle Corps, and on the 12th March of that year a meeting was held at Walton-on-Thames on the subject of the formation of the proposed corps. To the offer of service, the following reply was received from the Home Office.

"Whitehall, 2nd April, 1852.

"Sir,—Mr. Walpole directs us to inform you, in reply to your letter of the 1st instant, that the principles by which he has been guided with regard to the Volunteer Corps, have had respect to the nature of the bill he has introduced for the raising of the Militia, which being based on voluntary enlistment in the first instance, and failing that, on the ballot, would be materially impaired by a general adoption of volunteer corps, as in the first instance it is to be expected, that many of the volunteers for the Militia would be found among those for the Volunteer corps; and in the event of its being necessary to have recourse to the ballot, the burden of that measure would be considerably increased by the exemption of volunteers from its operation.

"These reasons he thinks you will on reflection admit as fully justifying the course he has laid down for his guidance on the subject; at the same time, he highly appreciates the zeal and spirit which has been manifested in many instances by those who, like yourself, have come forward to offer their services to the Government, which, in the event of the failing of the measure which his sense of duty to the State has led him to introduce, he would be glad to avail himself of, though for the above reasons he cannot recommend for the present acceptance of the Government. I have the honour to be, &c.,

Signed, G. A. PERCIVAL."

The famous Chartist riots appear to have been the mainspring of C. Rawson's action, in striving to promote a volunteer force. He had been in command of a company of special constables during the riots in 1848, and at the dinner given to C. Rawson by the R.R.B., when the National Anthem was sung, the words "frustrate their knavish tricks" were altered to "frustrate their Chartist tricks." In the list of names forming the committee given in the above extract, the honoured names of several noted old beaglers figure conspicuously, showing that beaglers were then (as they now are) ready for anything, from "pitch-and-toss to manslaughter."

Vincent Ashfield King.

"No man alive can love, in such a sort,
The thing he means to kill, more excellently."
                    Troilus and Cressida, act iv, scene 1.

"Ould King" (as he loved to call himself) is undoubtedly the most striking figure in connection with the Royal Rock Beagles. He was a prominent member in the inauguration of the pack, and took the lead at a very early date in the history of the Hunt, retaining the mastership from 1853 till his death in 1882, a period of thirty seasons.

V. A. King was one of the first members in 1845, a committee-man in 1846, chairman from 1849 to 1852, and then master till 1882, a total active membership of thirty-seven years. Our present senior member (T. Banner Newton) must remain with us till 1897 to equal this record; and among our honorary life members we have two well-known gentlemen, J. B. Morgan and J. A. Smith, who, in this year of jubilee, have been thirty-eight years connected with the Hunt, though not of late as active members.

V. A. King, from his connection and influence with the landowners in the northern part of Wirral, was of immense assistance to the promoters of the R.R.B. Hunt in inaugurating the pack, and obtaining the permission of the landowners and farmers to hunt the country. His father, George King, of Higher Bebington Hall, and his uncle, the Rev. Joshua King, Rector of Woodchurch, were the first landowners, after the Rev. R. M. Feilden, of Bebington, to give their consent.

The first mention of V. A. King in the records of the Hunt is that he was the 80th enrolled member; and that on October 28th, 1846, he was elected a member of the Committee, of which he became Chairman at the annual meeting in 1849. Up to this time V. A. King did not take an active share in the management of the Hunt, nor does he appear to have attended any of the Committee meetings, no doubt owing to his absence in Bombay; but after he was made Chairman, he had the Committee meetings at his office, and was always present, except during his periodical trips to India. During one of these absences the Master, C. Rawson, wished to resign, but was prevailed upon to retain the office till the return of V. A. King.

At the 8th annual general meeting, 18th August, 1853, V. A. King was unanimously elected Master ("and a right good master too"), and no Chairman of Committee was appointed after this date, but henceforth the Master was the head of the Hunt. For the two following seasons he was re-elected Master, but here the minute book of the club comes to an end, and no further record of the proceedings is extant. Tradition, however, says, that at the annual meetings the worthy Secretary, J. B. Morgan, was wont to say, "Our next business is the election of Master," when "Ould King" would burst in with: "Hold your blather; I'm master here." All that is definitely known is, that the oldest of the present beaglers found V. A. King the Master, and Master he remained to the day of his death.

During one of the periodical visits of the hounds to Llanfyllyn, at the invitation of Squire Dugdale, which visits were always of a merry and somewhat larky order, the members present took upon themselves to depose the Master, V. A. King, and elected our old and popular member, John Gibbons, in his place. The next day at the meet, Gibbons was invested by one of the young ladies with a toy tin horn, and he remained Master for a period of one hour, when he subsided into his proper place, and V. A. King resumed his duties with acclamation.

When King was made a member of the Committee he caused a careful record of runs to be kept by the Secretary in the Sport Book, and when he was appointed Chairman he kept the record in his own handwriting up to the end of 1856, with a break of two seasons when absent in India. It is characteristic of the man, that the first mention of himself in the Sport Book reads, "V. A. King was the only member out, in consequence of the rain." He was always noted for his indifference to the inclemency of the weather, and once at a meet at Llanfyllyn when, just as we were starting from the hotel, the rain came down in torrents, a luckless member said, "I say, "Master, surely you're not going to start in this rain?" The Master looked him over from head to foot and slowly back again for a moment or two, then in a withering tone, but with a friendly twinkle in his eye, retorted, "I'm not "aware, sir, that the hounds can't hunt when it's raining." As a matter of fact the hounds this time did not hunt, as the weather was so infernal, that we all went home wet to the skin, and without even finding a hare.

In the early days of the R.R.B., Woodchurch was a very frequent and favourite meet. Here V. A. King's uncle was Rector, and invariably welcomed the beaglers most hospitably, providing a capital lunch, and a sure find afterwards. On these occasions, during V. A. King's absence in Bombay, he was always remembered by the toast of his "health and success." The first meet at Woodchurch after his return was cancelled, on account of the death of Mrs. King, wife of the Rector. V. A. King records, 6th October, 1849:—

Woodchurch, 2 p.m. No meet, in consequence of the much-lamented death of Mrs. King. This is a kind sympathy on the part of the members, which here I cannot refrain from gratefully acknowledging.

October 20th, 1849, King writes:—

As this is the first time I have been out after an absence of two seasons, I may be permitted to bear testimony to the great improvement in the pack. The quick and sporting manner in which the hounds now do their work, in fact without need of the huntsman, is very striking.

And March 30th, 1850: -

Thus ended the season of 1849/1850, in which we have enjoyed most excellent sport, and, to add to this enjoyment, there has not been the slightest unpleasantness or ill-feeling among any of the members, for on the contrary there has been the best and kindest feeling among all of us.

The merciful feeling which King entertained for hares, and indeed for all animals, and which was so strongly marked in the later years of his mastership, can be traced in his records, as the following examples will show :—

And then, I almost regret to say, this sporting hare met her death from the hounds.
Found again, and had a beautiful run of an hour. Whipped off to save her life. This was one of the best runs of the season ; scent good and steady, and the pack never off it.

On this occasion two members only were out, which probably accounts for mercy prevailing over sport.

" During the run old Merryman broke his leg, and the poor old hound had to be destroyed. He met an honourable death where he should do, on the field."

As Master, King has been known to take the hounds away from a spot where he alone has seen a beaten hare go to ground, without saying anything about it to the more blood-thirsty sportsmen.

> "A proper man.
> Indeed, he is so : I repent me much
> That so I harried him."
> *Antony and Cleopatra, act iii, scene 3.*

When the Wirral Harriers started in 1868, a somewhat acrimonious correspondence (reference to which will be found on a previous page) passed between V. A. King, as Master of the Beagles, and J. R. Court, as Master of the Harriers. The tone of this correspondence on the part of the harriers was little calculated to conciliate a man of our Master's autocratic temperament. The idea of considering his beagles inferior to harriers would rouse all the combative spirit in his composition ; and we cannot be surprised that, for all the remainder of his life, he had a bitter feeling towards the harriers, although he had many warm and personal friends among their members.

A young woman, who lived at a farm-house near Raby, relates that, when she was a child playing about the roads, Colonel King several times said to her in passing : " Look here, my lass ! whenever you see any of them "harrier chaps passing this way, just you peg stones at 'em."

In later years his animosity softened down a little, but he never quite forgave their intrusion into his country. Some of the beaglers were also members of the harriers, and this was somewhat hurting to his feelings. The writer frequently, when riding homewards from hunting with the harriers on a Saturday afternoon, looked in to have tea with the beaglers at their " pub," when old King would invariably bawl out—" Hillo ! here's one of them " harrier fellers : turn him out. Oh ! it's only old Caine, we'll let him in ; " he's a good beagler after all."

V. A. King as Beagler.

"Now to our mountain sport ; up to yon hill ;
Your legs are young ; I'll tread these flats."
Cymbeline, act iii, scene 3.

As a beagler " Ould King " was perfect, and a model to us all. In his young days he was a good runner and kept well up with the hounds ; but those of the present members of the club, who had the inestimable advantage of being beaglers when he was Master, can only remember him as practically an old man, though one who kept up his stamina to the last, and tramped about the fields in a way which tired out many a youngster. His knowledge of the etiquette of sport was complete, and his word was law in all matters connected with the Hunt. His ready tact smoothed all difficulties that might arise with farmers or shooting men ; in fact, no one could resist his persuasive eloquence.

In the later years of his life, his beagles (and he could, without offence, call them " his beagles," including in that term not only the hounds but all the members as well) held the first place in his heart, and during the hunting season he would look forward to Wednesdays and Saturdays as his red-letter days. There can be no doubt that intense enjoyment began for "ould King" on Saturdays, from the time that he donned his familiar old green coat and horn, his check knickerbockers and thick boots, to proceed down to the Woodside landing-stage to welcome his beaglers, and was sustained to the time when he wished the last good night to the happy beaglers he entertained at dinner.

Who can forget the way in which our Master met the 12 o'clock boat from Liverpool ? On the approach of the boat to the Woodside stage, the beaglers on board gathered in a knot at the gangway, surrounded by a gaping crowd of the more curious passengers, and beheld their Master, clad in all his panoply of the chase, without an overcoat, standing in an attitude similar to that in his portrait, and with much the same expression on his face. When the boat arrived within hailing distance, he would call out —" Eh ! lads, I'm " that glad to see you "; to which our response would be, " Good morning, " Master." If there was any delay in mooring the boat, the pause became somewhat embarrassing, which the Master would relieve by some quip at the expense of J. B. Morgan or J. Gibbons, or one or other of his cronies.

As we landed from the boat, he would shake hands with each one of us as we came up the gangway, and march up with us, talking loudly in pleasant chaff, to watch us eat a sandwich at the hotel. Then ensconcing himself in the far corner inside the 'bus, where followed him the older members, such as Morgan, Roper, Green, Williamson, Gibbons, Newton, Stevenson, &c., he would hold them all well entertained, and smothered in tobacco smoke, during the drive to the meet. Arrived, the Master would slowly extricate himself from the bus, and greet the huntsman and hounds, the latter surrounding him, and fawning upon him as if they loved him : as, no doubt, they did. After "throwing off," he would tramp about with the hounds until they "found" and went merrily away, when he would exclaim, "There, my job's done. I've found you a hare ; now make the best of it." Settling himself down to " shanking it " after the hounds, although he never ran, somehow or other he managed to be about the right place, and saw most of the sport. The merry music of the pack in the distance, invariably drew from him the exclamation, " Oucks ! my little dawgs."

As evening drew on he would say, " Here ! I'm off to a sure find," and wend his way to the pub. (the beaglers' name for the house where tea is prepared) to enjoy his tea and " methody cream." Here, if sport had been fair, he would be supremely happy, rendering all around him equally so, with his jovial wit and sprightly badinage : and when the time of departure arrived he would say to the waitress—" Eh ! my lass, here's a shilling for my tea, " and sixpence for my gin, and sixpence for yourself ; and you're better worth " it than the gin is :" the girl, meanwhile, standing by wreathed in smiles and blushes.

On Saturday evenings, during the hunting season, it was the Master's custom to have three or four beaglers to dinner. Each member received an invitation once every season, the fortunate committee more often. The invitation was given verbally on the previous Saturday, if the intended diner was out, otherwise he received a note on the following Tuesday. The invitation was always given thus :—" Beagler —— will you do me the honour to " worry a gowse at my house next Saturday ?" No one ever declined this invitation who could by any possibility accept it. The charm of his hospitality was so delightful ; the welcome all beaglers received from Mrs. and Miss King (who idolized the husband and father, and entered heartily into all his pleasures) so cordial ; the home surroundings so beautiful, with the old oak furniture, old silver, and Indian curios ; the *camaraderie* of the beaglers so inspiriting—that an evening spent thus was simply fascinating, and one could only wish it to be repeated every Saturday night for the remainder of life. The great features of the dinner were, a good strong Indian curry with "Bombay ducks," and a noble roast goose, washed down with Bombay beer, a special brew of Allsopp which had been the voyage to India and back, thereby improving its flavour and quality. This beer was passed round the table in a famous old loving cup. After drawing the corks of two bottles, and pouring the contents into the cup, King would march round the table to the beagler selected for the honour of escorting Mrs. King in to dinner, and address him with, " Here's your good health ;" proceeding, after drinking from the cup, with " May your shadow never grow less :" this beagler would then respond in like manner, take a good pull at the beer, and hand the cup round to the others.

The Master always used the old Winchester grace :—

  Before dinner : *" Benedictus—Benedicat."*
  After dinner : *" Benedicto — Benedicatur."*

Our noble old Master made a pleasant picture, seated at the head of his dinner table. On these occasions he sported a handsome and genuinely old-fashioned rig-out, the following description of which may happily recall it to the remembrance of the beaglers who rejoiced in those good old days :— A short jacket of black velvet, with knickerbockers of the same, shoes with silver buckles, and red stockings with a red waistcoat, or black stockings with a white waistcoat, and, to crown all, a beautiful point lace neck-tie with hanging ends.

During the course of his long connection with the R.R.B., King was the recipient of several tokens of the esteem and affection in which he was held by the members. Once (the occasion is obscure) he was presented with a silver horn ; and in December, 1851, after he had been chairman of the committee for two years only, the eve of his departure for India was seized as an opportunity for presenting him with a massive silver tankard. This tankard may be seen at Point of Ayr to this day ; it is a sporting piece, with a coursing scene of a brace of greyhounds after a hare, a scene quite opposed to our Master's own views of sport, as he cared nothing for coursing. A farewell dinner was given to King, and the Master of the R.R.B., C. Rawson, wrote him as follows :—

            London, December 27th, 1851.

My dear King,—I cannot allow the 29th to pass over without your receiving my hearty good wishes for you and yours. I do indeed truly regret that I am not one of the party who are giving you a farewell dinner on Monday, but I shall be with you in heart, and I am sure not one of those who will be present will more cordially wish your happiness than I do.

You have indeed a good firm band of friends, all deeply interested in your welfare ; and, wherever you go, you appear to carry away with you the goodwill and friendly feelings of all you meet. I have heard you "spoken of from the East" as well as from the banks of the Mersey, and always in the same terms of respect and regard.

I am not singular, therefore, in feeling towards you a deep feeling of interest and regard, and though not present at this pleasing testimony to your being a "real good fellow," on Monday, believe me no one feels and knows that you are so better than I do.

Accept my sincere and hearty good wishes for yourself and yours; may your trip prove prosperous in every way, and on your return may we have the pleasure of dubbing you our *Master*, and run many a brilliant and successful campaign under your management.

God bless you, old fellow! and believe me ever your attached friend.

C. RAWSON.

In 1866, the beaglers commissioned an artist to paint a capital picture, in oil colours, of the hounds, in the charge of Williams the huntsman, and during V. A. King's absence they hung it in his dining room without his knowledge. On the return of the family, they used the room for two days without noticing the presence of the picture. The Master was so delighted with this mark of the affection of his beaglers that he had the picture let into the oak panelling above his sideboard, where it still remains as a permanent fixture.

On the occasion of his seventieth birthday, Colonel King was presented with a portrait of his wife, by the volunteer battalion which he commanded: and the beaglers took the same opportunity to present Mrs. King with a portrait of the Master, in his beagling costume. The volunteers would fain have reversed this order, and would have dearly liked to have the Colonel painted in his uniform. The beaglers, however, were first in the field, and it was only after hearing of their intention, and after all the arrangements had been made, that the volunteers followed suit with the portrait of Mrs. King. Many of us are proud to possess an etching of the portrait of the Master, which is a speaking likeness. A reproduction faces this chapter.

On Saturday evening, the 24th January, 1880, the R.R.B. Hunt gave their annual dinner to the farmers of Wirral, and the presentation of the portrait of the Master formed a pleasing episode in the proceedings. The secretary, J. B. Morgan, had the honour of making the presentation, with a few complimentary remarks, to which the Master made the following speech in reply:—

My dear friends, I rise with mingled feelings of pleasure and regret. My feelings of pleasure are to acknowledge the charming gift which you have just made to my dear wife; my feelings of regret are because I am quite certain I cannot find words to give expression to my feelings for your kindness. I wish to make a good speech, and I much fear I shall make a bad one.

You have given a great amount of pleasure by your gift. You have given pleasure to myself, by this proof of your love and affection for me; you have given pleasure to my dear wife, by presenting to her this excellent portrait of

V. A. KING.

her husband, painted by the hand of a cunning limner, Mr. Boadle; you have given pleasure to our dear child, for in years to come this picture will recall to her memory the happy days and good sport she has so often enjoyed with the beagles in company with her dear father; and, lastly, you will give great pleasure to many dear friends, who will see the picture when they assemble round our board, where, I hope, we dispense that Christian grace of hospitality in a true and proper Christian spirit.

I have been Master of the beagles since 1849, and this is not the first time I have received from the members a token of their regard for me. In 1851, upon my departure for India, they gave me a very handsome silver mug and salver. Some years later they gave me a silver horn. Fourteen years ago, they gave me a beautiful and faithful picture of the hounds, which has been an ornament to our dining room, and a pleasure to all who see it. And now you have made to my wife this very charming gift. When I think upon these gifts, I cannot help thinking also of those many dear friends who, having a hand in them, have passed from time to eternity; and that thought gives rise to chastened feelings in my breast. I ask myself what I have done to deserve all this kindness, this affection, at your hands, and I answer—nothing. If I have done my best to show you good sport; if I have tried to have the pack in good order, all this is nothing more than is my duty to do, and I do not even deserve thanks for it; but you have given me much more than thanks.

I have much to thank God for. He has blessed me with such health and strength that now, at the age of three score years and ten, I enjoy field sports as keenly as ever I did; and few things give me greater pleasure than a good day with the beagles. I always look on Saturday, when it does not freeze, as a red-letter day. I meet you on the landing-stage, and see your happy faces; then there is the pleasant talk on the drive out to the meet; then a charming afternoon of real good sport; last, but by no means least, is the tea and "methody cream" in a sweet little village hostel; and I hope those very worthy gentlemen the teetotallers will never be able to shut up that good old English institution, the village public-house.

The pack was established in 1845, and during all the long period which has elapsed since then, there has always been the best and kindest feeling among the members. I have made many kind and dear friends among them. The little pack, in the course of these thirty-five years, has given to many young men a cheap and innocent pleasure; but it has done more than this, it has encouraged a spirit of true manliness, and I hold that true manliness is one form of religion, for sure I am that any man who has the spirit of true manliness in him will never be guilty of any low debasing sin or pleasure. I have always felt that it is a great honour to any man to be placed at the head of such a force of manliness as the members of the beagles.

All I can say more are poor words, which do not express my meaning—which do not express my feelings—which do not express my gratitude—I thank you.

Copy of a newspaper cutting from Miss King's scrap-book. Source and date unknown.

ANTIQUITIES OF CHESHIRE.—XV.

Dear Sir,—From the extract below, from the old MSS., it would appear that the old hunters of the forest made a great to-do about very little. I wonder what the daring sportsmen of the present day would think of all this fuss over the killing of such a comparatively small animal.

I am, yours truly,

E. JAMES, M.A., T.H., E.W.S., &c.

YE KING AND YE COURTE GOE HUNTYNGE.

Sailing ouer ye Mere Sea from Litherpoole, ye King didde come bye ye ferrie to Wode Syde, where some of hys friendes didde meete him, and theye didde alle goe through ye towne, uppe to Uppetowne. Woode Kirke, Stortone, and rounde aboute to hunt ye wylde beastes, that didde roame inn ye fearnes and forrestes theyre. Indeed ye King didde hunt alle oure Oueralle. Some doe call it Wirral, bye reason that att one tyme, as is sayed—

> "From Blacon Hedde to Hillburee.
> Ye swirral didde swirle from tree to tree."

And ye huntsmann was alle ready, with a goodlie pack of houndes, close bye Arrowe, where ye King and hys friendes didde alle come together; ye huntsmann with hys horn and stoute whippe, and yeladd inn hys redde coate, and ye King and hys friendes inn greene, and alle of themme with strong shoes and swathynges of leathere, to save theyre legges from tearing, forr theye didde hunt afoote, and not lyke ye Courte folk, that didde bedeck themselves in fyne cloathes, and with bigge bootes and spurres, didde take horse, soe that, should ye wylde beaste tourne uppon themme inn ye huntynge, theye monght have ye better chaunce to flee awaye from him, forr should hee have done soe, it is dreddfulle to thynke what mought have come to happe.

And ye King was sore att oddes againste ye Courte folk forr going huntynge round hys huntynge groundes, rowsynge uppe ye beastes that hadd gone into ye forrest forr reste, and forr doing alle theye coulde to spoyle ye game, that hadd been hys and hys friendes forr soe many yeares. Soe, as hath been sayed, ye King and hys friendes (beeing brave and knowing no feare) didde hunt afoote and with Bigle-houndes.

Ye Bigle is soe called from hys littelnesse; this doeth seeme strange, yette it is soe. Hee is onely aboute a foote inn hight, and hys hedde is bigge and heavy lookynge, and hee is soe deep-mouthed that hys chappes or flewes doe sometymes hang downe lyke to an ould mann's bearde. Ye jowles of one olde hounde theyre were so bigge that ye grasse didde sweepe hys flewes as hee flewe along, yette allthough hys olde chappes hadd dropped soe, ye olde fellowe was not chapp-fallen otherways, butte as brave as ever, and didde keepe on with ye others righte well.

And beeing come to ye huntynge grounde, theye soughte inn many a seate that didd seeme lykelie to suite, to gette sighte of ye game, but didde not forr a long tyme; yette still beatynge aboute, att laste theye didde starte from hys layer one wylde beaste that didde tourne back hys greate eares and flee awaye att marvellous speede. An ye reeke beeing strong and lying well, ye houndes, that doe hunt bye ye nose and not ye eye, didde give tong, and setting off after hym, theye were soone inn fulle crye. Awaye theye didde goe, with theyre heddes well downe to ye grounde, and runnynge soe close togethere that one mought spredde a sheete over themme allmoste, as was sayed. Thenne ye heartie olde King didde crye oute inn hys gruff voyce, "Well done." "pretty," "pretty," "good littel bigles," and ye like.

And ye menn didde followe after, some of ye more lythe and sinnewy leapynge ouer dykes and bushes, and keeping well uppe to ye houndes, yette not too close; other, not runnynge soe fast, didde goe gapynge aboute to find gappes, or theye didde make themme, to get thorough; and againe, some fewe, newe to ye sporte, too olde or ouer fatte, didde cutte acrosse, neare wayes bye ye gates and soe on. And these didde as welle as ye other, forr that ye beaste doeth not often goe straighte forr long, butte doeth tourne aboute againe and againe to crosse ye reeke, and soe spoyle ye traile and gette awaye from ye dogges. It was a goodlie sighte to see ye houndes goe thorough ye bushes, and howe one fellowe fell ouer another, tumbellynge oute into ye dyke, and thenne on againe. And ye menn leapynge ouer, didde some fall on ye toppe, and some on ye bottom, butte didde soone gette uppe and awaye againe. And ye huntsmann, though following hotly, didde allwayes keepe coole, and neare to ye houndes, to steady and courage themme; forr att tymes some of ye yonger dogges would gette wide awaye, and thenne didde this coole master of ye houndes gette warme, and whippe ye truantes well to teache themme better.

Nowe, although theyre were not more than, mayhappe, fifty menn, and butte some score and half houndes att moste, that didde hunt ye wylde beaste, yette after going some miles and tourning often, hee was ouretaken and done to death. Then ye whipper-inn didde whippe hym onto hys bugle and blowe a blaste till ille was blue, and hys face was redde as hys coate; and ye menn inn greene coming uppe, ye King didde allso blowe hys silver horn, lyke as hee would straightwaye blowe it straighte. And alle didde gather round ye wylde beaste, that, thanks to ye goode King and hys brave menn, is nowe att laste ouercome inn hys mightie strength, and slaine.

Thenne hys scutte was cutte off and given toe ye King as a token of ye ouercoming. And ye King didde stick hys scutte inn hys hatte, and ye yeomann didde cutte hys stick, to beare ye dead beaste awaye, forr that it was hys, bye custome, beeing killed on hys holdynge. And afterwarde, ye beaste beeing first stripped of hys hyde, and thenne stuffed with sweete herbes and ye lyke, hee was roasted whole, and ye fearmer and hys folke didde greatly rejoyce.

Such was ye ende of ye beaste of ye Uppetowne wylds that hadd plagued ye whole nighborhoode, and hadd beene hunted forr yeares, butte hadd hitherto gettan awaye. And ye King and hys friendes didd retourne greatlie rejoycing att theyre fyne sporte, and ye chronicler didde thenne come awaye.

And the name of ye beaste was H-A-R-E.

Lieut.=Col. King as Volunteer.

" I do believe,
(Statist though I am none, nor like to be)
That this will prove a war: and you shall hear
The legions, now in Gallia, sooner landed
In our not-fearing Britain, than have tidings
Of any penny tribute paid. Our countrymen
Are men more order'd, than when Julius Cæsar
Smiled at their lack of skill, but found their courage
Worthy his frowning at: their discipline
(Now mingled with their courage) will make known
To their approvers, they are people, such
That mend upon the world."

Cymbeline, act ii, scene 4.

About the year 1859 England had been roused by a scare of invasion. Napoleon III, the Emperor of the French, was suspected of assembling troops at Boulogne with the idea of a descent upon the shores of Britain. This roused the military instincts of the nation to a feverish pitch of excitement; and companies of rifle volunteers were formed all over the kingdom.

In May, 1859, the present volunteer force was originated, and amongst the earliest formed companies was the 2nd Cheshire, or Oxton Company, of which V. A. King was the promoter and first captain; his captain's commission being dated 30th August, 1859.

In a speech made by Lieut.-Col. King on an auspicious occasion, to be referred to hereafter, he says :—

I well remember, in fact, I do not think I shall ever forget, a fine morning in May, 1859, just at the time when men's minds were deeply stirred about the risks of invasion and our defenceless position. On this morning I was quietly smoking my cheroot after breakfast, when my dear neighbour, Ledward, came in, and said, with a thrilling earnestness I shall never forget, " King ! I have had a deal of talk with many upon the necessity of a volunteer movement, and we all say that you are the man to take it up in this neighbourhood." Now, although I might well have felt that I had neither the talents nor the position to take the lead in so grand a movement as this, yet I can assure you there was an earnestness, aye, a solemnity, in Ledward's manner which so impressed me, that I did not hesitate one moment, but answered him in an instant, " Well ! I will ; I will do my best." From that day I hope I have done my best. It was very soon after this that my connexion with you commenced, and how well I remember that bright July morning when we met on Oxton Common at six o'clock, in dresses of all shapes and colours, and had our first drill.

Soon after the first formation of the Oxton Company, Captain King made one of a party of volunteer officers from all parts of the country, who went up to Hythe for a week's training in rifle practice at the Hythe School of Musketry. This party consisted of forty-two officers, and seven of them were from the companies which afterwards formed the 1st Cheshire Rifle Volunteer Battalion. At least four of these seven were beaglers. Captain King went thoroughly into the details of this subject, mastering it to such an extent that he gave a course of lectures to his company and others. The *Times* devoted a whole column to a report of his first lecture, from which the following extract is redolent of the enthusiasm of our old Master :—

Our gallant lieutenant (Horner) made twenty-nine points, I only made four, and, like all blockheads, was kept in the 3rd class ; but I have the satisfaction to say, I got out of it, and am now a 2nd class man. This practice lasted from Tuesday till Saturday, and I cannot describe to you the excitement of it. It exceeded anything I ever saw. Hunting, or cricket, or boating is nothing to it. I felt when I saw it, that there was no mistake about the volunteer movement ; and there is no reason why there should not be the same excitement, when the Cheshire companies march from their parade ground for ball practice, as there was at the barrack-yard of Hythe.

In the course of an important leading article in the same issue, the *Times* says :—

Captain King, of the Cheshire Rifles, has done the State some service in telling millions of his fellow-countrymen what is really done at Hythe. His picture is like an interior by some old Dutch cabinet painter,- precise, hard, and clear, with an attention to details which is refreshing without being pre-Raphaelite.

In due time, when the companies of Wirral had mastered their company drill, it became necessary to form them into a battalion. Captain King was unanimously chosen to take the command, his lieutenant-colonel's commission being dated 24th October, 1860. This occasion was seized by the Oxton company to present their late captain with a testimonial, consisting of an address and a handsome silver candelabrum, which was ornamented at its base with portrait figures of three members of the company—Ensign Cunningham and Privates Kingcome and Wilmot, the first two of whom were also well-known beaglers. Part of Colonel King's speech in reply to the address has been given above, and the further extract, as follows, will perhaps be of interest as conveying the first impressions of an active participator in the formation of the volunteer force of the country, given at a time when the facts must have been green in his memory. A great deal of controversy has since arisen, as to the individual or individuals to whom the honour of having originated the movement is due.

As the occasion appears to call for it, allow me to say a few words upon the start of the volunteer movement, some eighteen months ago. We have heard of various claimants to the honour of being the originators of this glorious movement, which has swept as a torrent over the country. Now, far be it from me to disparage the exertions and merits of anyone; but, when a man claims to be the originator of this movement, I cannot help thinking he must have a fair opinion of himself. No! depend upon it, God gives to few, to very few men, the mental power of directing the mind of a great nation. This is far too grand, too dangerous a gift to be given to many. According to my opinion, the originator of this great volunteer movement was the will, the mind, of a great and free people—the English nation. That I may have been an humble instrument, in this part of the country, perhaps it would be mock modesty in me to deny. I often feel that in the higher rank which I now hold I shall never have the happiness, the delight, I had in the command of the Second Cheshire. I can assure you, what helps to reconcile me to the loss of my command of you, is the knowledge that I leave you with three gentlemen as officers who, I am certain, will all do their duty to the very best of their ability; and I can pay them no higher compliment, when I say they are worthy to command the Second Cheshire.

These gentlemen were three good beaglers—Captain Horner, Lieutenant Roper, and Ensign Cunningham.

As lieutenant-colonel, King was a first-rate officer in every respect. He was a martinet as regards discipline, and although he unbent with his men in camp, and on social occasions when off duty, he was very strict when on duty, but with such ready tact that he was universally beloved and respected in his regiment. He understood his business thoroughly in all departments, and was a most excellent drill, working his battalion up to a first-rate pitch of efficiency. King was a very liberal commanding officer as regards the expenses of the corps. He gave handsomely to the prize funds of the battalion and of the county meetings, taking great interest in the shooting of his men. The expenses of the annual camp at Hooton, over and above the Government grant and the small shares contributed by the men, were always borne by the commanding officer.

It was in June, 1863, that the first summer camp was established at Hooton. Very good work was put in there in the way of drill and discipline, and also much enjoyment and healthful pastime fell to the lot of those volunteers fortunate enough to attend the camp. Many pleasant memories of the "camp weeks" exist in the breasts of those who formed the camps in Colonel King's time, and are still retailed to willing ears as occasion arises.

As the seventieth birthday of Colonel King approached, it was strongly felt in the two institutions with which he was so intimately associated, and whose existence was so peculiarly identified with his own, that the epoch should be marked in some suitable manner. It need hardly be pointed out that these two institutions were the Royal Rock Beagle Hunt and the 1st Cheshire Rifle Volunteers. The beaglers wished to present a portrait of their Master in his hunting rig-out, and the volunteers wished to present a portrait of their Colonel in full uniform. There was some sharp skirmishing over this matter, but the beaglers held their ground, being backed up by some good reasoning. It was felt that "old King" had been for thirty-five years a beagler, and barely twenty-one a volunteer; that the prime of his life had been passed with the beagles, and that he was, heart and soul, wrapped up in them. The volunteers therefore gracefully retreated and took up fresh ground. They decided to make the gift complete, and present to their beloved colonel a portrait of his wife. This was carried out on the 23rd Jan., 1880, the night before the beaglers made their presentation. Mr. Duncan Graham occupied the chair at the meeting, and made the presentation on behalf of the battalion. Colonel King replied in the following speech :—

My dear brother Volunteers,—It appears to me that words are weak, in fact powerless, when we want to express feelings and affections. These, if I may so speak, are too delicate, too refined, too exquisite, to be expressed in mere words. I feel this strongly at the present moment. I want words to express what I feel by the kind sentiments which have just been expressed by Mr. Duncan Graham to my dear wife and to myself; and I want words to express what I feel for this very exquisite gift. All I can say is comprised in three words, weak as they are, I thank you! But I have not yet expressed all my thanks. Your kind present could not have been in a more charming or more grateful form to me than the one you have chosen in the portrait of as dear, as loving a wife as ever man was blessed with. It will be an ornament and a joy to us in our happy home, and when we have passed away to our rest it will remain a priceless memorial to our dear child. I may honestly say of my dear wife that, in her daily life, she sheds all around her a pure Christian light. It has often struck me that dear woman does not get the credit she deserves in this world from her silent influences. Let me apply this to myself. I have been successful as a volunteer officer, and I say this success is due, in a measure, to my wife. She has always encouraged me to do my duty, and never allowed any pleasures of her own to interfere with that duty. In 1859, she went with me to the school of musketry at Hythe. For years she attended every drill. She never missed the county rifle meetings at Shotwick and Altcar, and cheerfully undertook the duty of selling "pool" tickets. Yes: I say any success of mine is shared by my dear wife.

I am disposed to think there is a great significance in the kind present you have made me; and its significance is this—it marks the great difference there is, and always must be, between the volunteer force and the regular army. Such a token of affection as that which you have given me would scarcely be possible in the regular army. No. The feelings between privates and their commanding officer must be very different to those between volunteers and their commanding officer. I have commanded you for twenty years, and I can honestly say that, in all that long period, there has always been the most perfect subordination and the best feeling in the whole battalion.

Mr. Graham has referred in very kind and flattering terms to my services as a volunteer, and you have recognised these services by your exquisite gift; but I cannot for a moment allow that I have any claim of merit. All I have done is purely and simply my duty. I confess I feel strongly, and almost painfully, that every man in the battalion has as much right to a testimonial as I have, for each and all have done their duty, and I have done no more. If I know my drill and attend to my work, this is nothing more than every English gentleman ought to do, who has the honour to hold a commission from his sovereign. If I have been kind and courteous to all those under my command, this again is nothing more than every Christian gentleman ought to be. I thank you, and may God bless you all!

Colonel King once said in a speech, that "as long as Old King lived, "if he were the only man that survived in the battalion, he would always "come out to Hooton, pitch his tent, and stop the usual nineteen days." Notwithstanding this, in the month of June, 1881, he severed his connection with the volunteer force. This deplorable event came about in this wise. The Government had published in the *Gazette* a list of "birthday honours," including therein some marks of distinction for certain volunteer officers. As Colonel King's name was omitted, and a "C.B." granted to an officer in the same county much junior to himself, he chose to look upon this as a slight from the War Office, and tendered his resignation in the following letter.

6th June, 1881.

Sir,—I have the honour to inform you that it is my wish to resign the commission which at present I have the honour to hold, and I will thank you to obtain the acceptance of my resignation. The reason of my resignation is this: that I observe that an officer, junior to myself in this county, has been preferred before me for the reception of a mark of honour from the Crown.

I do not complain of the advice which has been tendered to Her Majesty; but I can draw no other inference from the fact above stated than this: that my conduct and services have not been deemed satisfactory, and that it would be well, therefore, that some other gentleman should be appointed to the post which I have unworthily held for the past twenty-two years.

It would be convenient that my resignation should take effect from the 4th July next. My battalion goes into camp from 21st June to 4th July. As I pay a large share of the expense, my immediate resignation would render the camp impossible, and the result would be that a large portion of my battalion would not be efficient this year. When the camp is struck, the whole of our volunteer work will be finished for this year, and I have no wish to leave anything undone.

Feeling as I do in this matter, I could not take a course different from that which I have the honour to announce in this letter; but I think it only right to say that I am supported in the belief that no other was open to me by the strong feeling of my battalion, and by the general public opinion of this neighbourhood.

I have the honour to be, Sir, your obedient servant,

(Signed) V. A. KING,
Lieutenant-Colonel commanding 1st Cheshire Rifle Volunteer Corps.

The Under-Secretary of State for War.

Before sending this letter, Colonel King showed it to many of his friends, seeking their counsel and advice. Several of them begged him to suppress it, and to treat the slight, if slight it was, with dignified silence. It was pointed out to him that the great Brutus had once retorted to a friend, who remarked on the fact that his statue did not appear amongst the great men of Rome, "I had rather that men should wonder why I had not a "statue, than that they should wonder why I had." Colonel King's fellow citizens, even his political opponents, all knew that he well merited any distinction that could be conferred on a volunteer officer, and the reason why he was passed over on this occasion was freely discussed in the press. As this event occurred under a Liberal administration, the Tory papers sided with Colonel King and applauded his decision, while the Liberal papers rather condemned his action as being impulsive and not justified by the circumstances. Newspaper cuttings of all sorts on the subject have been preserved by Colonel King in his scrap-book.

To all Colonel King's friends, it will seem a pity that for so slight an occasion he should have thought fit to sever his connection with the volunteer force. Having been a leading spirit in the movement from the outset, it would have been a fitting complement to his career that he should have died in the service; and we may be sure that his successor, Colonel Cunningham, would gladly have waited for his promotion. Though severed from his old battalion, Colonel King did not withdraw his interest in its progress and success. He was permitted to retain his rank and the right to wear the uniform of the corps, and he continued to manage the Cheshire County Rifle Meeting, to which he had been a liberal subscriber from its inception.

In conclusion, it may without hesitation be said of Colonel King that few men, if any, have done more for the volunteer force than he has done. For the twenty-two years during which he was in command of the 1st C.R.V., he devoted a great portion of his time, and much of his means, to the interests of his battalion and volunteering generally. The writer of "Volunteer Notes" in the *Manchester Courier* wrote of him:—

His beneficence and generosity were unbounded, and although the seal of secrecy prevents us saying one word about his wide-spread private benefactions, we must be pardoned for chronicling the fact that the hard cash he expended upon the promotion of volunteer shooting and general efficiency falls little short of £10,000.

Colonel King's record of attendance at drills stands very high, nearly 94 per cent. of the "highest possible." Up to the time of his retirement, the total number of battalion drills amounted to 532, and Colonel King was present at 497, having been absent on only thirty-five occasions. He died a volunteer at heart, in less than fourteen months after his resignation from the force, and his last wishes were respectfully carried out, by his "lads," as he loved to call them, carrying the coffin to the grave. At the funeral the battalion mustered 400 strong, and relays of the men carried the remains of their beloved late commanding officer from his residence at Oxton to the parish church at Woodchurch.

V. A. King as Citizen.

"Cry, holla! to thy tongue, I pr'ythee; it curvets
very unseasonably. He was furnished like a hunter."
As You Like It, act iii, scene 2.

Having given a sketch of V. A. King in his more prominent aspects of beagler and volunteer, it now only remains to treat of him in his character of citizen.

The inhabitants of Birkenhead and Wirral of twenty years of age and upwards will have a familiar recollection of his face and figure, as he was always very much in evidence whenever anything of importance was stirring in the neighbourhood. He either presided, or was one of the chief speakers, at most of the public meetings held in Oxton or Birkenhead, on an endless variety of subjects. No question, political, social, religious, literary, agricultural, or commercial, seemed to come amiss to him, and he had, reverently be it said, his "finger in every pie."

His speeches show how well-informed he was on every subject he took up. He was a fluent and a ready speaker, and was possessed of oratorical powers of a rare order, although his gestures might be held, by those not accustomed to his manner, to be somewhat exaggerated.

He was genial and kindly in every relation of life, thoroughly cosmopolitan in his *bonhomie* with every class, high or low, rich or poor, and a general favourite with them all; in short, he was, what he always aimed at being, a bluff, hearty, English gentleman, of the good old Tory type. In controversy, he could always "give as good as he got," and many an opponent (he had few opponents except in politics) has winced under his satire, for with all his geniality, he possessed a bitter tongue when roused, and anyone who opposed him generally heard some plain truths, given in plain, unvarnished, unmistakeable Saxon.

Vincent Ashfield King was born at Everton, 26th January, 1810. He was the son of Mr. George King, a Liverpool merchant, who possessed a considerable property at Higher Bebington, where he afterwards resided, and where V. A. King was first initiated in the mysteries of sport. His boyhood and school days were spent in Liverpool, but he became associated with the Hundred of Wirral at an early age, his father possessing a cottage at Oxton, to which the family removed during the summer months. There was no steam ferry to Liverpool in those days, and King used often to relate how he remembered going over to school at Liverpool in a sailing boat; also how his father used to ride on horseback to church on Sundays from Oxton, over the Fender to Woodchurch, with V. A. King in front and his mother behind, on " pillion."

At the age of eighteen King went out to Bombay, to join his brother's firm (G. S. King and Co.), remaining there for some years. Somewhere about the year 1838 he returned to Liverpool, engaging in business in connection with the same firm, and making periodical visits to Bombay. During this period he resided with his father, at the Hall, Higher Bebington, and here we find him when he joined the Royal Rock Beagles, in 1845, a strong, hardy, active man of thirty-five, and a good runner with the beagles, as his contemporaries relate. Up to this time King had taken no active part in political or public life, but was quietly making his fortune, and qualifying himself for the brilliant and useful position he occupied during the later half of his life. In 1834 he had been enrolled a free burgess of Liverpool, and this is the only incident of a public character which has been recorded of his early life. When he entered public life, he formed the habit of cutting out and placing in his scrap-book all newspaper references to himself, whether favourable or otherwise.

In 1851 V. A. King married the daughter of the Rev. E. T. Tanqueray, Rector of Tingrith, Bedfordshire, the bride being also a niece of the Rev. Joshua King, Rector of Woodchurch. At the close of that year they went out to Bombay, and from the annals of the Beagle Hunt it may be gathered that they returned to England some time in 1853, as King was made Master of the Hunt in that year, and took the chair at the general meeting, August 18th, 1853. On their return from Bombay, Mr. and Mrs. King took up their residence at Oxton, at the well-known Point of Ayr, where they spent the remainder of their happy married life, cheered by the love and companionship of their only child, Miss Catherine King. These three were almost inseparable, wife and daughter always accompanying V. A. King wherever he journeyed, entering thoroughly and *con amore* into all his pursuits and pastimes, and helping and encouraging him in his public work.

The first time on which King was, so to speak, pulled out of his shell, and induced to take part in public affairs, was connected with the volunteer movement in 1859, as described on a previous page. From this time to the day of his death he continued to be one of the most prominent men in Wirral, and in 1860 was appointed a Deputy-Lieutenant of Cheshire.

As a churchman, King was a profound theologian of the high-church school, engaging readily in all polemical discussions. He was a lay-representative at the Diocesan Conferences, and a liberal supporter of all the charitable and religious institutions of the diocese. At various times he made many strong and effective speeches on the religious and controversial subjects of the day:—in favour of the "free and open church movement"; national schools as opposed to board schools; and the union of Church and State. He held broad views on Sunday observance, expressing them freely when the subject was mooted at the conferences. At the Chester Diocesan Conference in 1874, the Bishop had invited King to read a paper on "Systematic Almsgiving." Being a liberal and unostentatious giver, he was well qualified to speak on the subject, and a most exhaustive speech he made, occupying two columns of a closely-printed newspaper report. At another conference King read a paper on the "Influence of Cathedrals." This was a subject after his own heart, as he was well read and intensely interested in all mediæval matters, and an authority on ecclesiastical architecture.

Colonel King was treasurer of the Church Building Committee of Birkenhead, and besides being a generous contributor, he succeeded by his influence in collecting a large sum. He was mainly instrumental in the building and endowment of Higher Bebington Church; and as a fitting monument to his memory, his wife and daughter added a tower and spire to that edifice. For many years, King was in the habit of going to Liverpool every Sunday morning to attend St. Nicholas' Church, as he much appreciated its excellent musical service.

As a politician, King had taken no active part in the affairs of the nation until the first election of a Member of Parliament for the newly created Borough of Birkenhead. Previous to that time he had interested himself in local matters, had been a Poor-Law Guardian, and was a noted speaker at all local events and ceremonies.

On March 5th, 1861, he presided at the meeting of the late Mr. John Laird's supporters, and made, as he himself described it, "his maiden political "speech in this maiden borough." He described himself as "a Tory, a real "Tory, a fossil Tory, if you like." A verse from one of the election squibs of the period reads:—

> God bless you pretty maiden; your speech, in ev'ry part,
> Betrays, if not a Tory head, a right good Lib'ral heart.
> And, if these be the principles in which a fossil glories,
> Long life to fossil Tory King—the King of all the Tories.

Colonel King remained a true and hearty supporter of Mr. Laird during the three following elections, and after the latter's death in 1874, this support was continued to Mr. David MacIver. He also took an active part in the election of Mr. Henry Tollemache for West Cheshire in 1881, having himself declined an invitation to stand for the constituency.

THE FINE OLD FOSSIL TORY.

Come, gather round, my lads, awhile,
    And listen to the story
Of one without a taint of guile,
    The fine old fossil Tory.

What though his hair is passing grey,
    His step is light and youthful;
His eye is bright; his voice is clear;
    His face—ah! that is truthful.

He loves his country, loves his Queen,
    He loves his fellow-men—
Except the " Rads," he thinks them mean,
    But still he loves the men.

    .   .   .   .   .

No boaster he, no quarreller;
    Not quick to take offence;
Not skilful in immoral or
    Diplomatic fence;

But bluff and hearty, leal and true,
    He asks the same of others,
And, out of party, takes the view
    That all good men are brothers.

Go, see him in his English home,
    That English oaks environ,
Where oaken panels bind the walls
    As firm as English iron;

While English fare smokes on the board
    With hospitable glowing,
And " Pass the tankard " is the word,
    While English ale is flowing.

Then see him as he dwells in camp,
    Amidst his Volunteers—
Their loved commander. Hark, that tramp!
    And hark, those ringing cheers!

As, marching in their silver grey,
    The county " First " go by
The Roodee, with its proud array;
    " A King!" " A King!" the cry.

They say the age has passed him; well,
    The past age was his glory;
And Heaven preserve to England still
    The fine old fossil Tory.

                    B.W.S.H.

As a magistrate, V. A. King was indefatigable in his attention to the duties of the office, and was noted for the manner in which he tempered justice with mercy. It was almost a pleasure to an offender to be sentenced by him. He was created a county magistrate in 1869, for Cheshire, and a borough magistrate for Birkenhead in 1878.

In his seventy-third year, Colonel King, sportsman to the last, caught a chill when out otter hunting in the neighbourhood of Carlisle, and being ordered by his doctor to take a sea voyage, he paid a visit to the United States. The voyage did not do him much good, and on his return to this country, at the end of September, he became unwell, and after less than a week's illness, died on the afternoon of Sunday, 1st October, 1882. His funeral was the occasion of a great public demonstration of respect. It was estimated that not less than five thousand persons were present. The coffin was carried from Oxton to Woodchurch by relays of volunteers, and was borne from the church and lowered into the grave by a contingent of the numerous beaglers present, the huntsman with eight couple of the hounds being in attendance, in accordance with the expressed wishes of their late Master.

In closing this account of V. A. King, it must be freely admitted that it very inadequately expresses the feelings of regard, reverence, and affection for the Master, Colonel, and friend, developed in all those with whom he came in contact. His memory is ever green, and he will live long in the hearts of all beaglers and volunteers of his county. The following verses, by Mr. George Rae, of Redcourt, Claughton, are an eloquent tribute to a worthy friend.

VINCENT ASHFIELD KING.
IN MEMORIAM.

His voice is hushed that oft like clarion rung
    Above all uproar of the ringing cheers,
Which hailed the wit and sturdy sense it flung,
    In trenchant rhetoric to approving ears.

A readiness robust to give or take
    Hard knocks, political, with steadfast pluck.
He scorned foul hitting, even for party's sake;
    He barbed no shafts, to rankle where they struck.

Full half his prime he yielded up to nurse
    The growing movement for our home defence,
So far as in him lay, with brain and purse,
    Without requital and without pretence.

High-stomached ever with those high in place,
    When bald routine did vex his broader sense;
The laurels for the foremost in the race—
    So rightly his—did others recompense.

But lust of honours, or of orders rare,
    Ne'er stirred his pulses with a sordid beat;
Old England's welfare was his single care,
    The service high to which he bent his feet.

The charity was his that loves to give;
    His the right hand that never knew its left;
The alms that rendered life less hard to live,
    That helped the helpless and the sore bereft.

To propagate Christ's truth in every land,
    To bring some brightness to the darkened brain,
To give to all good works a helping hand—
    The labours these which called him, not in vain.

The genial humour and the joyous wit,
    That kept his table oft in merry roar,
The radiant eyes, with coming laughter lit,
    Unsparing Death, must these be nevermore?

> Our beagle "meets," when far the master's horn—
> Now mute—was heard across the autumn fields,
> A joyance held for us; but now, forlorn,
> The Hunt no more its former rapture yields.
>
> Dear friend, brave heart, our lives shall surely hold
> In loving memory thy goodness great;
> It never failed thy friends—that heart of gold—
> It never thrust the hungry from thy gate.

Louis Rudd Stevenson.

> "Then should the warlike Harry, like himself,
> Assume the port of Mars; and at his heels
> Leash'd in like hounds," &c., &c.
> *King Henry V, Introduction.*

After the death of our beloved old Master (V. A. King), some of the older members thought the time had come to terminate the existence of the Royal Rock Beagle Hunt, feeling that it would be impossible for any one to fill his place. The sentiments of us all were well expressed in Mr. Rae's poem, "In Memoriam":—

> Our beagle meets, when far the master's horn—
> Now mute—was heard across the autumn fields,
> A joyance held for us; but now, forlorn,
> The Hunt no more its former rapture yields.

The majority of the younger members, however, were not disposed to abandon the Hunt, feeling that to carry it on would be the best tribute to their old Master's memory. L. R. Stevenson here came to the rescue, and showed that nothing could be further from Colonel King's wishes than that the pack should be given up, and the country left a prey to the harriers. He was also able to assure the club that both Mrs. and Miss King would be terribly disappointed if the R.R.B. were not carried on with spirit, and also that both ladies had commissioned him to express their wish to become honorary members, promising to subscribe ten guineas.

Under these circumstances it was decided to carry on the Hunt, and at the annual general meeting in 1882, when these matters were discussed, it was unanimously resolved to invite L. R. Stevenson to become Master, and to lead us on to a brilliant future.

Looking back over the past dozen years, we cannot but be convinced that it would have been a "crying shame" if such a grand organization had been permitted to lapse. At the same time there can be no doubt that it was a very critical period, and Stevenson must have had many an anxious moment before he could persuade himself to "step into the shoes" of such a Master as "Old King." It was, however, the general feeling, that if the Hunt were to be carried on, Stevenson was the man to do it. He was an old and intimate friend and one of the executors of the late Master; he was popular in the district, with the farmers, and with the club; in short, he was the right man for the time and place. The only hesitation he had in accepting the post, was his inability to devote the time necessary for the details of kennel management, but when it was proposed that J. W. Macfie should be created deputy master, and take the kennel work off his hands, he hesitated no longer.

The next few years found the Hunt as flourishing as ever, and enjoying the appreciation of all concerned. The goodwill of the farmers was well maintained; an *entente cordiale* was established with that *bête noir* of the late Master, the Wirral Harriers; the kindly feeling of brotherhood among beaglers was encouraged and developed; a pleasant interchange of courtesies with other packs was inaugurated, our hounds being taken to Chirk to fraternise with the Llangollen Beagles, and Mr. Johnson's Malpas Beagles invited to give us a meet in our country. Under Stevenson's auspices the sociability of the club was fostered and brought to its present pitch of perfection. He inaugurated the pleasant custom of the annual dinner, at which the members meet to enjoy a festive evening and promote the feeling of fraternity among the Royal Rock beaglers.

L. R. Stevenson was born in London on the 15th October, 1840. He was the youngest son of Mr. William Stevenson (senior partner in London of the firm of Charles Tennant, Sons and Co.), who died in 1854. Educated at private schools in Ayrshire and Surrey, till fourteen years of age, Stevenson then went to Germany to acquire languages and prepare for a military career, as he had a strong desire to secure a commission in the Royal Engineers. This ambition was, however, over-ruled by his guardians, and in 1856 he became an articled pupil to Thos. E. Blackwell, C.E., and began the practical study of civil engineering at Bristol. Next year, Mr. Blackwell, having accepted the post of managing director of the Grand Trunk Railway, went out to Montreal with a staff of assistants, young Stevenson among the number. There for five years he was actively engaged in preliminary surveys in Upper and Lower Canada, and in the laying out and construction of railway works, including the great Victoria bridge over the St. Lawrence, at Montreal. The old hankering for a military career being revived by association with officers of all branches of the regular army then quartered in Canada, Stevenson, having attained his twenty-first year and become his own master, decided, at the expiration of his apprenticeship in 1862, to return home and enter the army. He passed the requisite examination, and was duly gazetted to a commission in the 3rd King's Own Hussars, then quartered in Dublin, serving as cornet and lieutenant with his regiment in various parts of the United Kingdom for the next six years. In 1868 his regiment being under orders to proceed to India, Stevenson retired from the army as senior lieutenant, an accident having rendered him unfitted for service in a hot climate. In the spring of that year his charger had fallen with him at Hampton Court, whereby he sustained a severe concussion of the brain and other serious injuries.

L. R. Stevenson had married in 1866, and on his retirement from the army he entered business life in Liverpool as an iron merchant, taking up his residence in Birkenhead, with his wife and infant son. Here he made the acquaintance of Colonel King and other beaglers, and, having been during his army career accustomed to hunt with foxhounds and harriers, he felt drawn towards the gallant little beagle pack, and joined the R.R.B. in 1869. Stevenson did not take any very active part in the management of the Hunt until he was made Master. He was on the committee, was indefatigable in attending the meets, and took great interest in the sport. On those occasions when Colonel King took the hounds to Llanfyllyn for two or three days' hunting, at the invitation of his old friend Squire Dugdale, Stevenson always made one of the party.

L. R. Stevenson was Master of the R.R.B. from 1882 to 1889. During his "reign" the sport was most excellent, many notable runs occurring of which no record was kept, but which are treasured in the memories of, and frequently referred to by those privileged to enjoy them. Stevenson resigned the Mastership in 1889, after filling the honourable post for seven seasons to the satisfaction of all. We were proud of him as head of the Hunt, and received his resignation with extreme regret. His portrait is among those of beaglers at Whitby.

John William Macfie.

"You twain
Rule in this realm, and the gored state sustain."
King Lear, act v, scene 3.

J. W. Macfie is the eldest son of the late Robert Andrew Macfie, Esquire, of Dreghorn Castle, Midlothian, who was the representative in Parliament for the Leith Burghs from 1868 to 1874, and who died 16th February, 1893. As detailed in Burke's *Landed Gentry*, the family were of the clan Macfie or Macduffie, which hailed from the islands of Colonsay and Oronsay, Argyllshire, but were dispossessed by the Macdonalds, and removed to Ayr and Renfrew. Early in this century Macfie's ancestors were in Greenock, where they became connected with the sugar interest, which they have since so worthily represented at Greenock, Leith, and Liverpool. Members of the family intermarried with the families of Marquis, Fairrie, and Thorburn.

J. W. Macfie was born 1st December, 1844, and in his boyhood resided at Ashfield Hall, in Wirral. Here he got his first introduction to sport in the shape of ratting with Skye terriers, varied with a little pigeon-shooting. Having learned to ride even before he could walk, Macfie had plenty of fox-hunting during his visits to Scotland, where his uncle, Mr. William Macfie, was well known with several of the Scotch packs— the Duke of Buccleuch's, the Linlithgow and Stirlingshire, and the Lothian. Young Macfie made friends with the huntsman of the Lothian (Atkinson) and frequently went with him to the kennels to look over the hounds. Another uncle, Mr. John Macfie, who was one of the early members of the R.R.B., often brought him out with the beagles; this must have been during the time when Jones was huntsman, Macfie being a boy under ten years of age. He must have known the R.R.B. for a longer period than anyone now connected with them, and remembers many of the ancient celebrities, having a special recollection of being "slanged" by Alfred Walford for over-keenness.

After his marriage in 1867, Macfie resided at New Ferry, and in 1870 he joined the R.R.B. as a member, when he was dubbed by the master (Old King), in friendly jest, a "pestilent Liberal and Psalm-singing Presbyterian." Many of us remember Macfie before he became troubled with rheumatism, and when he was one of the best runners with the hounds. He was always a good beagler, and dearly loved the glorious sport. He was well read in all the literature of hunting, and took great delight in watching the working of hounds.

In 1882, as described on a previous page, Macfie was elected deputy-master along with L. R. Stevenson. He undertook the kennel management, and made it a labour of love. The following extract from one of his letters will testify to his work —

When buying hounds, I found great difficulty in getting beagles of hound type. Each master had a different idea of what a beagle should be, some had hounds with heads and ears like fox-terriers, others like pups, and some like miniature fox-hounds. So, when I was asked to support a harrier and beagle show at Peterborough, I cordially entered into the idea, and have given my support and a cup there every year. From that show has sprung the Association of Masters of Harriers and Beagles, and the foundation of a Stud Book for harrier and beagle hounds. I hope, in time, this may result in a type as clearly defined for beagles as the foxhound show, supported in its infancy by Anstruther Thompson, has fixed for the fox-hound.

In 1889, when Stevenson resigned the mastership, Macfie was unanimously elected Master, but this post he only retained for one season, as he had left his house at New Ferry, and gone to reside at Rowton Hall, near Chester. It was with great regret that he gave up the hounds, and now he solaces himself by breeding hackneys, having nearly as many foals as he used to have puppies. Macfie has acted on the council of the Association of Masters of Harriers and Beagles ever since its formation, and helped to found the Polo Pony Stud Book Society. As a public man he has confined himself to taking an active interest in various philanthropic institutions. He has served on the boards of the Liverpool Savings Bank, the Northern Hospital, and the Chester Infirmary; and has been president and chairman of the Wirral Agricultural Society. A portrait of Macfie may be seen among those of beaglers at Whitby, and also at Raby, the latter taken when he was Master.

J. Gould Smyth.

"Though grey
Do something mingle with our younger brown; yet have we
A brain that nourishes our nerves, and can
Get goal for goal of youth."
Antony and Cleopatra, act iv, scene 8.

Smyth claims to have "seen more sport" with the R.R.B. than any one now connected with the Hunt. If W. E. Hall had still remained a member he would have been able to contest this claim, but in his absence we must yield the honour to our present good Master. Smyth joined as a member in 1877, but for three years previously he had been hunting regularly with the hounds, having been requested by Colonel King to carry a whip. He was then, and has remained, a noted runner, his previous training with the draghounds rendering it easy for him to become a good beagler. As one of the whips Smyth took great and active interest in all the affairs of the Hunt. He was a firm friend of W. E. Hall, and soon made himself familiar with the hounds, visiting the kennels with Hall and calling over the hounds by name till they got to know him. In the illustration of the hounds at Raby, Smyth may be seen with one of the hounds jumping up and fawning on him.

When Macfie resigned the mastership in 1890, J. Gould Smyth was unanimously chosen to be the Master of the R.R.B. He had acted as whip for fifteen years, had served usefully on the committee of management and on all the sub-committees appointed to arrange farmer's balls and club dinners. He has been re-elected Master every year since then, and if he remains a beagler to the end of his days he bids fair to rival the late V. A. King in the affection and esteem of every one connected with the R.R.B. Hunt.

Since Smyth took the mastership he has himself hunted the hounds and shown us very good sport. Being a good runner, he is always at hand at a check, and is smart at handling his hounds. He is exceedingly popular with all classes of sportsmen and with the landowners and farmers of his country. He is indefatigable in attending his fixtures, only occasionally absenting himself when he goes for a little deer-stalking or other shooting, with his friend, John Sherwood, in Scotland. On these occasions he hands the horn, as deputy master, to C. T. Dixon or J. Ravenscroft, allowing Davies, the kennel huntsman, to hunt the hounds in the field.

Smyth joined the Association of Masters of Harriers and Beagles, which his predecessor, Macfie, had aided in promoting. He put the R.R.B. pack into the Stud Book, every hound being eligible, and has since taken great interest in the work of the Association. At Peterborough hound show the R.R.B. have been fairly successful in winning prizes. At the show in 1895 Smyth got first prize for "champion bitch," and also for the "best couple of bitches." It is worthy of note that in this year all the first prizes for beagles came to Cheshire—the Cheshire Beagles winning for "champion dog" and "best couple unentered hounds;" and the Malpas Beagles winning for "best couple of dogs" and "best three couple of hounds."

J. Gould Smyth was born July 25th, 1851, at Miller's Bridge. His family came from Devonshire, where his uncle, Mr. William Gould Smyth, kept a pack of harriers for some thirty years. With this pack our Master, in his boyhood and youth, gained his great and noteworthy knowledge of hare-hunting. There also he had the chance of gaining experience in stag-hunting and various kinds of sport. On the death of Mr. W. Gould Smyth, the pack was bought by the Empress of Austria, who was well pleased with the hounds. Shortly afterwards, Miss Smyth received from the Empress a beautifully-mounted pad as a memento.

The Smyths are now well known in Liverpool and Wirral as a sporting and athletic family. The brothers of our Master have all been beaglers and good runners, and his son, who is now getting his athletic and scholastic training at Loretto, comes out with us during his holidays, and gives great promise of "leading the field."

CHAPTER VII.

THE HUNTSMEN.

"Nay, press not so upon me; stand far off."
Julius Cæsar, act iii, scene 2.

Since the first season of the R.R.B. up to the time of our present master, J. Gould Smyth, the hounds have always been hunted by the kennel huntsmen, and it has been of great importance to the sport to secure the services of a man fully qualified for the post. The club may be said to have been fortunate in always getting good men, two of whom died in the service, the others (except the first Davies and Cole, who both preferred farming) retiring on account of advancing years. With the exception of Kay, a Lancashire man, Cole, from Derbyshire, and our new kennel huntsman, Davies, all the R.R.B. huntsmen have been born and bred in Wales, which country seems to have been an admirable nursery for Hunt servants. The profession of huntsman seems to descend from father to son, and the best are those who have been brought up with hounds from the cradle. There are many qualities which go to make up a good all-round huntsman. He must be sober, patient, industrious, active, strong in wind and limb, punctual, civil and obliging, a good manager of hounds in the kennel and in the field, and a lover of the sport.

Thomas Kay.

"'Tis double death to drown in ken of shore."
Poems—Lucrece.

Kay was the first huntsman of the R.R.B. He is described by Mr. Rawson as a rough Lancashire man, and was recommended by Captain Hopwood. Mr. Turbett says that he came from Chowbent, and that his dialect was unintelligible, even to the hounds! Kay was appointed as kennel huntsman to look after the hounds, and was only expected to hunt them in the absence of the master, Tinley Barton. There is no record of his antecedents, and as he was huntsman for the first season only, there is not much record of his qualifications, but he appears to have given satisfaction to the Committee. He was engaged 29th August, 1845, at a weekly wage of one pound, with house, his uniform to be scarlet coat, green waistcoat, white breeches, and leggings. After hunting the first season, Kay gave notice on May 26th, 1846, to resign his situation, on the ground of his family requiring his presence at home. His resignation was accepted, and Mr. Okell was empowered to apply to the gentleman who recommended Kay to put the R.R.B. on the track of a successor. On June 15th, 1846, before his notice of resignation had expired, poor Kay met with a melancholy end in the discharge of his duty. The minute book records :—

On this day our huntsman, Thomas Kay, whilst bathing the pack on the Rock Ferry slip, slipped into the river, and was unfortunately drowned. His body was found the same evening. He leaves a wife and nine young children.

Mr. Rawson has furnished a graphic account of this tragic incident. He writes :—

In the first season, when taking the hounds to bathe from the end of the Rock Ferry pier, Kay fell into the river. All the pack swam to him, and had he only put his arms and hands on a lot of them, they would have held him up till succour came. When he sank, the dogs landed on the pier, and hunted his back trail full cry all the way back to the kennels, to the surprise of his poor wife at hearing the hounds hunting in sorrow.

This extraordinary story is vouched for, and fully believed in, by Mr. Rawson, though other surviving contemporaries have lost all recollection of the circumstance, which must at the time have made a great impression. Our late huntsman, Cole, thinks it quite a likely thing for the hounds to hunt the back trail in full cry. It is also quite possible that the hounds might have brought Kay ashore, as very little supports a man entirely immersed in water. The Committee of the R.R.B. resolved that—

In testimony of the respect which the Hunt feel for their late huntsman, Thomas Kay, and with the wish to in some degree mitigate the sad bereavement to his wife and large family, the Hunt take upon themselves the whole expenses of his funeral ; and as many of the members as are able are requested to follow the remains to their last resting place at Bebington parish church.

It was also resolved that a subscription be at once raised, for the relief of his poor widow and family. Four committee-men and a few other members attended the funeral. The subscription realized £75.

At the first farmers' dinner, Kay was called in to favour the company with a song. He gave them—

    Smiling May! Smiling May
    Deck'd all out with flow'rets gay—

and so on for fifty verses, taking nearly three-quarters of an hour for its delivery. Tinley Earton says that at the next annual dinner they excused Kay from obliging with his song ; but this is an instance of the treacherous character of memory, for poor Kay met with his death before the second dinner.

L

Humphrey Jones.

*"But I will tell you at some meeter season.
The business of this man looks out of him."
Antony and Cleopatra, act v, scene 1.*

All that can be ascertained about the antecedents of this almost perfect huntsman is, that before he came to the R.R.B., he was for some years huntsman with Mr. Green, of Newtown, Montgomeryshire, by whom he was highly recommended.

When poor Kay had sent in his resignation, shortly before his unfortunate death, the Committee of the R.R.B. had taken steps to supply his place. Six applicants from various districts were forthcoming, one of whom, Robert Clegg, was selected, being highly recommended by Captain Hopwood, who had also previously nominated Kay. At an interview with the Committee, it was found that Clegg had never had entire charge of any kennels or pack of hounds, and was therefore not sufficiently experienced for the situation.

The sudden death of Kay somewhat "forcing the hands" of the Committee, they decided to ask Jones to come for a month on trial. He came 21st June, 1846, and on the 20th July was appointed huntsman, at a wage of sixteen shillings per week, with house, coals, and clothes. At the end of his first season, he had given so much satisfaction that his wages were raised to one pound per week, and at every subsequent annual meeting of the members, he was called into the room to receive the expression of their satisfaction with his management of the hounds and his conduct generally.

The qualifications of Jones as a huntsman appear in very many notices recorded in the sport books of the Hunt. He was a speedy and tireless runner, and a most agile leaper, usually carrying, in addition to his whip, a pole with which he was able to clear hedges and gates, flying them in his stride. In many of the records of notable runs, he is mentioned in some such manner as follows:—"Only Jones up with the hounds." "Only Walford and Jones saw anything of this run."

On days when scent was poor and hunting slow, Jones was very painstaking in his casts, and was noted for his success in keeping on the line of the hare up to a kill. In his days the total of kills was very large. His management of the hounds in kennel was also highly commended, and his command of "dog language" was so unusually excellent, that the members, at their annual dinners to the farmers, used to have him in to give an exhibition performance of "view halloos," "tally-hos," "gone-aways," "who-hoops," and various forms of rating and encouraging hounds in the field.

Jones was apparently rather severe on his clothes, for after two seasons he had to have a new rig-out. On September 23rd, 1848, when hunting, the committee sent him home early in the afternoon, "as it turned "out very wet, to save his new red coat." He was very fond of taking out a large pack, usually eighteen or nineteen couples. The account of a run, 26th October, 1848, finishes up thus :—"Lost, a very sporting run, "the result would have been different had not Jones taken out every dog "in the pack, puppies included." The Sport Books give several accounts of hares jumping into the arms of Jones, and his speed and agility must have been quite abnormal, as one record reads—

Found a hare, which gave us a good day's sport, occasionally getting away with a considerable reprieve, at length being caught by Jones himself to prevent the hounds from eating her. Not being hurt, she was turned down again, when she gave us an excellent run till dark, and actually got away at last. Jones considers this a kill, so book it accordingly as "Kill No. 16."

It would appear that if no members turned up at a meet, Jones either assumed or was allowed the privilege of "throwing off" on his own account. The Sport Books record several runs that Jones had by himself; and on one occasion, the meet being at Thingwall Mill, it is noted that "the hare took "into Arrowe Park after an hour's run, and there being only two strangers "present, Jones whipped off and took the hounds home." Jones was thirty years of age when he came to the R.R.B.; he hunted the hounds for eight seasons, and must have overdone himself with running, as he died suddenly on his sofa at the kennels on the afternoon of 11th January, 1854. There had been no hunting for a fortnight previous to the day of his death, on account of a severe frost, which lasted till 19th January. His portrait appears with that of Mr. Rawson.

EXTRACT FROM THE MINUTE BOOK.

Our huntsman Humphrey Jones died very suddenly on Wednesday, 11th January, 1854, at 7-30 p.m. He had been a faithful servant to us for seven years and a half, and was in every sense of the word an excellent, worthy man. He was buried at Bebington Church on 16th January, seven of the members attending his funeral.

IN MEMORY OF
HUMPHREY JONES,
HUNTSMAN OF
THE ROYAL ROCK BEAGLES.
WHO
DIED 11TH JANUARY, 1854.
AGED 38 YEARS.

THE MEMBERS OF THE HUNT HAVE PLACED THIS STONE OVER HIS MORTAL REMAINS, AS A MARK OF THEIR RESPECT FOR THE MEMORY OF AN HONEST, FAITHFUL, AND VALUED SERVANT.

John Davies.

"Thou wouldst else have made thy tale large."
Romeo and Juliet, act ii, scene 4.

Very little information is obtainable about this huntsman, as although the Master (King) kept up the Sport Books for a year or two after the appointment of Davies, his accounts of proceedings became of a very meagre character, and Davies is only once mentioned in the records.

On the death of Jones, the committee of the R.R.B. advertised for a huntsman in *Bell's Life*. Davies was selected out of many applicants, mainly because he was recommended by Mr. George Green, of Newtown, Montgomeryshire, who must have been a good trainer of hunt servants, as he had already supplied the R.R.B. with an excellent specimen in Jones. On February 7th, 1854, John Davies was appointed huntsman to the R.R.B, at £1 per week, with house, coals, candles, clothes, &c.; and on the 9th February it is recorded—"Davies, our new huntsman, was out for "the first time, and seems to understand his work well." Davies had a farm at Caersws, Montgomeryshire, and, not wishing to give it up altogether, he resigned his situation and returned to his farm after one season.

John Vaughan.

"By this, far off she hears some huntsman's holla."
Poems—Venus and Adonis.

Considering that many of the old beagiers now surviving hunted with the hounds during the time that this man was huntsman, it seems extraordinary that no one can be found who remembers him.

He came from Newtown, in Montgomeryshire, in 1854, probably at the recommendation of Mr. Green, and he remained huntsman for nine years, retiring in 1863, on the plea of old age. He went to live in Holywell, where he was heard of, a few years ago, as still living, notwithstanding a lapse of nearly thirty years since he retired on account of his advanced age.

Charles Williams.

"Thither I must, although against my will;
For servants must their masters' minds fulfil."
Comedy of Errors, act iv, scene 1.

This well-known and much respected huntsman was the son of David Williams, who for thirty years hunted a pack of harriers belonging to Mr. Rowland Jones, of Llanidloes, Montgomeryshire. These hounds were hunted on foot, and Charles Williams gained his experience in hunting, and his great knowledge of the management of hounds, under the tuition of his father. He was appointed huntsman to the R.R.B. in June, 1863, and remained with us for twenty-three years, gaining the good-will and esteem of all who came in contact with him. He was a general favourite, and gave entire satisfaction to the authorities of the Hunt. He showed good sport, and was indefatigable in his attention to the hounds in kennel. Williams was a little over forty years of age when he came to the R.R.B., and he proved himself a good and hardy pedestrian. He was always a good walker, and keeps it up to this day in spite of his seventy-three winters. In April, 1886, he retired from the post, receiving a handsome presentation from the members of the Hunt, and taking with him the hearty good wishes of all. He said he was "sorry to leave the hounds, but being in his sixty-fifth year, he "found he could not keep well enough up with them." Williams had fairly good "hound language." He used to talk to his hounds in Welsh, and they appeared to understand him very well. Being invited to record some of his dog language, he furnishes the following, which is very much the same as all huntsmen use. It would have been more interesting to have had some of his Welsh expressions.

See ho! Spying a hare on her form.

Ses! ses! Calling hounds to feed.

Hoy gone! Casting when at a check.

Ho! ratter! In full view. This is something like our old friend Dixon's "Have-at-her!"

When hounds had over-run the scent, Williams would say "They've "over-runted it." This was no doubt a cross between over-running and over-hunting.

A portrait of Williams is among the Whitby group. Williams does not claim the authorship of this old and typical hunting song, which he has preserved. He is willing to leave the credit to his successor, Cole.

SONG IN HONOUR OF MR. ROWLAND JONES AND HIS HARRIERS.

Come all you gallant sportsmen, come listen to my song,
A few lines I will relate to you, I won't detain you long;
It's concerning of a hunt that took place the other day,
With Rowland Jones' harriers—it's them that bears the sway.
It was on the top of Cefnmawr, near to the black well,
There was a game old hare, who many years did dwell;
She had been hunted by the beagles and coursed by greyhounds fair,
But none of those great sportsmen could kill this old game hare.
The tidings came to Rowland Jones, -glad for to hear the news,
Says he "I'll come and kill that hare any day you choose,
With six couple of my harriers and a few of Newtown footmen,
And if ever she is put up, she'll never be put up again."

They put her up upon a farm that's called Tynypwyll.
The footmen good never stood at hedges, gates, or filth ;
But straight through Brynypentre she led them such a chase,
And they never broke their cry till they turned round Viswlais.
Hunted her over the top of Cefnmawr, down by Vechan brookside,
Where she, standing on her hind legs. Tom Harper heard her say :
" Oh ! these cannot be the same dogs that used me to pursue ;
Oh, no ! these are Rowland Jones' harriers—I must bid this world adieu."
It was on the top of Newaddfraith, old Traveller took sight,
Says he " I'll be in with thee, although it's dusk of night."
And straight through Tynybitfield fold, (mark ! what I say is true.)
And they never broke their cry till they killed her on the view.
So now this old game hare is dead and gone, and I must end my song,
I hope there will be more before it's very long.
For our hounds they can kill hares whilst there's marrow in their bones.
Here's a health to all good sportsmen, and long life to Rowland Jones.

Jonathan Cole.

"Tear him for his bad verses, tear him for his bad verses."
Julius Cæsar, act iii, scene 3.

Cole was born 3rd February, 1849, at Hayfield, in Derbyshire. His father, William Cole, was a keeper in the neighbourhood, so that Cole from his boyhood was familiar with various kinds of sport. At that time it was the custom in the locality for farmers and others to keep what is called a "trencher-fed pack ;" that is, a pack of hounds not kept together in kennel, but distributed among the various votaries of the sport, each of whom brought his lot to the appointed place of meeting. Cole's father kept five couple of these hounds at his house.

This was Cole's first introduction to hounds, and when he was twenty years of age he took his first hunting situation, as whip to the Rossendale Harriers, a pack hunted on foot. He served under the famous huntsman, Harry Mitchell, for three years, then went as huntsman, first to the Halifax and Calder Vale Harriers, which he hunted for five seasons, and afterwards to the Holme Valley Harriers for ten years.

In 1886, when Williams was retiring from the R.R.B., Cole heard of the vacancy through Mr. John Foster, of the Penny-ghent Beagles, and sent in his application. He remained with us for seven years, and we found him a very good huntsman, though not a fast runner. Being nearly forty years of age when he came to the R.R.B., his running powers did not improve as the years went on, but as the Master, J. Gould Smyth, preferred to take on himself the duty of hunting the hounds in the field, Cole had merely to bring the hounds to the meet and be ready to take them home.

During the season 1890-91, Cole managed to arrange with some of his friends at Hayfield, that the R.R.B. hounds should be brought over for three days' hunting in that district. On 9th March, the Master, J. G. Smyth, with some of his whips (J. Ravenscroft, W. H. Legge, Stuart Smyth, and N. Caine), took advantage of the opportunity. They enjoyed some very good sport on the second day, but the weather was very unpropitious on the last day. This was exceptionally unfortunate, as the village was *en fête* for the occasion, a general holiday, with all the mills closed, and hundreds turning up at the meet. We were a long time in finding, and, immediately we did find, a blinding snowstorm and mist prevented all chance of sport. In the evening Cole was in his element. All the sport-lovers of the place assembled in the tap-room of the hotel, and Cole held a sort of court, leading the revelry of song and mirth in fine style, convincing his cronies (and possibly himself) that the hounds belonged to him, and that he would certainly bring his hounds again to Hayfield in the coming season. He also sang a song of his own composition, which was very well received by the assembled company. Here it is :—

It was near to Naby town, my boys, as I have heard them tell,
There was an old sporting hare that us-ed for to dwell.
She had been run by greyhounds, the Wirral hounds as well,
But never a one amongst them could kill this old hare.
        Chorus—To my fal de lal, &c.

Macfie being our Master, and hearing of the news,
He says, " I can kill that champion hare on any day I choose.
I'll take ten couple of beagles and a few gentlemen,
So we'll go a-hunting there, and then, oh! then, oh! then."

When we came to the place where this old hare used to lie,
We threw out our beagles, and bid them for to try ;
Such questing and such music as you seldom ever knew,
As though they had been running her all in full view.

This old hare laying so snug, and hearing of the sounds,
She thought within herself it was time to leave the grounds ;
If they'd been those Wirral Harriers, with them I'd sport and play,
But it's Cole with his beagles, and he'll take my life away.

Then right round by Hinderton, she led a gallant chase,
Our men they ran most vig'rously, the spoils for to embrace.
We had Trimbush, Lady, Driver, who held up the chase so gay,
But Wasteful was a fast young bitch, and led them all the way.

Then right round by Thornton Hough, they rattled her about,
Till they brought her to the place again, whence first she went out,
Down upon Tom McAlroy's farm, where she had meant to steal away,
But Lingerer was too quick for her, and caused her for to stay.

It was ten couple of beagles that caused this old hare to die,
The average of their height is just sixteen inches high.
The equal of these hounds, is not to be found
Nor never better hunters seen upon Old England's ground.

Then here's a health to all hunters of every degree.
Long may they live, and happy may they be,
Likewise to the Royal Rock Beagles, they are the men who bear the fame,
For their hounds they bring them glory and honour to their name.
                                                Chorus, &c., &c.

It is whispered that the second verse of this song originally stood as—

The Master of the beagles hearing of the news.
Says, " I can kill that champion hare any day I choose,
I'll take ten couple of beagles, and of runners two or three."
The huntsman Mister Jonathan Cole, the master was Maclie—

but Cole being somewhat chaffed about it, has amended the verse as above.

In the season of 1892-3, Cole found that his eyesight was becoming defective, so that he had to take to spectacles, and just before the commencement of the season 1893-4, having an offer from his old master of a position as bailiff, he resigned his post with the Royal Rock Beagles. His portrait appears in the background of the Raby group.

Frank James Davies.

"Take thou no scorn to wear the horn;
It was a crest ere thou wast born.
Thy father's father wore it,
And thy father bore it.
The horn, the horn, the lusty horn,
Is not a thing to laugh to scorn."
                        As You Like It, act iv. scene 2.

Our present huntsman was born 12th September, 1872, at Crookham, Hampshire. During Davies' boyhood his father, James Paynter Davies, was huntsman to the Hadlow Harriers in Kent, and in 1879 he was appointed huntsman to the Todmorden Harriers. These two packs were hunted on foot. Davies may be said to have lived all his life with hounds. By helping his father in the kennels he acquired an unusual amount of kennel knowledge and experience in the treatment of hounds. In 1892, the elder Davies was appointed huntsman to the Anglesey Harriers, hunted on horseback, and for the season 1892/3 Davies "whipped up" to his father, and during the rare occasions of the latter's absence or illness he took full charge of the hounds.

On the sudden resignation of Cole from the R.R.B., at the beginning of the season 1893/4, our Master heard of Davies from Rice Roberts, Esq., of Anglesey, and, notwithstanding his youth (he was only twenty-one years of age), it was felt that his exceptional experience and capital recommendations quite justified us in giving him a trial in the responsible position of kennel huntsman to the Royal Rock Beagles. His career is before him, and we all hope he will succeed in establishing himself with us, and make as good a record as any of his predecessors.

CHAPTER VIII.

THE MEMBERS.

> "Come, I'll question you
> Of my lord's tricks, and yours, when you were boys.
> You were pretty lordlings then."
> *Winter's Tale, act i, scene 2.*

Looking over the names of those who have joined the Royal Rock Beagles during the fifty years from the inauguration of the club to this year of Jubilee, many familiar names of local repute will be noticed. There is some occasion for surprise that a score or more of names of beaglers can be picked out from among the earlier members, whose sons at the present day know nothing of beagling, and have even forgotten that their fathers were ever members of the Hunt. On the other hand, as many names can be found of men whose sons either have been or are now members of the R.R.B., and in at least one case a grandson of an old member is now "one "of us." A feeling of good fellowship has always existed among the members of the R.R.B. No sooner is a man admitted to the club as a member, than he is welcomed by all. During the hunting season they are all brother beaglers wherever they may meet, and in the off time they may still be found together at golf, tennis, rowing, or other athletic pursuits. Taken altogether, the R.R.B. are, and always have been, a body to be proud of in any community. The severity of the work connected with the sport demands that no delicate or infirm person should take part in it, and although advancing years are no bar to the true enjoyment of the sport, they must be accompanied with good health and a fair amount of activity.

Since the formation of the Hunt, over 500 men have joined the club, and, without being invidious, it is possible to select a certain number who, with one accord, would be dubbed the celebrities of the Hunt. A short account of some of these will be of interest to present and future beaglers. They may be classed as ancient, mediæval, and modern celebrities; the first class being taken from the members who joined before 1860, the second from those between 1860 and 1875, and the third from later members.

If, in fifty years, 500 members have joined the Hunt, we may take it that the average number of vacancies each year will be ten, and as our numbers are limited to sixty, a generation of beaglers is comprised in six years. All members of over six years' standing may therefore be called old beaglers. A glance at the list for 1894 will show that exactly half of the members are in this category. This seems rather a short life, if a merry one, and it will be curious to enquire into the causes of the vacancies in this swiftly-changing roll of members.

Death during membership will not account for more than two per cent. of the vacancies; and resignation on account of ill-health is comparatively unknown. Some few leave the club because they can come out with the hounds so seldom that it is hardly worth while continuing their subscription; others resign to follow other sports, golf more particularly: now and again we have resignations on account of advancing years. There can be little doubt, however, that the greatest number of vacancies are caused by members leaving the neighbourhood.

In the event of the death of any member of the Hunt, it is customary, if the funeral is fixed for a hunting day, to cancel the hunt fixture, as a mark of respect for the deceased beagler. The same thing is done in case of the death of a member of the royal family, or of any particularly great and distinguished public man. The old records of the Hunt contain precedents:

October 6th, 1849. Woodchurch. No meet, in consequence of the much lamented death of Mrs. King (wife of the rector). This is a kind sympathy on the part of the members, which here I cannot refrain from gratefully acknowledging. (Signed) V. A. KING.

18th November, 1852. The fixture for the day, the kennels as published, it was decided in committee should not take place, it being the day of the Duke of Wellington's funeral. It was, however, decided a bye-day, for the convenience of a few members, should take place at Thurstaston, the meet there the previous week not having taken place.

For this breach of etiquette surely they deserved a blank day.

Chronological List of Members of the R.R.B.

"We are men, my liege."
"Ay, in the catalogue ye go for men;
As hounds, and greyhounds, mongrels, spaniels, curs,
Shoughs, water-rugs, and demi-wolves, are cleped
All by the name of dogs: the valued file
Distinguishes the swift, the slow, the subtle,
The housekeeper, the hunter, every one
According to the gift which bounteous Nature
Hath in him closed; whereby he does receive
Particular addition, from the bill
That writes them all alike; and so of men."
Macbeth, act iii, scene 1.

1845.
J. Higginson.
R. Hemingway.
G. J. Wainwright.
W. Robinson.
J. Okell.
G. Comer.
J. Stephenson.
J. B. Amey.
W. W. Perry.
C. Hemery.
R. Christie, Jun.
J. W. Harden.
W. Stockley.
W. F. Foster.
A. L. Edgar.
Frederick Lyon.
H. Walford.
C. Rawson.
R. J. Tinley.
G. A. Tinley.
Captain Barton.
S. Vertue.
W. Parkinson.
E. Mengins.
J. T. Raynes.
H. Jenkins.
J. Budd.
W. Pike.
Jos. Aspinall.
H. Aspinall.
T. B. Sands.
Richard Barton.
A. Barton.
J. Carter.
R. J. Hardman.
T. A. Bushby.
A. Walford.
S. Willoughby.
H. Watson.
— Whittaker.

1845—Continued.
W. Watson.
T. H. Irwin.
R. J. Ramsden.
— Jamieson.
W. Cole.
F. Kulenkamp.
T. Sleddall.
T. Lutwyche.
J. Matthie.
H. Mollineux.
H. Williams.
B. Southern.
D. Bellhouse.
F. Duncan.
C. H. Steele.
E. Lane.
H. Barton, Jun.
T. Clint.
J. Herd.
M. Richardson.
D. Carmon.
T. Barton.
W. Comer.
G. A. Brown.
J. Black.
C. Higginson.
F. Clarke.
A. Turneur.
W. G. Baldwin.
B. Kinnear.
A. Aikin.
T. Morewood.
J. Thompson.
J. M. Wooley.
H. Wilson.
Bolton Littledale.
B. Parkinson.
J. Scott.
V. A. King.
H. Royds.

1845—Continued.
— Martigny.
F. O. Bateson.
W. Brancker.
A. Lyon.
F. Matthias.
J. F. Williams.
— Lowe.
J. A. Scott.
H. Hassall.
J. Dixon.

1846.
W. C. Young.
G. Johnson.
J. Haselden.
— Thorpe.
C. Jenkins.
W. Barber.
Ed. Morgan.
J. Hossack.
F. Peel.
A. Findley.
W. Bower.
G. Goore.
J. Boyd.
— Read.
John Haselden.
W. Hewett.
G. Green.
G. Pym.
James Bower.
C. Cameron.
G. Hardman.
W. T. Maur.
F. Whittall.
W. Lyon.
W. H. Lake.
T. W. Sherland.
W. V. Willis.
A. Higgins.

1846—Continued.
O. Burchardt.
P. Kelham.
C. Stewart.
T. Littledale.
G. A. McKenzie.
W. Tobin.
W. F. Gray.
S. A. Greaves.
A. Potter.
F. Cole.
Jerome Smith.
W. A. Park.
J. P. Younghusband.
W. Clayton.
W. Caytor.
A. Powles.
E. A. Watson.
E. Budd.

1847.
John Scott.
F. Hollins.
F. Stacey.
F. St. John.
James Blake.
T. Sill.
W. T. Hall.
L. L. Bird.
T. Flint.
P. F. Currie.
J. Haselden.
Weir Anderson.
W. Chambres.
W. Critchley.
S. Shannon.
H. Greenham.
W. Sheppard.
W. B. Kewley.
B. Haigh.
T. S. Eddowes.

1848.
J. Cummings.
H. Tristram.
E. B. Bilborough.
S. Morgan.
J. B. Best.
R. Jones.
E. Corrie.
J. Bateson.
W. Aspinall.
W. Watson.
G. Aman.
J. B. Neilson.
E. Reynolds.
M. A. Grey.
R. Brocklebank.

1849.
J. Willink.
H. Cox.
J. Coupland.
John Saunders.
John Ravenscroft.
Robert Heath.
R. E. Heath.
F. Maxwell.
N. Duckworth.
W. Tarbet.
James Turbett.
G. E. Taunton.
H. Smith.
E. H. Satterthwaite.
Jos. Ewart.
E. P. Dickson.

1850.
Wm. Hind.
J. Grey.
J. Tomlinson.
W. Morecroft.
J. Sharman.
J. Barron.
S. Rickman.
Jas. Pownall.
T. B. Sands.
H. Sillam.
W. Pritt.
A. Ellis.
C. B. Banning.
M. Constable.
F. Reynolds.
Robert Patterson.
W. Pilkington.

1850—Continued.
W. H. Jackson.
J. Munns.
F. Thornley.

1851.
S. Perrott.
G. Swainson.
H. Craig.
J. Gray.
W. Gibson.
Geo. Jevons.
A. Dudley.
E. Harvey.
H. Barton.
J. H. Worthington.
W. Horner.
Paggan Hab.

1852.
J. G. Brown.
Jos. Crosfield.
C. Thompson.
A. Middleton.
W. W. Smith.
Duncan Graham.
W. Lyon.
Gordon Ross.
E. Rayner.

1853.
J. F. Lawrence.
J. Middleton.
E. Pryce.
G. Potter.
J. A. Smith.
James Fairrie.
B. Wrigley.
R. Moon.

1854.
— Garratt.
J. Hadwen.
J. B. Shaw.
W. J. Briggs.
E. Mottlerkamp.
E. E. Bateson.

No records till 1862.

1857.
J. B. Morgan.

1860.
T. B. Newton.

1861.
W. Williamson.

1862 or earlier.
John Bouch.
C. Bateson.
J. Bower.
G. R. Clover.
J. Crowe.
H. Cotesworth.
R. H. Coddington.
C. Cotesworth.
A. H. Cowie.
C. G. Cowie.
P. W. Curry.
H. Dixon.
G. C. Dobell.
Hugh Duckworth.
R. Edwards.
H. Tootner.
G. L. Fosberry.
S. Field.
J. Enthoven.
W. Griffiths.
H. Graham.
J. Gifford.
Rev. E. Green.
S. Gath.
E. C. Houghton.
A. R. Houghton.
J. Harbridge.
J. Haddock.
R. Hinshaw.
L. Hornblower.
A. Hope.
R. G. Hamilton.
H. Jefferson.
W. Jackson.
Charles Inman.
Fredk. Jevons.
C. Kingcome.
Seps. Ledward.
W. Mossman.
J. P. Mellor.
P. Mussabini.
T. Maxwell.
A. C. Mozeley.
Henry Oulton.
A. Potter.
James Poole.

1862 or earlier—Continued.
W. Paton.
George Rae.
J. S. Reede.
R. Roberts.
Jas. Robinson.
G. S. Robinson.
J. B. Spence.
Hugh Smythe.
J. P. Sheppard.
Samuel Stitt.
A. Stoddart.
R. J. Strafford.
R. Tetley.
J. B. Thompson.
J. H. Thomas.
G. R. Unsworth.
S. Wood.
W. Wignall.

1862.
James Green.

1863.
Edgar Musgrove.

1864.
John Gibbons.
F. Borthwick.

1867.
J. H. Macrae.
Edward Smith.
Desbh. Walford.

1868.
J. C. Cunningham.
C. S. Lemon.

1869.
Henry Loxdale.
J. M. Semple.
Rev. J. C. Macdona.
L. R. Stevenson.

1870 or earlier.
F. Boteler.
B. Bower.
Stuart Brown.
W. Boult.
C. H. Bolton.
R. R. Dobell.

THE MEMBERS.

1870 or earlier—
Continued.
Geo. H. Eaton.
A. Hartley.
R. Jones.
W. Joynson.
S. Maples.
E. Pictet.
A. J. Roberts.
A. Ryley.
James Roper.
J. A. Sellar.

1870.
W. Bewley.
J. N. Darbishire.
E. S. Holland.
T. H. Ismay.
J. T. King.
J. Langdale.
J. W. Macfie.
W. Nickels.
Lionel Peel.
E. Porter.
C. Rawdon.
H. Somerville.
R. S. Tipton.
W. Williams.

1871.
T. R. Bulley.
A. C. Beazley.
G. R. Livingston.
L. Mills.
W. Nevett.
W. Nixon.

1872.
C. T. Dixon.
Benedict Jones.
R. Livingston.
C. J. Livingston.
J. Walter.

1873.
H. Tennant.
J. H. Beazley.
F. E. M. Dixon.
F. Gardner.
J. D. Newton.

1874.
H. J. Sillam.

1874—*Continued.*
G. Bold.
Edward Joynson.
G. F. Lyster.
Jas. Porter.
G. R. Rogerson.
H. Barker.
J. Briscoe.
R. W. Dean.
W. E. Hall.
Thos. Littledale.
C. Chandos Pole.
J. C. Robinson.
J. H. Winsloe.
A. E. Yarrow.

1875.
H. W. Draper.
J. E. Gray Hill.
R. Leitch.
T. Percival.

1876.
W. S. Caine.
N. Caine.
C. Gatehouse.
M. Horan.
J. Leitch, Junr.
J. Mawdsley.
W. Pickford.
W. A. Todd-Naylor.
S. H. Woodhouse.
C. R. Wilson.
W. Wainwright.

1877.
R. Heap.
H. W. Hind.
G. Leatham.
C. Haddock.
A. C. Kent.
J. Gould Smyth.
E. K. Layborn.
C. S. Pain.

1878.
F. C. Hartley.
M. Clover.
E. Evans.

1879.
H. R. Bouverie.
A. Culshaw.

1879—*Continued.*
A. Hutton.
E. C. Kendall.

1880.
J. A. Duckworth.
G. H. Horsfall.

1881.
Meadows A. Frost.
J. D. Irven.
D. Layborn.
R. Marquis.
T. H. Thornley.

1882.
H. Brooke.
W. H. Legge.
D. C. Scott.
B. L. Tarleton.

1883.
G. Holt.
J. Urmson.
Jos. Ravenscroft.
C. B. Royds.
G. Herne.
J. Fairrie.
G. W. Jevons.
E. Lyon Keates.
E. Beazley.

1884.
C. Phillips.
C. S. Watson.
W. C. Hutton.
J. Tetley Nickels.
R. Cavan Robertson.
R. A. Young.

1885.
A. J. Brown.
F. C. Beazley.
J. G. Forman.
J. W. Bell.
S. Castle.
T. S. Hannay.
S. C. Smyth.
G. A. Solly.

1886.
D. A. Bingham.
G. A. Hastings.

1886—*Continued.*
C. G. Cowie.
G. H. Eaton.
W. C. Gardner.

1887.
R. A. Barker.
G. Cowie.
E. C. Dempsey.
C. K. Hall.
H. S. Hall.
G. Holtzwart.
H. B. Kent.
A. Ker.
J. M. Laird.
P. O. Lawrence.
A. Lawson.
John Lawson.
G. Nicholson.
H. B. Scott.
J. J. Shallcross.
P. M. Smyth.

1888.
J. G. Churton.
Geo. Irvine.
S. A. Williamson.
A. H. Wrigley.

1889.
H. Latham.
J. Turbett.
G. H. F. Duncan.
F. Rogerson.
C. E. Byrne.
R. E. Fox.
W. C. Cross.
A. C. Callender.

1890.
A. Wrigley.
R. E. Langlands.
F. G. Williamson.
J. W. Williamson.
J. A. Pownall.
F. Brocklehurst.
A. W. Bibby.

1891.
R. E. R. Brocklebank.
W. H. Cochran.
C. MacIver.
A. D. Holland.

1892.	1892—Continued.	1893—Continued.	1894—Continued.
E. Bateson.	J. Heap.	C. W. Laird.	T. C. H. Castle.
Capⁿ Blennerhasset.	G. W. Morrison.	H. W. Draper.	P. V. Churton.
M. A. G. Dowie.	M. Schintz.	A. G. Wood.	F. Edmondson.
W. Edmunds.		T. Royden.	R. Edmondson.
J. H. Gair.	1893.	R. Beckett.	H. C. Neilson.
F. Holt.	H. O. Cowie.		H. Todd.
M. L. Mills.	H. C. Duncan.	1894.	C. J. Williamson.
D.C.F. Pennefather.	D. B. Halhed.	C. R. Anderson.	G. D. Wilson.
J. MacDonald.	R. Jackson.	Thos. Brocklebank.	C. W. Wyatt.

Ancient Celebrities of the Hunt.

"If speaking truth
In this fine age, were not thought flattery."
Henry IV, Part I, act iv, scene 1.

The deeds of these gentlemen are recorded in the Sport Books of the Hunt, which were well kept for the first ten years by H. Walford and V. A. King, and are also celebrated in song by C. Rawson, who had the knack of hitting off the peculiarities and attributes of his friends. It is to be deplored that so few of them are alive at this day. From the life-tables of insurance companies it may be gathered, that out of one hundred men of the commercial class aged between twenty-five and thirty, about twenty should survive for fifty years. How many of the first hundred members of the R.R.B. are now alive? As beaglers are presumably all robust and healthy men, of active habits, we should expect the result to beat the presumption of the life-tables calculated on averages, the bad with the good. It can be ascertained that a dozen of this hundred are surviving, and it may well be that many others are still to the fore, though it is very difficult to trace them in the changes of a large commercial community like that of Liverpool.

Several of the ancient celebrities of the Hunt are shown in the picture of the beaglers at Beeston, painted in 1848 by Herr Trautschald. A reproduction of this picture is placed opposite this page. Beginning at the left, the three figures above are those of Robert Christie (left), C. Rawson (centre), and William Bowman. The two seated in the foreground are William Watson (left) and Robert Tinley. The central figure with the long stick is that of William Foster, with his hand on the shoulder of Thomas Arthur Bushby; William Lyon comes next, and then on the right the two Walfords—Alfred Walford with the seat in his hat, and Henry Walford with his long boots. The following song was composed by C. Rawson, *à propos* of this picture :—

ANCIENT BEAGLERS AT BEESTON.

BEAGLERS AT BEESTON.

(R. CHRISTIE.)
Ah! there's bland Christie, with his winning smile,
   In Christendom you'll find few better faces,
But, by the holy Moses! that profile
   Smacks of sham spectacles and shagreen cases.

(W. WATSON.)
And, shure, the t's Mister Watson sitting there!
   And mighty handsome is his picture drawn,
I wish you saw him follow hound and hare,
   I wish you heard him singing "Molly Bawn."

(W. BOWMAN.)
And who are you, my little broad brim, pray?
   That look as if you'd led these sporting people!
Who'd think that you'd been sitting through the day,
   Smoking your pipe, on Bunbury church steeple?

(W. FOSTER.)
Why smile so pensively, I beg to ask?
   You're always foremost in the jocund laugh,
I fear you're coveting that empty flask,
   You dog! you wish you'd had the "premier" quaff.

(T. A. BUSHBY.)
But see! that brow of pride and eye of fire,
   Actæon treading in the covert shades,
(His trowsers turned to keep them from the mire)
   Seeking the goddess and her sylvan maids.

(W. LYON.)
And you, my merry, joking punchinello,
   You think a Beeston "meet" is only a burletta,
You'll find there's more to do, my jovial fellow,
   Than cross your legs and whiff your cigaretta.

(ALFRED WALFORD.)
By Jupiter! but that's a splendid chap,
   On hardest days he's never known to yield,
He's got the certain token in his cap,
   That he's the boy to lead the beagle field.

(R. TINLEY.)
That's you, Bob Tinley! that I swear by jingo,
   You've laid yourself most gracefully at ease,
That eye belies you, or you've sucked all the stingo,
   And thrown the bottle to the R.R.B.'s.

(HENRY WALFORD.)
Behold Old Noll! the painter could not draw him,
   He said "he seemed so like a midnight rake,"
But I, and these green coats, that better know him,
   Declare in him there can be "no mistake."

Last in the group, but first in every heart,
   On thee the pen and pencil strive in vain,
Thy perfect picture is beyond their art,
   We'll never, never see thy like again.

Another song, composed by C. Rawson for the occasion of a dinner to the farmers at Beeston Castle, refers to a considerable number of the old members of the R.R.B. in their more convivial aspect, and, as the song is of great length, it may conveniently be divided, the latter portion being more appropriately placed after the description of the visits of the hounds to Beeston.

THE R.R.B. AT BEESTON.

You ask me to sing, but my boys I'm afraid.
A very bad choice you will find you have made ;
Still my shocking bad singing may cause you a laugh,
And mirth gives a zest to the liquor we quaff.

I never could boast that I'd musical jaws,
Nor e'er hoped to rival friend Walford's " jackdaws,"
Nor like Greenham, " The great Mogul's* accident " sing,
Nor come the pathetic like our Ching-a-ring.

Were I to attempt " Down among the dead men,"
You'd cry " Demme ! if ever we ask *him* again " ;
And Christie would cut me for ever, I know.
If I were to spoil " Slither down a rainbow."

Instead of fine singing, I'll give you a toast ;
Let us drink to the pack that's a pride and a boast,
From the Mersey's wide shores to the banks of the Dee :
Here's success and long life to the famed R.R.B.

The enjoyment they give can't be purchased with wealth ;
They've created good fellowship, given us health,
And his heart must be cold who's not pleased with the sight
Of the good-humoured faces around us to-night.

As long as we live we can never forget
The runs we have had and the friends we have met ;
What can e'er efface, midst life's future pursuits,
Our " By-gum's " good legs and our " Cromwell's " black boots?

And who can forget, when he thinks of the pack,
Bob Tinley and Cameron perched on a stack ?
Whilst Christie and Findlay, on top of a gate,
The return of the hare most patiently wait.

See, Walford is leading—then Hewitt and Clarke ;
D. O. Bateson and Hemery will run till 'tis dark ;
And we must confess without envious bias,
There's no better runner than Mister Matthias.

The great " Ching-a-ring," too, is in a good place ;
Our chaplain has run till he's black in the face,
Whilst Tobin is smoking behind them so far,
And Lyon's enjoying a paper cigar.

---

* NICKNAMES OF SOME OF THE ANCIENT MEMBERS.—" The Great Mogul " : H. Greenham. " Ching-a-ring " : T. A. Bushby (probably). " By Gum " : A. Walford. " Cromwell," or " Old Noil " : Henry Walford. " Evergreen " : J. Okell.

And who could forget the next figure that comes,
He's in a good place, but how queerly he runs!
Is it K ng? with his jacket so scrimpy behind,
A. King? no an emp'ror, the best of the kind.

There's Stockley, to who's introduction we owe
The kind welcome we get when to Beeston we go.
I must, too, our punch-maker, Parkinson, mention,
And those two artful dodgers, Cromwell and St. John.

Alfred Walford.

"I go, I go; look, how I go;
Swifter than arrow from the Tartar's bow."
Midsummer Night's Dream, act iii, scene 2.

This noted sportsman was one of the leading spirits in the early days of the Royal Rock Beagles, and although he was not prominent in the organization of the club, he made himself exceedingly useful in the management of the hounds, in the kennels, and in the field. Being a famous runner and a first-class sportsman, he was an invaluable whipper-in to the hounds, and when fortune favoured the R.R.B. with a good straight run, he was always well to the front, and in at the death. The Sport Book many and many a time records "only A. Walford and Jones up at the finish."

A. Walford was one of the first members, in fact, the thirty-eighth, and was elected to the Committee in 1846, retaining this position till his resignation in 1867. For a couple of seasons, during the period when C. Rawson had given notice of his intention to resign the mastership, and V. A. King was still absent from England, Walford acted as Deputy-master, and carried the horn. Some little interest attaches itself to this horn. It was the property of C. Rawson, and was of peculiar shape, as shown on Rawson's portrait, with a silver-mounted belt. When King became Master he used the modern straight horn, and C. Rawson's curved horn remained in the possession of A. Walford, whose son, Desborough Walford, presented it to L. R. Stevenson, when he was elected Master after the death of V. A. King. The horn is now in the possession of J. Gould Smyth as Master, Mr. Rawson desiring it to remain the property of the Hunt.

A. Walford's portrait may be seen in the picture of the hounds and a group of beaglers at Beeston. He always wore long white cord trousers, not breeches. One day, he accidentally jumped on a hare in a fence, and put it in the capacious pocket of his coat. It was the occasion of the annual dinner to the farmers, and coming home the 'bus upset; on regaining their feet and inspecting damages, the beaglers were horrified to see Walford's white trousers covered with blood, and thought he was fatally injured; but soon it was discovered that he had fallen upon the dead hare in his pocket, badly crushing it in his descent.

All his beagling days, Walford was a keen sportsman. Bad weather did not deter him. On rainy days, when only two or three were out, he was sure to be one of them. Sport Book, September 18th, 1847:—

Hoylake. Meet at 1-30 p.m. A most blustering, wet morning, frightening all but three members—Walford, Pyke, and Johnson.

At one of the Beeston meets in 1853, Walford was the only member who took the trip. He proved a worthy representative of the R.R.B.

A splendid morning, and our good friends all alive, but much disappointed at only Mr. Walford showing up. A large muster on horseback. Our first run a magnificent thing of an hour; six miles straight, giving most of the steeds quite enough, the land being dreadfully deep. The scent being so good, the hare had no chance; the hounds not at fault for a moment, and killed her in style. Then enjoyed Mr. Cawley's hospitality, after which, about two o'clock, turned out in torrents of rain; again had a splendid run of an hour and a half, and killed our hare in style.

In 1852, at the annual dinner to the farmers, Walford filled the chair, in the absence of the Master, and enlivened the company with his well-known song, "The Little Jackdaw," following it up with this moral—

> Let this be our maxim, 'tis the best I can put,
> Hunt the Royal Rock Beagles for ever on foot;
> And may he who would ride, meet the fate of this bird,
> And we all be present to see him interred.

When the huntsman Jones died, Walford hunted the pack for the rest of the season, showing great ability, and giving great satisfaction to his brother beaglers. After his resignation he always kept up his interest in the old pack, and his friendship with Colonel King and the old members. Many of the present generation of beaglers were familiar with his appearance on 'Change, and can remember his clean-shaved, keen, sporting face. He would probably have remained an active member for the rest of his life, had he not suffered from some affection of the hip joint, caused by a chill received through slipping into the Fender.

Alfred Walford has left two sons and several grandsons in the Hundred of Wirral, all fit to be good beaglers, and we all regret that we have not now a Walford in our ranks.

Henry Walford.

"I can keep honest counsel, ride, run, mar a curious tale in telling it, and deliver a plain message bluntly."—*King Lear, act 1, scene 4.*

This devoted beagler was one of the first members of the R.R.B., being the eighteenth on the register. At the time of the formation of the pack he resided in Rock Ferry, and interested himself most heartily in all the arrangements. In 1846, the second year of the Hunt, H. Walford was appointed Secretary, *vice* J. T. Raynes resigned, retaining the office till 1855. His services were much appreciated by the members, so much so, that in 1850, at one of the Beeston meets, he received a testimonial. The Sport Book records this event as follows :—

At 5 p.m. we sat down at the Tollemache Arms, to the number of forty, with our kind friends, Bird, Cawley, and Davenport as our guests. After dinner, a silver coffee pot, cream jug, and sugar basin, were presented to our most excellent and worthy honorary secretary, Henry Walford, from a number of the members, as a token of their regard for him, and a mark of their sense of his services.

H. Walford was a great favourite with the beaglers, always having a large following in the field, attracted by his wit and funny stories. By his cronies he was nicknamed "Oliver Cromwell" or "Old Noll," as he claimed descent from Oliver Cromwell, the latter's daughter having married one of his ancestors, Colonel Desborough. The names, Oliver and Desborough, are retained as family names in the present generation of Walfords. Walford's portrait is in the Beeston group, distinguished by his long boots. Whenever C. Rawson perpetrated poetry, H. Walford was remembered.

> What can e'er efface midst life's future pursuits,
>   Our By-gum's good legs, and our Cromwell's black boots.
>
> Behold "Old Noll"! the painter could not draw him,
>   He said he seemed so like a midnight rake;
> But I, and these green coats, that better know him,
>   Declare in him there can be "no mistake."
>
> Last in the group, but first in every heart.
>   On thee the pen and pencil strive in vain,
> Thy perfect picture is beyond their art,
>   We'll never, never see thy like again.

H. Walford remained an enthusiastic beagler to the day of his death in 1859. He was buried in Wallasey Churchyard. On his death-bed, he asked the Master, Colonel King, to have an annual meet of the hounds at Wallasey, and to have the hounds "whipped" over his grave, saying, "the "hounds will cry over me if no one else does." The "whipping" here desired was in the sporting sense, not meaning flogging. The members of the R.R.B. subscribed for a stained glass window, which was put up in Wallasey Church to his memory.

D. O. Bateson.

" Is not this your son, my lord?"—King Lear, act i, scene 1.

This gentleman is one of the few surviving original members of the R.R.B., and in the early days was a well-known and prominent figure in the Hunt. He was a good and persevering runner with the hounds, and no doubt his fourteen years' sport with the beagles laid the foundation of the remarkably good health he has enjoyed during his life. Bateson joined the club in 1845, and was elected to the committee in 1849, which office he retained till 1855. He sent in his resignation in 1859, on account of his marriage in that year, as Mrs. Bateson claimed that his Saturday afternoons should be spent in her company—"not in running after his horrid old dogs." He was appointed in 1852, along with A. Walford and H. A. Gray, as a sub-committee to fix on an alteration in the dress of the Hunt. The result of their deliberations is not recorded, but our present uniform is probably the outcome.

April 9th, 1847. D. O. Bateson made one of a party of seven beaglers who accompanied the hounds to Denbigh, on the invitation of Mr. Robyn. They had a fine time of it for a couple of days, and Bateson has a vivid recollection of their doings on the occasion. A description of the sport they had with the hounds will be found in the chapter devoted to records of notable runs.

Bateson relates that the party consisted of the Master (C. Rawson), V. A. King, R. Christie, W. Parkinson, A. Findlay, J. Hossack, and himself.

We arrived after dark, and were much disgusted to find the hotel occupied by a party of Welshmen, engaged in celebrating the coming of age of one of the notabilities of the neighbourhood. They had got the town band, and we thought it well to engage it also, after the festivities were over. In due time we proceeded to our dinner, after which we announced that we would utilize our band by having a dance. Accordingly the younger members descended to the bar to engage the barmaids, others ascended the stairs and brought down the chambermaids; in fact, all the females in the house were requisitioned, and right good dancers they proved themselves. In the midst of the fun, it was noticed that V. A. King was standing disconsolate and partnerless, until a sudden inspiration seemed to strike him; he rushed off, but in a few moments returned to the ball-room, leading in triumph the hotel cook, and with her commenced the most erratic waltz ever witnessed. The lady had cooked two big dinners that day, and not having had time to make herself presentable, her appearance and movements were not such as would have passed current at Almack's.

The next day, after hunting, we entertained our host to dinner, and also provided a supper for the keepers and shepherds of the neighbourhood. After dinner we descended to the bar to join these sportsmen, none of whom spoke English, which seemed no bar to their conviviality. Parkinson was especially popular with them, making speeches in broad Lancashire, which so pleased the

Welshmen, that they passed a resolution to make him member of Parliament for the shire at the next election.

It was now getting late, the wind was blowing, with the rain coming down, as it can among the mountains, but despite of this, two of us (King and Bateson), who were to sleep at a friend's house, had to find their way home. The night was pitch dark, our host was mounted on his pony, and he alone knew the road. However, off we set, all going well for a time, when suddenly both man and horse disappeared from the scene. The night being so dark, it was some little time before they could be found; at length both were dragged out of the ditch, when it was found that the equestrian had been stunned by the fall, and could no longer direct his friends. Here was a pretty situation. It was next to impossible to find the way back, and to go forward along an unknown road an extremely risky proceeding. After consideration of the pros and cons it was decided to trust to the pony, give him his head, and follow as best could be done. In the space of a few minutes the gate was reached, into which the pony turned, when the lights of the house became visible, much to the delight of the way-worn travellers.

D. O. Bateson has now a good representative in the R.R.B. in his son, Ernest Bateson, who joined the club in 1892, but previous to that date had been out with the hounds several times, and had made one of the party who went to Chirk for a few days' hunting in 1891.

John Okell.

"Let me play the fool:
With mirth and laughter let old wrinkles come."
Merchant of Venice, act i, scene i.

This gentleman is distinguished among beaglers as the partner with whom Tinley Barton, as previously noticed, hunted the Wirral country with three couple of hounds, before the R.R.B. were inaugurated. He took an active part in forming the pack, and was the fifth enrolled member of the Hunt. Although he only remained in the club for the first season, he was very useful on the committee during that time, and was mainly instrumental in finding the first two huntsmen, Kay and Jones. Having thus got the Hunt well under way, Mr. Okell disappears from the records as regards beagling, but as he was a keen rider to hounds, he hunted regularly with the Hooton foxhounds, and was present at the dinner given to Sir William Massey Stanley, an account of which will be found on a later page.

Even in his young days "Johnny Okell" received from his confrères the nickname of "Evergreen," and to the day of his death, some ten years ago, he was well known along the line between Ledsham and Birkenhead as a well-groomed, well-preserved, elderly gentleman. It seems possible that the epithet "Evergreen," applied to him in 1845, gave the bent to his mind which led him in his later years to take such infinite pains to hide all the ravages of time. A story is told of him that one day on the Stock Exchange, of which he was a distinguished member, one of the wags startled his fellow-members by saying. " Poor Johnny Okell dyed this morning."

Though in his young days a keen sportsman, J. Okell gave up hunting at an earlier period of life than is usual with those whose time and means permit the enjoyment of the sport. He, however, kept up his interest in the R.R.B., which he had assisted in starting, and always maintained his friendship with his old friends, the beaglers.

Bolton Littledale.

"What an arm he has! He turned me about with his finger and his thumb, as one would set up a top."—Coriolanus, act iv, scene 5.

B. Littledale was one of the first members of the R.R.B., and was the best runner of his time with the hounds, leading even A. Walford and the huntsman Jones. Our brother beagler, Fairrie, who knew him with the R.R.B. in 1851, says that he was without doubt the best runner that ever was out with the hounds, and that he jumped at anything, no matter what was at the other side. He always came out hunting wearing an old swallow-tail dress coat, with any old trousers he had, never wearing the uniform of the club. He does not appear in the records of the Hunt, except that he was elected to the Committee in 1849. When he retired from business he went to reside in Cheshire, hunting with the Cheshire hounds, with which he had a great reputation as a hard and straight rider. He was a noted preserver of foxes, and received the honour of the "green collar" of the Tarporley Hunt.

Robert Christie, Jun.

*" I am no orator, as Brutus is;
But as you know me all, a plain blunt man:
That love my friend; and that they know full well
That gave me public leave to speak of him."
—Julius Cæsar, act iii, scene 2.*

Robert Christie was a member of the R.R.B. for the first four seasons. He was the twelfth enrolled member, but did not take any active part in the administration or management of the hounds. None of his exploits are recorded in the annals of the club, but he was chiefly distinguished for his kindly and genial manner, which rendered him a favourite with everybody. He was particularly useful at the annual dinners to the farmers, when he contributed more than his share to the harmony of the evening, and was always the life and soul of the party at the club dinners and other social functions. His favourite song was " Slither down a Rainbow,' which title opens up possibilities of a good song, and it is a pity that no copy of the words is forthcoming. Christie was not a keen follower of the hounds, if we may judge from the reference to him in Rawson's poem.

> Whilst Christie and Findlay, on top of a gate,
> The return of the hare most patiently wait.

Christie's portrait will be found in the copy of the picture presented to C. Rawson.

> Ah! there's bland Christie with his winning smile,
> In Christendom you'll find few better faces—
> But, by the holy Moses! that profile
> Smacks of sham spectacles and shagreen cases.

At the dinner given to C. Rawson, Christie was Vice-Chairman, and had the honour of being selected to make the presentation of the picture to C. Rawson. His speech is given in the account of this interesting event, included in the notice of the Master, C. Rawson.

The Rev. W. Banister.

"Very reverend sport, truly, and done in the testimony of a good conscience."
Love's Labour's Lost, act iv, scene 2.

The chaplain of the Liverpool Workhouse was the first and only chaplain ever appointed to the R.R.B. As previously explained, C. Rawson, being then a young man, felt the serious responsibility of having so many young men under his charge in the field, and at the annual dinners of the club; he felt that he would like to have the support of a chaplain. Mr. Banister, being of an active and kindly disposition, readily assented to fill the post, which he retained for about eight seasons, often going out with the pack. Mr. Banister figured in the great meet at Beeston, celebrated in song—

> The great Ching-a-ring, too, is in a good place,
> Our chaplain has run till he's black in the face.

He severed his official connection with the R.R.B. in 1852, but till the day of his death always had a friendly interest in the Hunt, and occasionally turned up at a meet to see the hounds throw off. On resigning, he sent the following characteristic letter to the secretary:—

December 23rd, 1852.

My dear Mr. Secretary,—Having resigned the chaplaincy of the workhouse, and of Her Majesty's forces, I have yet hitherto deferred that keenest trial of my resignation—the severance of my professional connexion with the Royal Rock Beagles. But as I am so shortly to take up my abode at a long distance from the Hundred of Wirral, I feel that respect for the Hunt, as well as for my own character, obliges me to surrender honours gained rather by favour than merit.

I will thank you, Mr. Secretary, to inform the Hunt how much satisfaction I shall have in remembering friendships formed on a gatepost and cemented in a ditch, and which, proof against thorns and "Fenders," will ever be guttapercha'd on my memory's soul.

I must also add how much I now regret that idleness and engagements have robbed me of the recollection of many a good run, and, as my last official act, beg to admonish each member to avail himself of every opportunity of improving his health and temper by beagling gallantly on the fields of Upton, Landican, and Greasby.

Wishing you the best of sport, believe me, dear Mr. Secretary, without dodging,
Ever yours faithfully,
WM. BANISTER.

Mr. Banister was about twenty-seven years of age when, in 1844, he left a curacy in Essex to take the chaplaincy of the Liverpool Workhouse, and in 1852 he was appointed chaplain of the St. James' Cemetery, in Liverpool, where he was himself buried, 23rd January, 1892, aged 76 years. During this long connection with Liverpool he gained the esteem of all who knew him. He took an active part in the administration of the Hospital Sunday scheme, and the District Provident Society. Mr. Bannister was also an active member of the Liverpool Microscopical Society and the Naturalists' Field Club, of which he was secretary for twenty-five years.

EXTRACT FROM "THE MEMORIES OF DEAN HOLE."

Is it right for a clergyman to hunt? If I were a bishop, and that question were put to me by a priest, I should answer: If you can assure me that you can spare a day's holiday in the week, without neglecting any of your duties, reducing your charities, or getting into debt, you have my permission to hunt, on one immutable condition—that you ride straight to hounds; and if I hear of your craning and shirking, I shall withdraw it at once.

William Chambres.

"Oh! the blood more stirs,
To rouse a lion, than to start a hare."
King Henry IV., Part I, act i, scene 3.

Major Chambres was better known as a volunteer officer and civil magistrate than as a beagler; but having joined the R.R.B. in 1847, and on his resignation having been made an honorary life member, he enjoyed the distinction of being connected with the R.R.B. for a longer period than any man who has ever been on the register. He was a distinguished volunteer. He raised the Wallasey Company, now the 3rd Company of 1st Cheshire, his name being the first enrolled, and his captain's commission being dated 5th September, 1859. When his company was incorporated in the battalion under Colonel King, he was promoted to the rank of major, in December, 1861. Colonel Cunningham writes of him:—

Major Chambres held an almost equal share in the love and respect of every man in the battalion with his contemporary, the late Colonel King, and it is somewhat singular that both passed away at the same age—73 years. Up to the last, Major Chambres took the warmest interest in his old comrades and the affairs of the battalion, and his many acts of generosity and kindness will never be forgotten.

Major Chambres was a deputy-lieutenant and high sheriff for Denbighshire. He was made a county magistrate for Wirral in 1867, and was most indefatigable in his attendance on the bench. Mr. Eskrigge said of him:—

Mr. Chambres as a magistrate was ever eminently just, but at the same time his justice was tempered with mercy. To everything in the nature of meanness or cruelty he was stern to the last degree; but where there was any excuse to be found for the delinquent he was the first man to see it and to give it its due weight. He was a noble-living, courteous Christian gentleman. Whether the late Major Chambres was speaking to, or brought into contact with, men in high or low station, his courtesy was the same.

A brother magistrate was once brought before him for the offence of jumping on to a ferry-boat after the gangway had been withdrawn. Major Chambres felt it to be his duty to fine his friend; but to salve the wounded feelings of the irritated "beak," he assured him that he left the court without a stain upon his character.

Major Chambres encouraged his family to be fond of sport, and in later years he might often be seen, accompanied by his daughters, riding with the harriers. His eldest son for a few years joined the R.R.B., and doubtless his son Algernon Chambres, who is well known to most beaglers, would have joined us long since, had not his predilections towards horsemanship bound him to the harriers.

James Turbett.

"But wherefore do you hold me here so long?
What is it that you would impart to me?"
Julius Cæsar, act i, scene 2.

About the year 1848, when a very young man, Turbett came over from Ireland to learn business in Liverpool. He took lodgings at Rock Ferry, and being the son of a good old Irish sportsman, he naturally made the acquaintance of some of the beaglers. These invited him to the early morning meets in September, 1849, and getting imbued with the love of sport, he despatched the following letter to his father, in order to raise the amount of the subscription, he then being on a fixed allowance:—

2nd October, 1849.

My dear Father.—I write to make the following request: that you kindly send me a present of £3, being subscription to a pack of beagles that hunt on foot. I was at a meet at 6 o'clock the other morning: had an excellent run, which I enjoyed. I was delighted with the hounds, and all connected with the sport: the members were all perfect gentlemen. I have heard the Hunt are very particular in selecting members. The exercise is grand. I can arrange an occasional day's absence without interfering with office business.

His father, himself a sportsman, readily responded, and sent him the cash by return of post, when Turbett was duly elected a member of the R.R.B., 15th October, 1849. He had the honour of being proposed by

Bolton Littledale, and seconded by V. A. King. He remained a member for a few years, and hunted regularly, thus gaining his well-known knowledge of hounds and hare hunting by studying that most excellent huntsman, Jones. After Turbett's return to Ireland to join his father's business, he kept a private pack of beagles, which he hunted himself, and he still often recounts amusing stories of his experiences. One of his "yarns" is to the effect that he once took out his beagles along with a lot of tall draghounds. They got on a fox, and went nearly ten miles over bog and hill. Turbett, gamely following on as best he could, asked a peasant woman if she had seen any hounds pass by. She replied, "Och shure! and indeed I did, sorr, and the little "pups were mortal tired."

After an interval of thirty-five years, Turbett came to reside at Thornton Hough. Still hale, hearty, and enthusiastic for sport, he rejoined the club, and was heartily welcomed by all whenever he appeared in the field. A few years ago he bought a house at Gresford, thence hunting with the Chester Beagles and the Llangollen Beagles, becoming a familiar figure with both packs, and gaining the honourable title of "Mr. Jorrocks."

Turbett is the only one of the old members contemporary with the originators of the R.R.B. Hunt who is still able to appear in the field, and we all hope to see him out with us for many years to come. It was with much regret that in 1892 we received his resignation of membership, thus severing the link which bound the present members to the forerunners of the Hunt. He had not been a member for a sufficient number of years, to have earned the compliment of being made an honorary life member.

Other Ancient Celebrities.

"If I could shake off but one seven years
From these old arms and legs, by the good gods,
I'd with thee every foot."
Coriolanus, act iv. scene 1.

Among the first members there are many names worthy of selection for special mention in connection with the R.R.B., but the information now to be gained about them is very meagre; suffice it to register some few of them.

J. T. RAYNES was the first secretary of the club, a post which he filled to the entire satisfaction of all his fellow members for the first season, after which he gave way to Henry Walford.

T. A. BUSHBY is one of the few surviving original members. He was conspicuous with the choice spirits of the early days of the pack, and his portrait is among the "Beaglers at Beeston," celebrated in Rawson's poem, along with that of R. J. Tinley, who afterwards became the well-known Liverpool Volunteer, the late Colonel R. J. Tilney.

HENRY HASSALL has not left a record of his doings with the R.R.B., but he has left sons well-known in the hunting fields of Wirral; his youngest son, Alfred, being one of the chief supporters and managers of the Wirral Harriers.

The same may be said of HENRY ROYDS and JOHN RAVENSCROFT, both of whom have left sons, now distinguished members of the R.R.B. Joe Ravenscroft has been a very useful member, having been an active and painstaking whip from the time he joined in 1883; and he is now an efficient coadjutor to the present Master in the management of the kennels. In the field he is a noted hare-finder, almost rivalling in that respect our old friend, W. E. Hall. C. B. Royds has not yet proved himself a working member, as he has never filled any official position; but he is a great favourite with the members, and at the annual dinners of the club he does his part in contributing to the general harmony of the evening.

Our old friends J. A. SMITH and JAMES FAIRRIE come into the category of ancient celebrities, having joined the R.R.B. in 1853. They must have been much younger men than their immediate contemporaries; the former, J. A. Smith, being still on our books as an honorary life member, and Fairrie having only a year or two ago left us, after having rejoined in 1883 as an active member. Fairrie in his younger days was a famous all-round athlete. He was a first-rate amateur boxer, an accomplished figure skater, a brilliant oarsman, and a prominent gymnast. If lawn tennis had been introduced in his day, we should have heard of him in the forefront. With all his proficiency in athletics, Fairrie did not neglect field sports; he thoroughly enjoyed fox-hunting, beagling, fishing, steeple-chasing, and other sports, and what he undertook he entered into heartily, making himself master of the various details. He studied the literature of hunting, and is now an acknowledged authority on the subject.

Mediæval Celebrities.

"Now, by two-headed Janus,
Nature hath framed strange fellows in her time."
Merchant of Venice, act i, scene 1.

Most of these beaglers are familiar to us all at the present day, and some of them are still the senior members of the Hunt. With the exception of, perhaps, Morgan, Semple, and Joynson, none of them took any prominent part in the affairs of the Hunt, but they are chiefly celebrated for the length of time during which they have been connected with the club, and for the intelligent interest they have displayed in the sport and in the social functions connected therewith. They were a jovial lot of fellows, and even now that they have mostly severed their connection with us, they are always enthusiastically welcomed when they appear in the field. It was in their days that the pleasant trips to Llanfyllyn took place, graphic accounts of the doings at which still filter down to our modern ears, and make us long to have been present at the various episodes. Some of us can claim to have taken part in the later visits to this charming place, and the recollections of them are treasured up among our most cherished memories.

Joseph B. Morgan.

"He bears him like a portly gentleman."
Romeo and Juliet, act i, scene 5.

This gentleman naturally claims the first place among the mediæval celebrities of the R.R.B. Hunt, inasmuch as the early date (1857) at which he joined the club would almost justify his inclusion among the ancient celebrities, and also as his father, Mr. Edward Morgan, was one of the earliest members, joining in 1846.

Morgan was elected to be the secretary and treasurer of the R.R.B. Hunt in 1863, a post which he worthily filled for twenty years. During this time he was the active manager of the affairs of the club, and directed matters at the kennels, under the supervision of the Master, V. A. King, ably assisted for part of the time by W. E. Hall, who resided near the kennels. At all the social functions of the R.R.B. Hunt, Morgan took a prominent part. He was hearty and jovial with the farmers at the periodical farmers' dinners, greatly helping to make the festivities go off with proper éclat. He was a welcome member of any party of beaglers who had the good fortune to accompany "Old King" in his visits with the hounds to Llanfyllyn, his ready wit drawing out King's repartee, to the intense enjoyment and amusement of the others. Many are the jokes and the stories he could, "an he would," retail about the doings on these occasions. When Morgan in 1888 sent in his resignation as member of the R.R.B., it was unanimously resolved to elect him an honorary life member. Long may he remain at the head of the list of members!

In 1890, J. B. Morgan received the distinguished honour of being elected Mayor of Liverpool, being the second beagler who has attained that high distinction. The first was Sir James Poole, a member of the R.R.B. in 1862, who was knighted during his year of mayoralty.

Extract from the "Liverpool Daily Post," November 14th, 1890.
CONGRATULATIONS TO THE MAYOR.

Congratulating him upon his elevation to the civic chair, a deputation consisting of the following gentlemen, members of the Royal Rock Beagle Hunt, waited upon his Worship, Mr. J. B. Morgan, yesterday afternoon:— Colonel W. Chambres, Colonel J. C. Cunningham, Messrs. H. W. Draper, J. Gibbons, C. Gatehouse, C. Tempest Dixon, B. L. Tarleton, A. Barker, L. R.

Corbet Lowe. H. Hind. O. Leatham. J. Newton. J.W. Macfie.
H. I. Bouverie. V.A. King. N. Caine. I. R. Stevenson. Charles Williams.
H. E. Scott. H. Barker. J. Gibbons. W. Williamson. J. Gould Smyth.
H. W. Draper. Miss King. N. Caine, Jun.
W. E. Hall. S. Abbott.

Stevenson, C. S. Watson, W. H. Legge, E. Beazley, J. H. Beazley, J. G. Churton, W. C. Cross, J. Green, J. W. Macfie, R. Marquis, and D. C. Scott. Mr. J. Gould Smyth, the Master, said that, on behalf of the members of the Royal Rock Beagle Hunt, of which his Worship had been a member for so many years, he tendered their sincere congratulations, and trusted his Worship would have health and prosperity during his year of office, and that everything might go well with him. The Mayor, in reply, thanked them very sincerely, and said that it was with the greatest pleasure that he saw them. His regret was that he did not see associated with them some of the old faces. His first call on his way home after his election was upon Mr. J. A. Smith, with whom he spoke of old "beagle" days. He very much regretted that for some years he had been prevented, owing to his business engagements, from going out with them as much as he would have liked.

During his year of office, the Mayor, Mr. J. B. Morgan, gave a special sporting banquet at the Town Hall, at which Prince George of Greece who had that day arrived in Liverpool, occupied the seat at the Mayor's right hand. To this feast he invited, together with the representatives of all the leading sporting and athletic clubs of Liverpool and district, the Master and several of the members of the Royal Rock Beagle Hunt, who spent a thoroughly enjoyable evening, and were certainly both vociferous and hearty in their appreciation of "Old Joe's" profuse hospitality.

On a notable occasion Morgan once acted as huntsman. Charles Williams was unwell, and unable to take the hounds to the meet, which was at Prenton Bridge. Morgan proceeded to the kennels to get out the hounds, starting gaily off with young Williams behind to whip up to him. When the party arrived at the Half-Way House, all the hounds broke away and made straight for home. Not to be beaten, Morgan, with his usual pluck, returned to the kennels, and donning the huntsman's red coat, which was too short in the sleeves and far too tight for him, he again started off. This time the hounds followed him in their usual manner, and he arrived safely at the meet, where he displayed excellent qualities as a huntsman.

T. Banner Newton.

"But I am constant as the northern star."
Julius Cæsar, act iii, scene 1.

This constant gentleman occupies the proud position of being the "Father of the Hunt." Joining in 1860, he has, in this year of jubilee, been a subscribing member for thirty-five years, a period much longer than that attained by any other individual who has ever been connected with the Hunt, save and except our late revered old master, V. A. King, whose record with the R.R.B. boasts of no less than thirty-seven years of good service. Newton has merely to remain with us three years longer to surpass King's record, and render his position almost unassailable, the next possible claimants being

L. R. Stevenson, nine years behind him, and J. W. Macfie, ten years, while C. T. Dixon is twelve years in arrear. We all hope that these three good members will keep in the running, though we nearly lost Stevenson in 1893, he having sent in his resignation, but happily recalled it at the last moment.

Newton has always been a good sportsman, though never a great runner with the beagles. For many years he has had an excellent bit of shooting in the neighbourhood of Ormskirk, where he has spent his Saturdays during the season. He often came out with the beagles in "Ould King's" time, but of late years we do not see him so often as we would like. We have a portrait of him in the Raby group.

Many of the charitable institutions of Liverpool feel the good service of T. Banner Newton. He was Honorary Treasurer to the Children's Infirmary for many years, and the Savings Bank has been long under his management.

Septimus Ledward.

"And then go to my inn, and dine with me."
Comedy of Errors, act i, scene 2.

This "fine old English gentleman" was a member of the Royal Rock Beagles in 1862, and for many years remained in the club. Most of the present beaglers only knew him in his capacity of host, as it was his custom in the later years of his life to have a luncheon meet once a season, at the beautiful place he had built at Frankby. Here, in the large enclosed space of moor and mere, were plenty of hares, and a whole afternoon's hunting could be had without crossing the boundaries. Most of the hunting could be witnessed from the lawn in front of the house, and here, after luncheon, some of the older and less active beaglers would assemble, refusing to budge all the afternoon, notwithstanding the noble example of their still older Master (King), who tramped after his hounds in his usual indefatigable style. It is to be feared that Mr. Ledward somewhat encouraged these delinquents, as he liked to have a chat about old times with his cronies. The mere at Frankby, when frost stopped hunting, was a place of resort for frozen-out beaglers, Mr. Ledward making them welcome for skating, and hockey on the ice, a game which is now called by sporting authorities "bandy," and which under the circumstances is the next best thing to beagling.

To Mr. Ledward belongs the credit, as enlarged upon in a previous chapter, of having induced Colonel King to become a volunteer, and he always retained a strong interest in the force.

We never go on Frankby now, mainly because Greasby and Thurstaston, in the immediate neighbourhood, afford us better meets, but Mr. Ledward will always remain in our memory as a good friend to beaglers.

Other Mediæval Celebrities.

"Go bid the huntsmen wake them with their horns."
Midsummer Night's Dream, act iv, scene 1.

There are a few more beaglers, whose merits and position in the Hunt demand that they should not be passed over without reference under this heading. Our old friends JAMES GREEN and JOHN GIBBONS were members for thirty years, and well deserved the compliment paid them on their resignation of being made honorary life members. The former, unfortunately, in later years did not often go out with the hounds, and was therefore little known to the majority of the present members; but Gibbons to the last often came out to the meets, and was always present at the annual dinners, where his quaint and caustic remarks enlivened the proceedings.

JOHN U. CUNNINGHAM, who joined in 1868, was a noted runner in his time, and excelled in negotiating high and strong hedges by rolling over them. He succeeded Colonel King in the command of the 1st Cheshire R.V. Battalion, and retains the command to the present day. Though he is no longer a member we trust his son will some day take his place in our ranks.

> Turn out the guard at once,
> And wake up Ensign Cunningham;*
> Don't stand idling there,
> But do your best at running, man.

JOHN M. SEMPLE. This man also, in his time, was a noted runner, untiring at any distance. He joined in 1869, and was soon appointed by the Master to be one of the whips of the Hunt. This post he filled satisfactorily to everyone, never shirking his duty, but being particularly fond of going after "skirters or lingerers." He was a favourite with all, from the Master to the newest member, and all were sorry when the exigencies of business caused him to relinquish his Saturday afternoon's beagling.

G. H. EATON was a good beagler when he joined in 1870, but after some years he left the club and did not rejoin till 1886, thus losing his seniority. But for this interval he would now have been junior to only two members, Newton and Stevenson. Since he went to reside at Raby House, where he rents the surrounding shooting, there has always been a good supply of hares in the vicinity, and whenever we meet there, which we frequently do, there is a double certainty of what "Old King" used to call "a sure find," that is, a hare for sport, and afterwards a hospitable welcome to a comfortable tea. On these occasions, regardless of the weather, there is a goodly company of young ladies, and the daughters of our host eagerly follow the chase, taking keen and intelligent interest in the sport.

* Old camp song.

Alderman JAMES ROPER, somewhat late in life, joined the R.R.B. in 1870 or earlier (the exact date is not ascertainable). He was not an enthusiastic beagler, but attended the meets, and enjoyed himself in a quiet way, by strolling about and seeing as much as he could of the sport. He was a great friend of the Master, V. A. King, and of the older members, displaying great hospitality to the committee and others. At the inauguration of the Volunteer force in 1859, Roper was made lieutenant in the Oxton Company formed by King, who was its first captain.

W. JOYNSON was a member for a few years, about 1870. He was the keenest hare hunter ever known with the R.R.B., and was hardly satisfied without a kill. He contributed many accounts of runs to the *Field*, under the pseudonym of "Little Jelly Dog." An account which he wrote of a run from Liscard, January 21st, 1874, will be found among the notable runs. Joynson took unflagging interest in the kennel work, devoting much of his leisure to visiting the kennels, and becoming acquainted with the hounds.

Modern Celebrities.

"Would any but these boiled brains of nineteen, and two and twenty,
hunt this weather? They have scared away two of my best sheep."
Winter's Tale, act iii, scene 3.

As we approach the present day, it becomes more and more difficult to single out names of members of whom it is possible to write such information as is not well known to most, if not all, of their brother beaglers. Some are known for their running powers, others for their social excellencies, and again others for their hunting experience; but there are a few men whose long connection with the Hunt, and efficient service in the administration of its affairs, render it not invidious to give them special and individual mention.

The club is tending to become composed of younger men than has been usual at any time in its past history. The older members are dropping out, golf proving an attraction now, which was not so much in evidence in past times, when beagling was about the only out-door winter sport for middle-aged men, who did not hunt with foxhounds, or shoot. Still, at the present time, one-third of the members of the club are over forty years of age. The interest in the sport is well kept up by the members: quite thirty or forty, out of the complement of sixty, turning up at the Saturday meets.

William E. Hall.

> "Rose-check'd Adonis hied him to the chase;
> Hunting he loved, but love he laugh'd to scorn."
> *Poems—Venus and Adonis.*

Billy Hall (as he is familiarly known to the R.R.B.) was born at Brymbo Hall, near Wrexham. When he was a young man, his father came to reside at Rock Ferry, in order to put his sons into business in Liverpool. W. E. Hall went into a cotton broker's office, but, finding that he did not care for business, and being independent of it, he soon gave it up and became absorbed in his pet hobbies—beagles and rose-growing. During his residence at Rock Ferry he became "infected" with the love of roses, through his visits to his namesake, Mr. T. B. Hall, of Larchwood, who was, and is, famous as the champion rose-grower of the district, winning first prizes at all the flower shows held in the neighbourhood for many years past. After the death of his father, W. E. Hall resided with his sister at Woodhey, near Bebington, and on her marriage to one of our good beaglers—H. K. Hall—he went into rooms at Higher Bebington, near the kennels. Here he earned a great reputation as a rose-grower, winning many prizes; he also devoted himself to the hounds, taking all the trouble of kennel management off the hands of our worthy Master, V. A. King.

Hall was an indefatigable beagler, hunting at least three days a week with the Chester Beagles and the R.R.B. He was an appointed and efficient whip with both packs. He joined the R.R.B. in 1874, and hunted with them for some sixteen seasons. It may be said of him that he was, perhaps, the most useful member that ever joined the Hunt; he paid almost daily visits to the kennels, nursed the hounds when they were sick, and walked with them to the meets, also home with them, after hunting, to the kennels. It was at his instigation that the van we now have was purchased, and it is open to anyone to surmise that his idea was to save his own legs as much as to spare the hounds.

In 1889, during one of the excursions with the hounds to Chirk, when we were hunting with the Llangollen Beagles on the hills, Hall had the misfortune to stumble in getting over an awkward mountain wall, with a low wire running along the top. He came down rather heavily on some loose stones at the foot of the wall, and put his elbow out. This accident gave him considerable trouble for many months, and seemed to deprive him of his customary keenness for beagling. He resigned from the R.R.B. and went to reside in Shropshire, occasionally, at long intervals, returning to his old haunts, and receiving an enthusiastic welcome from his old friends the beaglers whenever he appeared at a meet. Rumour sometimes announces that he is about to return to reside in Wirral, and this gives rise to eager anticipations that he will once more rejoin us at our sport.

As a beagler, Hall was as "good as they make 'em." To few people is it given to have such an eye for spotting a hare on its form; he could see it when others could not, though the position was pointed out, indeed it is very difficult for any but a trained eye to distinguish a hare on its form, as it seems to have just the colour of its surroundings. Hall knew all the hounds by name, and could distinguish them at any distance; even walking home with the hounds in the dark he would address them by name, when others could only discern light-coloured moving patches, which probably were hounds, as they were known to be in the immediate vicinity. Sceptics on these occasions have been heard to remark that he called the names hap-hazard, trusting to the ignorance of his companions. Hall's portrait is among those of beaglers at Whitby, and also at Raby.

C. Tempest Dixon.

> "And, starting so,
> He seem'd in running to devour the way,
> Staying no longer question."
> *King Henry IV, Part II, act i, scene 1.*

Dixon is one of the best known and most useful members of the Hunt, having been a beagler for over a quarter of a century. Previous to his joining the R.R.B. in 1872, he had, for a couple of seasons, been invited by the Master (V. A. King) to come out and carry a whip. Since 1890, Dixon has been our indefatigable treasurer, and, *ex officio*, has a permanent seat on the committee.

Temp. Dixon, as he is known to his friends, comes very near to being the senior member of the Hunt, as there are only three names before his on the list in order of seniority. Having carried a whip from the first, he is now the senior whip, and in the absence of the Master he acts as his deputy, taking charge of the hounds in the field. He has all the elements of a master in his sporting composition, and, in fact, when our present Master was approached by a deputation inviting him to allow himself to be nominated for the post, he replied that he would like the office, but only if Dixon found that his business would prevent him from taking it. We all look upon Dixon as a model beagler, *vide* his portrait in the Raby group. He is quick in spying a hare on her form or stealing away in the distance, and as a runner he is well to the front whenever there is a good run. His cry of "Hold hard!" is familiar to us, and quite ready when anyone is pressing too closely on the hounds. A very amusing circumstance occurred a year or two ago, when Dixon was out with the Cheshire Beagles. He was running well in front, when some one from the rear called out, "Hold hard!" Those of us who knew Dixon were interested to see how he would take this outrage. He seemed at first unable to realize that the remark had been addressed to him, then, speechless with indignation, he glared witheringly at the offender for a moment or two, and quietly resumed his course, muttering smothered blessings on his head.

Dixon's knowledge of sport in all its branches is so marked, and his opinion on all matters connected therewith carries so much weight with the sportsmen of his district, that a few facts of his early life will be of great interest to his many Wirral friends. He comes from a sporting family of Yorkshire, where they have been well known for a long period. Several of his relations were noted foxhunters. His cousin, Mr. Tom Hodgson, was at one time master of the Quorn, then of the Badsworth, and finally hunted the Holderness hounds. Another cousin, Mr. John Dixon, of Astle in Cheshire, was joint Master of the Cheshire Hounds, along with Mr. Smith-Barry.

Tempest Dixon was born near York, 5th March, 1848, and when a boy, used to spend his holidays with his uncle, Mr. John Swan, of Askham Hall, near York, where sport of all kinds was rife. Here Tempest Dixon, along with his younger brother Frank, who is well known to us all as a brother beagler, used to go out in the dead of night, previous to a hunting day, with the earth stoppers. From these men he gained large funds of animal lore about bird and beast, game and vermin.

In shooting, Dixon was accustomed to the gun from his early youth. He inherits his skill from his father (who was a noted game shot), and can do his share with most sportsmen, being a welcome guest in good shooting parties. In fishing, he has had a varied experience, but does not take to it as a speciality. Most other sports he knows, but does not pursue. Dixon's father lived in the Highlands, at Grantown on the Spey, and there Tempest Dixon had much experience in shooting and fishing.

Daniel C. Scott.

"O, you shall see him laugh, till his face
Be like a wet cloak ill laid up."
King Henry IV., Part II, act v, scene 1.

This very popular member of the R.R.B. is well known to us all as our indefatigable secretary. He has been connected with the Hunt for thirteen years, and a slight sketch of his career as a sportsman will be interesting to his numerous sporting friends.

Dan Scott was born in London, 12th March, 1848. His family came to Liverpool in 1850, and to Birkenhead in 1853. His uncles Charles and Alfred Cowie were members of the R.R.B., and with them he had several chance days with the hounds during his boyhood. About 1868 the Birkenhead Drag Hunt was started by George Bole, William Cowie, and others, some score of young men having a good run every Saturday afternoon during the winter over the Bidston and Leasowe marshes. In the second season Scott joined them and became one of the most enthusiastic members. This Hunt has been a good nursery for beaglers; Smyths, Ravenscrofts, Cowies, and Beazleys having all in their time taken up the sport. The interest in the Hunt was somewhat fluctuating; during one season Scott and the Master, Pierce Russell, were the only two members who ever went out, taking it in turns to hunt the hounds.

Dan Scott joined the R.R.B. in 1882, and in 1888 was elected secretary to the Hunt, an office which he has filled ever since to the entire satisfaction of all concerned. He enjoys the work, finding it, as he himself expresses it, " extremely congenial to his tastes." On the occasion of his marriage in 1893, the members of the R.R.B. Hunt made a presentation of a handsome silver tea and coffee service, with a salver and an illuminated address. This gratifying present he received with as much pleasure as his friends experienced in giving it, and in wishing him long life and happiness.

His brother, H. B. Scott, was for a few years a member of the R.R.B., but of late has preferred to join the Cheshire Beagles in order to get the whole day's sport.

Dan Scott is fond of all kinds of sport that come in his way. He has had his turn at shooting, fox hunting. beagling, &c., and of late years has taken to golf and tennis. At local athletic sports he used to be to the front, acting as handicapper, starter, and judge. Scott's portrait appears in the centre of the group at Raby.

Herbert W. Hind.

"Didst thou not fall out with a tailor for wearing his new doublet before Easter? with another, for tying his new shoes with old riband?"—*Romeo and Juliet, act iii, scene 1.*
"What, Patch-breech, I say!"—*Pericles, act ii, scene 1.*

Herbert Hind can boast of as long a connection with the R.R.B. as anyone now in the Hunt. When he was about ten years of age, his father, an old member, gave him a green waistcoat with the club buttons, which he sported with extreme satisfaction whenever he could get out with the hounds. Hind joined the R.R.B. in 1877, and is thus one of the senior members, being eighth on the chronological list of present members. He has served on the committee, and taken great interest in the affairs of the Hunt, doing his utmost to promote sociability among the members. Of late years he has taken enthusiastically to shooting, so that we have frequently to regret his absence from our meets. His sons, during their holidays, take kindly to our sport, and we hope one day to have a Hind of the third generation in our ranks.

Herbert Hind's father was rather a fox-hunter than a beagler, hunting with the Cheshire and with Sir W. M. Stanley's Hooton pack. It will be considered a curious circumstance by present beaglers that the first fox he saw found was from Fir Grove, Claughton, then a fox-cover, but now a residential property.

At one of our recent annual dinners, our esteemed brother-beagler, Pickford, made a clever and humorous speech, in which he passed in review the characteristics of various beaglers. Among others, he singled out for words of commendation our friend Herbert Hind, whom he dubbed "Censor to the Hunt," and this title Hind has since appropriated, with the approval of all concerned. It is noteworthy that in the portraits of Hind in the groups of Whitby and Raby, taken eleven years apart, the attitude is precisely the same.

Edward Evans, Junior.

"I am thoroughly weary.
I am weak with toil, yet strong in appetite.
There's cold meat i' the cave; we'll browse on that,
Whilst what we have kill'd be cook'd."
Cymbeline, act iii, scene 6.

This old friend is now better known as a politician than as a beagler, and of late years he may more often be found on the golf links than in the hunting field, but he has always been interested in the club, and many of the members have enjoyed his hospitality at special beagle dinners. To him we have also been indebted for several good days' sport at Bronwylfa, near Wrexham. His father, Mr. Edward Evans, of Bronwylfa, has resided there for many years past, and having the shooting rights over a considerable extent of ground, he has been able to extend to the R.R.B. an invitation for an occasional winter day's sport over the farms and moors of the neighbourhood. These have always proved most enjoyable days, although we have been frequently unfortunate in the weather. Frost or fog has dogged our steps, and prevented us killing more than one of these mountain hares, which one lost its life through taking to the reservoir and failing to swim across. An early start by train from Birkenhead, and a pleasant drive from Wrexham to Bronwylfa, brought us to a hospitable welcome from Mr. Evans, with a party of sportsmen and ladies invited to meet us. No time was lost in "throwing off," and a good days' sport up the hills found most of us tired out by three or four o'clock in the afternoon, and straggling back to the house to try the resources of the establishment for tubs and hot water. Afternoon tea and a game at billiards whiled away the time till dinner was announced. We mustered a goodly number, as many as twenty at one time enjoying the hospitality of Mr. Evans, who entered heartily into the whole thing, and we may well believe he enjoyed it as well as we did. After dinner, speeches, toasts, and sporting songs, with a coster ditty from Mr. Arthur Evans, brought us to the drawing room for a little real music, before driving back for the train for home. We were a merry party, and woke the echoes with three ringing cheers for Mr. Evans and family as we took our departure.

E. Evans, Junior, joined the R.R.B. in 1878, and in 1893 was appointed a member of the committee, his record of attendance at which is nil. Although he now rarely presents himself at any of our meets, we are glad to see that his daughters take an interest in the sport, and frequently honour us with their presence. His son might by this time have been a beagler, but up to the present evidently prefers the game of hockey, and is strongly suspected of a tendency to join the Wirral Harriers.

Other Modern Celebrities.

"We single you
As our best-moving fair solicitor."
Love's Labour's Lost, act ii, scene 1.

T. H. THORNELY is a son of one of the ancient members of the R.R.B. His father, F. Thornely, did not long remain a member, as he was one of the prime movers in the inauguration of the Wirral Harriers, with which he hunted regularly for the remainder of his life. T. H. Thornely is one of our noted runners, his long, strong stride gaining for him the *soubriquet* of "our ostrich." In a good straight run he is always well to the front, but with a twisting hare he does not seem to care to run "cunning," and appears to be waiting for a chance to let himself out. At our annual dinners he sometimes favours us with a song, which is always highly appreciated.

A. C. BEAZLEY joined the R.R.B. in 1871. If he had remained with us, he would now have been one of our oldest members, fourth on the list. We have had several Beazleys (J. H. and Edwin A.) through our ranks, and we all regret there is no representative of the family now on the register. They were all extremely popular and good sportsmen.

W. PICKFORD, Q.C., joined us in 1876, and left Liverpool in 1892, having been a steady sportsman with the R.R.B. for sixteen seasons. Though absent, he will not be forgotten by those who knew him. He entered thoroughly into the enjoyment of the sport, and although residing at Mossley Hill, on the far side of the Mersey, he did not dissociate himself from the sociability of the club, but always attended the annual dinners, and also frequently accorded his hospitality to the committee and others by *recherché* dinners at his club. His clever speeches were a notable feature at the annual dinners. His portrait appears in the group at Raby, and also in that of the Cheshire Beaglers.

Of good runners we have a fair average in the R.R.B.: BROCKLEBANK, COCHRAN, G. COWIE, LEGGE, STUART SMYTH, and SCHINTZ, who have not been previously mentioned. These are all sportsmen, and not simply cross-

W. Pickford. J. Laird. E. Beazley. C. S. Watson. N. Caine. R. A. Barker. J. W. Macfie. Miss Macfie.
A. Kee. H. Brooke. S. Castle. J. T. Fairlie. H. Latham. W. H. Legge. C. Gatehouse. C. B. Royds.
E. Bateson. C. Phillips. W. Marctis. W. E. Hall. T. B. Newton. J. Cole. Miss King.
C. K. Hall. H. Hind. J. Gould Smyth. H. E. Kent. T. Holt. C. T. Dixon.
J. Gibbons.

country runners; they enjoy the hunting of the hounds on slow-hunting days, and only long for the rare days when a good straight run gives them a chance of leading the field.

> What biting thoughts
> Torment th'abandon'd crew: old age laments
> His vigour spent; the tall, plump, brawny youth
> Curses his cumbrous bulk; and envies now
> The short pygmean race he whilome kenn'd
> With proud insulting leer. A chosen few
> Alone the sport enjoy, nor droop beneath
> Their pleasing toil. —*Somervile.*

We once had a member who paid his subscription for two seasons, and although he lives in Liverpool, yet he never to this day has seen the hounds. In mercy let us withhold his name.

List of Members, Season 1894=1895.

Newton T. Banner- 1860	Solly G. A. 1885	Schintz Max 1892
Stevenson L. R. . 1869	Cowie C. G. 1886	Beckett R. 1893
Macfie J. W. 1870	Eaton G. H. 1886	Cowie H. C. 1893
Dixon C. T. 1872	Hastings G. A. . . 1886	Draper H. W. . . . 1893
Caine N. 1876	Barker R. A. . . . 1887	Duncan H. C. . . . 1893
Gatehouse C. . . . 1876	Cowie Gilbert . . . 1887	Halhed D. B. . . . 1893
Smyth J. Gould - - 1877	Hall C. K. 1887	Jackson R. 1893
Hind H. W. 1877	Kent H. B. 1887	Laird C. W. 1893
Evans E. 1878	Ker A. 1887	Royden T. 1893
Thornely T. H. . . 1881	Churton J. G. . . . 1888	Anderson C. R. . . 1894
Brooke H. 1882	Callender A. C. . . 1889	Brocklebank T. . . 1894
Legge W. H. . . . 1882	Pownall J. A. . . . 1890	Castle T. C. H. . . 1894
Scott D. C. 1882	Brocklebank R.E.R. 1891	Churton P. V. . . . 1894
Ravenscroft Jos. . 1883	Holland A. D. . . . 1891	Edmondson F. . . 1894
Royds C. B. 1883	Bateson E. 1892	Edmondson R. . . 1894
Phillips C. 1884	Gair J. H. 1892	Neilson H. C. . . . 1894
Watson C. S. . . . 1884	Heap Jos. 1892	Todd H. 1894
Castle Septimus . . 1885	Holt F. 1892	Williamson C. J. . 1894
Hannay T. S. . . . 1885	Mills M. L. 1892	Wilson G. D. . . . 1894
Smyth S. E. 1885	Morrison G. W. . . 1892	Wyatt C. W. . . . 1894

CURIOSITIES OF THE ABOVE LIST.

T. B. Newton's years of membership alone nearly equal the united years of the whole of the junior half of the club. The united years of membership of the ten senior members nearly equal the united years of the whole of the other fifty members; the average standing of the first being twenty years, and of the others four years. Only seventeen members are of over ten years' standing. More than half the members reside at Oxton, Claughton, or Birkenhead; only seventeen are dispersed about the Hundred of Wirral, the others mostly coming from the Liverpool side of the river.

CHAPTER IX.

NOTABLE RUNS.

"A right description of our sport, my lord."
Love's Labour's Lost, act v, scene 2.
"O, for a horse with wings!"
Cymbeline, act iii, scene 2.

In the following pages will be found a selection from the records of some of the good runs enjoyed by the R.R.B. during the first few years of their existence. They were mostly written by Henry Walford, but were evidently inspired by Alfred Walford, who was a famous sportsman and runner. These accounts are intensely interesting to us modern beaglers, as serving to remind us of our own sport over the same country. The names of places and topographical allusions are familiar to us, and we can readily trace out the line of the runs described.

FRIDAY, 1ST JANUARY, 1847.

Thingwall Mill, 11-30 a.m. The dogs found beautifully in about a quarter of an hour, to the west of the mill, changed hares in the second field, went away for Irby cover, through the cover with bewitching music right across to Pensby cover, and through it also, then in the direction of Irby cover again; doubled to the left; after very beautiful hunting took her to the back of Mr. Broster's (Irby Hall)—here a splendid burst right across the road in the direction of Frankby; doubled to the left over Irby Common, then over two fields on to Thurstaston Common, near to Caldy, where we lost, after a run of one hour and three-quarters. Found immediately to the north of Irby, took straight for Arrow Hall, doubled to the right in a fallow of Mr. Neilson's, went across the road into the Irby cover, took her through the corner of it straight on end for Pensby, and after very pretty hunting lost in a fallow where the scent was very cold; run one hour and a quarter. The dogs put up a hare beautifully in a field close to Mr. Hancocks'; went at a terrible pace for Irby cover, took her through it with glorious music, then to Pensby cover, right through it at full cry on to Mr. Urmson's, through the garden, along the road, and almost up to Thingwall Mill; doubled to the left for Irby cover, through it again, then straight away in the direction of Barnston; a fresh hare got up right amongst the dogs in a stubble, called them off after running over one field, got them on the old scent, right away to Barnston. When close to Barnston Dale she turned a little to the right, in the direction of the common, and were obliged to whip off at 4.30 p.m., as it was quite dark, after a run of one hour and three-quarters. Thus ended what was reckoned, by Messrs. A. Walford and King, to be the hardest day the R.R.B.'s had ever had, the sport during the whole of it of first-rate order. Four members out; 16½ couples.

NOTABLE RUNS.

SATURDAY, 2ND JANUARY, 1847.

New Hall, 1 p.m. Found close to the house, went right for Mr. Mostyn's plantation. While the dogs were in this, the foxhounds came close to, and for fear of spoiling the sport of the "scarlet coats," the R.R.B.'s were drawn off the cover, which was done without difficulty as they came to "horn" immediately. Found again near the house; she went first in the direction of Ashfield, then into the plantation, then towards Barnston, doubled back to Thornton on the road, up this in the direction of Ashfield, doubled again down the road towards Thornton, and was lost near a cottage, the inmates of which, it is charitably supposed, chopped her, as she was dead beat. The hunting very good, and scent excellent. Six members out; 14 couples.

SATURDAY, MARCH 6TH, 1847.

Capenhurst. After viewing the meet at Hooton and the presentation of a gold horn to Mr. John Stanley, we proceeded to Capenhurst, where about forty of us sat down to a splendid lunch, given, with his accustomed kindness and liberality, by William Parkinson, Esq. Just as we were turning out, we witnessed Sir William Stanley's hounds run into their fox close to Capenhurst. After they had left we soon found. Unfortunately the hares were too numerous for us, and completely beat the dogs. They never ceased running from one o'clock till five. The scent was good and the hunting perfect. No three hares could have lived through such a run, could we have kept to them, but as we were feeling assured of a kill, the pack would come across a fresh hare, whilst the old one escaped. It was calculated that we must have run nearer twenty-five than twenty miles. We only required a kill to have made this day's sport perfect. Thirty members; 14 couples.

THURSDAY, MARCH 11TH, 1847.

Barnston. Partook of an excellent lunch, provided for us at the hospitable house of our worthy Master, Mr. Tinley Barton. Could not find anything till we reached New Hall. Found in the long cover, drove her from the end across the back of the Hall, through the park down to the lower covers, and from thence back to the large cover. This ring she made five times with hardly any alteration. We viewed her at last fairly used up, hardly able to run, in fact she was nearly coursed down by a spaniel pup belonging to the keeper. Had the pack left the cover in time to view her they must have killed her in two minutes; unfortunately she reached the cover, and the scent having greatly fallen off, we could never again get her up, and she was far too much used up to move unless trod upon. This run lasted an hour and a half. Showed some splendid hunting, nothing hardly short of a miracle could have saved her. We were greatly grieved during this run at the conduct of one of our members, and record the circumstance as a warning to him and others. Just as we viewed the hare for the last time, completely done and nearly in the jaws of the spaniel, we were electrified by hearing this excited member shout to the Master, who was close to the hare, " Kill her, Tinley! d―― n her, kill her!" Comment is needless. Surely, surely, such a scene will never again occur with the R.R.B. Fourteen members; 12 couples.

FRIDAY, APRIL 9TH, 1847.

Left Denbigh at 7·30 a.m., and reached the public house at ―――― about nine. Turned out and made for the low land below Mr. Robyn's house at ――――. Found in some rushy ground, and away flew puss for the mountains behind the Hall. The pack passed gallantly up the side of the mountain, picked her well through the heather, and after a wide ring, drove her through the plantations near the Hall to the low ground again, where she squatted. They soon had her up again, and took her twice the same ring, till they lost her in a hard dry road, along which she had taken for nearly a mile. This run lasted two hours, and was first-rate. After partaking of a capital lunch provided for us at the Hall by Mr. Robyn, we again found below the house. Puss took the same course as the former had done, affording us some glorious sport for an hour and five minutes, when the hounds came up with her on the summit of the mountains, and after some beautiful coursing in view, ran into her in the open, after as perfect a hunt as can be conceived. The working of the pack was brilliant throughout the day, and elicited the warmest approbation from all. Seven members; 14 couples. Kill No. 29.

Henry Walford, who wrote the account of this and the next day's sport at Denbigh, was not one of the seven members present, but probably got the necessary information from C. Rawson, as the style is not that of V. A. King. The latter would not have "shirked his fences" in the shape of the Welsh names, but would have negotiated them somehow or other.

D. O. Bateson has furnished an account of the "good time" they had on this occasion, which will be found in the chapter concerning the Ancient Members of the R.R.B.

SATURDAY, APRIL 10TH, 1847.

Turned out about 9 o'clock. Found in the low ground at some distance from the Hall. As usual, puss, after a ring in the valley, made straight for the mountain; was again hunted back to the low ground and back to the hill. After an hour and a half's sport, we lost her again on the dry hard road which saved our first hare yesterday. Soon found again, but after some first-rate sport for an hour, lost on the same road, and almost exactly in the same spot. Lunch was again provided for us by our kind host, Mr. Robyn, to which ample justice was done. Did not find again till nearly three o'clock, when we put up a hare close to the river Elwy. We had two perfect rings in the valley, when puss gallantly faced the mountain. She now made a gallant run of it, no more doubling or turning. For four miles she went as straight as an arrow, along the very summit of the mountains. Finding, however, her pursuers were not to be shaken off, she turned towards home. The scent became worse and worse as the evening came on; the pack came to a check close to a wall, where, after losing much time in casting, we found she had gone through a hole just large enough for her, and the scent had then become so cold, that we were obliged to whip off, after a two hours' run. We must have followed her nine miles at least. This finished our two days' glorious sport in Wales. We cannot say too much in praise of the kind, hospitable reception we have met with from Mr. Robyn. The country is exactly suited for beagles, and it is to be hoped we shall be able to avail ourselves of Mr. R.'s invitation to visit him again in September. The seven members who were fortunate enough to accompany the pack were—Mr. V. A. King, Mr. D. O. Bateson, Mr. A. Findley, Mr. Hossack, Mr. W. Parkinson, Mr. R. Christie, and the chairman, Mr. C. Rawson—all of whom thoroughly enjoyed the trip. Fifteen couples.

SATURDAY, SEPTEMBER 25TH, 1847.

Moreton Village. Met at Mr. Parkinson's. Knocked about for two hours all over his and the neighbouring farms, and did not come upon a quest. Drew off towards Upton, and found a capital hare at 3-30 in some turnips, several members having previously got disgusted and toddled off home. They never made a greater mistake in their lives, for we had an hour and a half's first-rate sport. She first made for Greasby, headed back, and came down almost to Moreton, then back again and into a small cover on the Upton property, where we fell in with a leveret and killed after a run of a few fields. Again got on our old hare, and after a run back to where we first found her, she made straight for Greasby cover, which was full of rabbits, and we had to whip off. Tried for another in making back for Moreton, without success. The " real dealers " in the sport tolerably well " gruel'd." Twenty members. Kill No. 1.

SATURDAY, OCTOBER 16TH, 1847.

Met at Seacombe. Turned out near Wallasey Bridge, drew the covers near Mr. Ripley's house and round by the church. After an hour's beat, at last found in a turnip field belonging to a farmer called Maddocks. Away she went towards the Copper Works, across part of the pool, and along the pool; then away across to Mr. Littledale's farm buildings, and back to the turnip field where first found. She took the same round again, almost exactly, till back to a field near the same turnip field. Here we had a check of about ten minutes till she started up in the middle of the pack and again made to the pool, across an arm of it, and tried to get back to Mr. Littledale's. She squatted in a stubble, but they soon put her up and drove her into a ditch, where they at once ran into her, after a gallant run of an hour and thirty-two minutes of as good hunting as ever was seen, greatly to the delight of all who were out.

The above account is interesting as relating to a part of the country which has not been visited by the R.R.B. for many years, and which probably does not now hold a single hare. W. Joynson wrote the following account of a meet in the same country in 1875, which was published in the *Field*.

A real live hare is a great rarity in the township of Liscard, but as there was news of one knocking about, Col. King was kind enough to allow the pack over for a search after it. Thursday, January 21st, at 10-30, they arrived, but it rained so steadily and blew so stiffly, that the prospect of a good "tow-row" was remote, did we even succeed in finding. However, a start was made towards Earlston, where there was a seat from which she had been put only a few days previously. The grounds were drawn blank, but the pack opened merrily upon an adjoining clover root, which told us plainly she had been feeding there in the early morning: they could not, however, carry the quest beyond the shelter of a high wall, and we now began to look over every inch of ground. After some further delay, the hare was found sitting on a field of Mr. Littledale's, between Sea View Road and Wallasey Church, and the pack, being close by, were quickly after her, full cry. She made straight for St. Hilary Brow, where there was a slight check, but the line was recovered by the windmill, and then, without much dalliance, we passed down by Mosslands to the Birkett. Following the water for some distance, we ran over an uninclosed country, and from all appearances were making straight for Hoylake, but going eventually right-handed, we pointed for the upper end of Wallasey village, on the way to which the pack went through a dirty drain and came out as black as sweeps, presenting the most comical appearance, in fact, they looked so much alike that it was impossible to tell " t'ot her from which." Near the Leasowe road we were puzzled by one or two counters, but crossed at Spragg's brewery, and then took a journey through the shades of the market gardens, where I fear the early produce suffered some little damage. We were soon on the grass again, and back for the flats, where, leaving a block of cottages called Twenty Row on our right, we headed straight for Sutton's farm at Leasowe, up to which they rattled at such a rate that most of us were distanced, and could only follow their cry. The hare now considered herself far enough, and began to think about her "'appy 'ome," which, like the recruit, she was destined to see "never no more;" and so the pack came back towards us. Unfortunately a dog as big as a camel got view of her, and stretched her legs till near the top end of the Birkett, where we got rid of him and laid the pack on again. Along the left bank and then across the water they fairly raced for a mile over a grass country, without a hedge to stop them, and, following in the rear, the question became "to swim or not to swim;" but nearing Wallasey Pool we were just able to see the pack take the water like otter hounds, and, after a momentary pause, break into full cry up the hill towards the windmill. The scent had held so well that there were no checks to speak of, and the pace was so telling that nothing short of a horse could live with it, and so the hare, which ran so bravely, fell to the pack close to Mosslands, after a splendid hunt of one hour and eight minutes. The luncheon so kindly offered to us at this hospitable house was most acceptable, and I am sure we did most ample justice to it.

I find from old records that a hare was found by the Royal Rock Beagles on the 17th October, 1846, close to Mr. Littledale's house. The account says: "She made straight into the grounds in front of the house. They hunted her from this, when she made direct for Mr. Ripley's house near the church, round the stone quarry, and into the little gorse covert near Mr. Ripley's house. Being driven from this, she made straight back for Seacombe, down the road towards the bridge, where we whipped off, it being dark."

The pack are as staunch in 1875 as they were in 1846. At any rate we accounted for our hare, and I should like to see many such runs over Wallasey flats; but in these days one would be almost as likely to find a hare in Trafalgar Square. LITTLE JELLY DOG.

MONDAY, FEBRUARY 14TH, 1848.

Beeston Station. Turned out at 9.30. Soon found near the Castle, and after a capital run of three-quarters of an hour, ran her into a canal, where a boatman picked her up. Soon found again, and after an hour and a half's run, we lost near the cover, and then went off to Mr. Bird's house, where we received that warm and hearty welcome that never fails us, from our kind friend, Mrs. Bird. After partaking of her bountiful hospitality, word was brought us that our old hare was returned to her old form. We soon found her, and after half an hour's splendid sport, killed her fairly in the open. Every hound did his duty perfectly. Many of us then ascended the Castle, and when we were there posted, a hare that was set for us was started. For three-quarters of an hour we witnessed every turn of the hare, every double she made, and every check they came to. She never went 300 yards from the foot of the hill, and was during all that time never out of our sight. Seldom could such a scene be witnessed as we saw on this occasion, and the truth with which the pack hunted their game pleased everyone. Finding herself hard pressed, she made straight off for the new park, which, however, she could never reach, but was fairly run down in the open, after as glorious a run as ever was witnessed. Altogether a most delightful day. Fourteen members; 17 couples. Kills Nos. 28, 29, and 30.

SATURDAY, OCTOBER 14TH, 1848.

Barnston. Mr. Sutton had most kindly prepared a most hospitable lunch. We then turned out, making to the direction of Irby. After nearly an hour's perseverance, we were repaid by kicking up a most sporting hare in the gorse bush in the pasture below Irby, which took a straight-ahead line for Pensby, crossed the road and made a considerable ring, coming round into the pasture in which we first found, making the same ring again, with the exception that she this time took us down towards the Dee, coming up again behind Thurstaston, and back to her old quarters. The hounds had now got so well on her, and it was such a splendid scenting day, that we looked upon this as kill No. 6, and no mistake. In coming to our old beat, after an hour and a half's run (three-quarters without a check), the "dodgers" viewed her, and kindly (?) lifting the hounds, threw them off the scent. They got on the road, and we could make nothing more of her, after a most sporting run of near two hours. We tried back towards Barnston, but did not again find, having seen but one hare the whole day. Twenty-five members out ; 19 couples.

THURSDAY, 30TH NOVEMBER, 1848.

Greasby, 11 o'clock. This did not prove a very sporting day ; such a profusion of rabbits, it spoiled the sport. One small hare fell a prey to the hounds, and a dozen rabbits. Four members present, and 22 couple of hounds. Kill No. 12.

THURSDAY, FEBRUARY 15TH, 1849.

Queen's Ferry. Started from Sutton, a small party of four members. On our arrival at the ferry, found Mr. Crockford's keeper in attendance, with an invitation from that gentleman to go upon his land. We crossed the ferry and immediately proceeded to business : found in the first field we entered, a fallow, and had a few beautiful rings till she made for high ground, and got upon the numerous tram roads, and we lost her. We found again in that neighbourhood and could not get her away. We kept at this sort of work till 4 o'clock, and gave it up. Mem.—Not to go to Queen's Ferry again. Not a beagle country.

About four years ago the R.R.B. went to Hawarden by invitation, and enjoyed a good day's sport. The Wirral Harriers for the last three years have regularly met at Queen's Ferry, with great success.

THURSDAY, DECEMBER 9TH, 1852.

Brimstage, 2 p.m. Almost immediately viewed a hare on foot, which made through the stock yard and orchard, and on towards New Hall ; we came to an unaccountable check, and could make no more of her. Looked for another. Dairymaid poked one out of a hedge close to the farm ; this hare we could not carry in the least, though only a few yards in front of the hounds ; went along the bottom under Brimstage. Some labourers having seen a hare go into the plantation at the Clatterbridge workhouse, we put the hounds through it, and knocked her out : she took to the pits and along under Brimstage to the road, and up it near a mile to the turning to Bebington and Neston ; here she took to the fields, skirting the road down almost to the toll-bar, crossed the road on to the Poulton side, going almost down to the hall ; got into the road and came up to the four-lane-ends ; up a few hundred yards on the Raby road, and then into the rough fields to the left, over the bog, and into the road leading to Bromborough ; here she doubled, and made, like a fox, back to the four-lane-ends, and into the pits under Brimstage, and again into the plantation where we first found her; through this and along the flats to the Brimstage road, and again back under Brimstage to within a field of the plantation where we first found her; here she was viewed quite used up, but it had become quite dark, being a quarter to five o'clock. The best thing of the season; the hare must have gone over at least 12 miles of ground. Twelve members; 19 couples.

SATURDAY, DECEMBER 18TH, 1852.

Hooton Station, 1 p.m. A large muster of members, who were doomed to see very little. In a quarter of an hour got upon the quest of a hare; gradually got warmer, and the hounds took her at a rattling pace to the cover near the station. Got her out in view; she took up towards Willaston Mill, and away to the right for Raby, where she altered her course; back again through the wood, and over the rails up to the Eastham road; doubled back and crossed the rails between Bromborough and Spital, striking through the wood down to Poulton Hall, over the hill in front of the house, crossing the swamps to Clatterbridge, crossing the road into Brimstage, and away almost to Bebington Church. About the most severe run on record with the hounds. We lost our hare six miles from where we found her. Only three members and Jones living with them out of a numerous field, Jones being close at home, shut up for the day. Eighteen members; 17½ couples.

"He was quick mettle, when he went to school."
Julius Cæsar, act i, scene 2.
"Your hands, than mine, are quicker for a fray :
My legs are longer, though, to run away."
Midsummer Night's Dream, act iii, scene 2.

Mr. Charles W. Smith, the late Master of the Cheshire Beagles, has kindly furnished the following account of a notable run with the R.R.B., some thirty years ago. He and his friend Henry Lyon (son of an old member of the R.R.B.) ventured, in their salad days, before Smith had dreamed of being a Master of Hounds himself, to perpetrate a hoax upon the R.R.B. Hunt. It is quite a pity the Sport Books of the Hunt were not kept up at this time, as it would have been interesting to read what the authorities had to say about this affair.

I see it was in 1865 that myself and Henry Lyon (eldest son of Fred. Lyon, Esq., of Mollington Hall) ran that drag. We started from the kennels at Bebington, and ran a bee line to Mollington Hall, in the park, where, I remember, we both got up a tree. In about twenty minutes or so the hounds came tearing along. Distance, I should say, nine miles. We were both great runners in those days,[*] and used to hunt every Saturday with the Rock, as, being in Liverpool, we could get away; besides, the Chester Beagles did not hunt regularly on Saturdays then. We were about twenty years of age, and the run, I remember, was the talk of the Hunt. I never told Mr. Alfred Walford about the drag, till some three or four years afterwards. He was much amused. I need hardly say the "field" did not arive till about an hour afterwards, and then only two or three came up. Signed,

CHARLES W. SMITH, Master of Cheshire Beagles.

---

[*] H. Lyon won the "Crick" when at Rugby, for a thirteen mile race across country. C. W. Smith was a noted runner in the North of England ; during the years 1865 to 1868 he was a crack amateur at any distance from one to two miles, flat or across country.

Our friend Dixon, who writes under the *nom de plume* of "Storm," furnished to the *Field* newspaper an account of a run which is well remembered by many of the present beaglers, is still often referred to, and a repetition of which is earnestly longed for whenever we meet at Ness.

Saturday, 6th March, 1880, Ness. Did not throw off till half-past one. Soon found between the village and the Dee; she gave us a ring-up over the hill at the back of the village, and then took straight for the river. As the tide was out, we ran her three and a half miles over the sands. She swam two or three large sheets of water on the way, and then tried the main channel of the Dee; but the tide must have been too much for her, as the hounds carried the line right into the water, and we could also prick her to the edge. We took seven couple of hounds over in a boat to the other side, but they could not own to it; so we concluded that she must have been carried away by the tide.

It will be in the recollection of many then present how the hounds were nearly carried away by the stream in attempting to swim the channel, and many of the beaglers waded in breast-high (our present Master was nearly up to his neck, rescuing a hound, "Old Roper," which was drowning), in the vain attempt to reach the Welsh shore. It was only about a stone's throw from the town of Flint. When the boat was hailed and some of the hounds put in along with the huntsman and two or three beaglers, old Williams got into a desperate funk and characterised the proceedings as only worthy of a lot of mad school boys, and not hunting at all. However, he was brought safely back, after finding nothing on the other side, though W. E. Hall affirmed that he could prick the hare out of the water and up the shore towards Wales. We must assume that this hare was drowned, as the strong current would have carried her down at least half a mile before she could land.

> "O, I am scalded with my violent motion."
> *King John, act v, scene 7.*

The most notable run of modern times is undoubtedly that famous run which took place five years ago, in the year of mastership of J. W. Macfie. Finding at Pensby, near Barnston, and killing near Hadlow Road, makes this a run to be treasured in the memories of all those fortunate enough to have participated in it. The fact that every hunting day enjoys the potentiality of such another run, gives the intense enjoyment of expectancy to beagling; and a small share of moderate sport is enough to prevent disappointment,—when the expectation is not fulfilled—from damping the ardour of the beagler.

Considering the importance of this famous run and the goodly muster of members who enjoyed it, and who, more or less, appreciated its various phases, it will perhaps not be considered too monotonous if three several accounts of the run, from different points of view, are here presented to the reader's notice. The first was written by the Master, J. W. Macfie, and communicated to the *Field*. The second by C. T. Dixon, who being throughout the run in the most forward position, is the best authority as to the exact course of the hounds. The third was written by the compiler of this book, who had the luck to be among those who were up at the kill, being one of the three whips mentioned in the Master's account, Dixon and D. C. Scott being the others. The two ladies who gallantly struggled on to the end, and who deserved to have been in at the death—five or ten minutes alone separating them from this desirable result—were the Misses Gertrude and Hilda Bevis, who frequently hunt with the Cheshire Beagles, and are among the lady subscribers to that pack of hounds.

Extract from "The Field," January 18th, 1890.

ROYAL ROCK BEAGLES.

In this season of big runs with hare hounds, it may be interesting to some of your readers to hear what an old fashioned pack, as a correspondent called the Royal Rock, have been doing, so I venture to send an account of last Saturday's (Jan. 11) sport. The meet was at the Glegg Arms, Gayton, and one o'clock. A very good muster there was of members, ladies, and boys from school, looking fit and keen. There was a longish draw before a hare was found, hid, after a wild night, behind a gorse bush on Carnsdale House Farm, Barnston. The hounds being on the other side of the hedge she got well away, and it was a minute or two before they were quietly laid on. Scent did not seem too good, and the hounds had a little difficulty at first in settling to it; however they stuck to it and ran towards Barnston Towers a field or two, and turned up through some small crofts towards Heswall. Seeing someone in her way, she turned and ran on to the clay lands of Gayton; and the hounds fairly raced over Gayton and past Backwood on to Leighton Hall Farm, and turning east ran past Westwood, the residence of the popular Master of the Wirral Harriers, and over the Neston Road, on to and over a wheat field. Here the first check occurred, owing to the hare having dodged a little. After the hounds had had their try, the huntsman, Jonathan Cole, by a judicious cast, hit off the line near where puss left the wheat field, and the danger from too many enthusiastic and over-zealous friends and fresh hares was got over. The little pack streamed away past Thornton Hough and Stanacres, crossing the Raby road at Raby Vale, and bending towards Raby Mere. On and on was the cry, over Hargrave and Raby House Farm, leaving Willaston village on the right, and over the Hooton road, to within a field of the Parkgate railway, where as bold a hare as ever stood up before hounds gave up its life. One hour and fifty minutes, with only one check (of fifteen minutes) worth mentioning, crossing ten public roads and several field lanes; five miles as the crow flies from find to kill, by measurement on the Ordnance Survey Map. About a dozen of the field were up at the kill, among whom were three of the whips, several members, some youngsters from school, and two of the ladies immediately after. It being now late, and a long way from the fixture, the order was given for home, and all went their different ways, well satisfied. This little pack, which has hunted the Hundred of Wirral for nearly half a century, has enjoyed its full share of the good sport that has been going this season, and has had some rare runs with straight-necked hares. AN OLD BEAGLER.

NOTABLE RUNS.

C. T. DIXON'S ACCOUNT.

The meet of our little pack, on January 11th, 1890, was at the Glegg Arms, Gayton, and as we had an exceptionally good run, we will endeavour to give a few particulars of the day's sport, for the benefit of those who had not the good luck to be out; among whom, we are sorry to say, three or four of the best men with these hounds must be counted. Some forty to fifty members and visitors, among the latter a goodly show of the fair sex, welcomed the Master; and as Jonathan Cole, the huntsman, and thirteen and a half couple were ready, we threw off about 1-20 p.m., and first drew a fallow alongside Barnston Towers (the residence of our good friend, John Sherwood), then up towards Heswall Hill. We then took a turn, over part of the common and on to two fallows, towards Barnston village; hereabout the hounds spoke to a quest, and though they kept hitting it here and there, leaving no doubt that a hare had been on the move, it was not until our worthy Master was fortunate enough to beat out a gorse clump with his "wee stick," that his keen eye had spotted as a likely place for a hare to lie up in after the storm of the previous night, that up she jumped, and one of the right sort, as the following will prove. "Gone away!" soon brought the hounds, which, as puss had got away without a view, were laid on quietly by the huntsman, and the moment they touched the line it was plainly seen what the scent was like, as they raced away at once and took us towards Barnston Towers. The hare, evidently being headed at the road, turned to the right and up over the hill, as if going for Heswall village, then, bearing to the left, she made a point straight as if for Ashfield, keeping two fields on the Dee side of the Hoylake and Chester road all the way till abreast of Westwood, when she turned sharp to the left and crossed the above-named road, passing on the left of Westwood, where some splendid hound-work was done by the little pack, as she made some very sharp doubles. Fresh hares also were on foot, but they did not leave the line, and took it across the road into Mr. Kynaston's farm-yard, then through the orchard and into the gardens, where she happened to be turned at the lodge gate. She made several doubles in the grounds, eventually going out through the orchard again, and away pointing for Raby. The hounds were a bit at fault in the garden, and this being the first check from the start, let up a considerable number of the field.

A judicious cast round the big meadow at the back of the house put us on the line again, and hounds ran as if going for Thornton, but doubled to the right down by the stream side for some distance, then crossed it and up through Stanacres (Mr. Grainger's) and forward, pointing straight for Raby Mere, passing on the right of W. H. Cochran's house and over the road by the bridge in the dip at Raby Vale; then on for some three hundred yards, and then turned sharp to the right. Here a jolly farmer (Mr. Milton—a good friend to sport), out on his land on a good useful sort of a nag, could not resist showing the way over several fences in good style; indeed some of us felt as if we would rather be in his position than on "shanks' nag," as hounds were running breast high. The line taken from here lay nearly straight for Lydiate, but when about a field past Raby House (G. Eaton's), puss had doubled sharp to the left and crossed between there and Willaston Mill. At this point George Eaton, one of our good members, who always has a hare for us, being about with his son, joined in, and having stolen a march on the rest of the field, the hounds being a long way ahead, led us well for a mile or so. Here it seemed as if puss were going to the left of Hooton, but bore away a little to the right down to within two hundred yards of Hooton Station, where she got on the high road. A field or so back from here we saw a resident of these parts (a light weight) on a good-looking pony; he evidently wished to see more of the run, but his mount was not of the same mind, as we left him the wrong side of a fence and ditch, which from appearances seemed likely to give him amusement for the rest of the afternoon. Puss now ran the road for a considerable distance towards Willaston village, Driver and Baneful, two trusty hounds, speaking to it nearly all the time. Once she turned off the road to the left and got on the grass, the hounds ran breast high again, and it was plain—bar the chance of changing hares—that we were getting on good terms with her, as she commenced to make short doubles. The hounds worked splendidly, and came up to her clapped on a field close to the railway near Hadlow Road Station, put her up, but she was so beat they ran into her in the open a field ahead of any of the hunt. She was saved, and having had her mask and pads taken off was given to the hounds, and richly they deserved their worry, as the run from find to kill was one hour and fifty minutes, with only one real check. Not being good at distances, those who know the country can judge for themselves the ground covered; from point to point it is five miles. We were very glad to see some of the young contingent going right well; there were also one or two veterans who took a good place in the first flight.

During the latter part of the run, a keen sportsman (S. Comerford) who is well-known with hounds, and also " between the flags," joined us. We hope he enjoyed the sport, as he took a good line of his own and went well, though on this occasion on the same class of nag as the rest of us.

We cannot finish this without saying how pleased we all were to see one of our whips (J. Gould Smyth) out for the first time after his illness, and with him his son Charlie, who is a " chip of the old block," without doubt. STORM.

[NOTE.—The absent runners referred to above, were Joseph Ravenscroft and Stuart Smyth, who were away in South America.]

ACCOUNT OF THE SAME RUN BY N. CAINE.

On Saturday, 11th January, 1890, the hounds met at Gayton. After drawing over a few fields to Pensby, the Master (J. W. Macfie), with his well-known leaping-pole, beat up a hare out of a bush beside a pit hole. The hounds were then quietly put on the line, and went away with a good scent towards Gayton old mill. Some people scattered about (who wisely kept quite quiet) turned the hare towards Heswall, but after passing them she made her point towards the mill. The hounds here came to a check in a turnip field, but soon finding the line with a good cast by the huntsman (Cole), they went away at racing pace, almost straight for a mile and a half, towards Ashfield. They then swept sharply to the left to Westwood, where the hare had evidently made a turn for home, but was headed by a chance passer-by, and continued her line past Thornton Hough. The hounds came to a check at Westwood, for about a quarter of an hour, and we had a narrow escape of being put on to a fresh hare by a zealous county police officer; but the Master kept the huntsman to his cast, the hounds presently took up the line, and went merrily along the stream through Raby Vale for nearly two miles, then turning sharply to the right went over the rise past Willaston mill, leaving it half a mile on our right hand. Before crossing the high-road between Willaston and Hooton there was a short check, but a little judicious assistance by the senior whip (Dixon) put the hounds again on the line, and they hunted steadily to a kill, within a field of the Parkgate railway, a quarter of a mile from Hadlow Road station.

This run, from point to point, was four and seven-eighths miles, as the crow flies, and with the turns was fully nine miles, occupying one hour and forty minutes from find to kill. By this time those of the field who had come up to the finish had had enough, and went their various ways, well satisfied with the day's sport. The county policeman above mentioned did not live to the finish, though he started keenly from Westwood, and, as he became exhausted, shed his garments one by one, leaving his cape at one cottage, belt and leggings at another.

The most recent notable run with the R.R.B. was on 12th Dec., 1894, from Prenton Bridge to Heswall Church, and back to Barnston for a kill. Our friend, Tempest Dixon, communicated the following account to the *Field* :—

ROYAL ROCK BEAGLES.

As this pack, now just on its jubilee, is showing rare sport, perhaps a short account of its doings last week may interest some of your readers. On Wednesday, the 12th instant, the meet was at Prenton Bridge, over the Fender. This valley has always been looked upon as the cream of the country hunted over by this pack, and noted for its stout hares, and on this occasion it kept up the traditions of the past ; but alas ! a railway now being made right through it makes us sceptical as to the future. At the trysting place there were some seven members and a few friends to meet the Master and his eleven and a-half couples ; and, keen as ever, he threw off on the stroke of 12 o'clock to draw the land up towards Monk's Farm, Woodchurch, which he did without finding; but just as he was turning to try lower down in the valley, a message came from the farmer "to try his big field well, as there be two or three hares thereabout, he knew :" and right he was, as hardly had we got into the field when up one jumped, and the little hounds drove her in view down to the Fender, but here she made a sharp turn and came back to the right, then, turning to the left, she crossed the Woodchurch road and pointed as if going to Landican village, then edging off to the right crossed the Barnston road by Thingwall Hall, running up towards the mill, but on the brow of the hill turned left-handed, and went straight as if for Barnston, but just after passing the big dip going into the village, she took another turn to the right and headed for Heswall Common, keeping Higher Pensby on the right, the little hounds driving her along merrily all the time ; once on the common there was some very good hound work ; for although on the heather scent was good, in the sandy lanes, of which there are many, only some of the old hounds could own to it, but with the help of one or two view halloas we managed to work on over the common and down nearly to the church ; to this point the distance from the find is just four miles. Here she clapped in a garden and was very nearly clopped, but managing to get out of the drive gate, she took us in full cry right up the road, through no end of villages (all doing their best to mob her) and on to the common again, over which we had some slow hunting, but once off it, the hounds carried a grand head and were going their best pace, and as we had a grass country in front, it looked as if they were going to get their well-earned reward, which they did just at the church end of Barnston village, where they hunted up to their hare on a wheat-field and ran her in view, old Craftsman pulling her down. This point from where she was put out of the garden is quite one and a-half miles straight. The time of the run from the find was an hour and thirty-one minutes, and was as good a beagling run as anyone could wish, as although the pace was good almost throughout, yet the hounds never got right away from the field. After the trophies had been duly cut off, the hounds had their worry. May we have many more such runs, and may our worthy Master take home the mask of many such good hares, to be used as this one was, so whisper sayeth, to blood the last olive branch! The only regret was that not more of our young members were there to enjoy the good run. As we should have had to go quite five miles back, and hounds being handy for home, the Master decided not to draw again. STORM.

Mr. Turbett relates, from his diary of 1874, that, on Thursday, 26th Nov. in that year, he was present at Broxton, at a joint meet of the R.R.B. and the Chester Beagles. Each pack furnished a number of hounds, Mr. Bagnall, of the Chester, was Master in the field, and Howarth, the Chester huntsman, hunted the hounds. In the evening, there was a dinner at the Broxton Hotel, at which Col. King, of the R.R.B., presided. There is no record of the sport on this interesting occasion, the only item of intelligence being that snow lay on the hills.

CHAPTER X.

LUNCHES, &c.

> "*Nay, gentlemen, prepare not to be gone;
> We have a trifling foolish banquet towards.*"
> *Romeo and Juliet, act i, scene 5.*

On those occasions when the Hunt is invited to partake of the hospitality of some kind friend to lunch, or it may be to tea after hunting, it is understood by etiquette to be "open house" for all the members, and any stranger who is out on a member's invitation; but no casual stranger should venture in, unless specially invited by the host or by the Master of the hounds. Up to the last dozen years it was quite a common practice for the R.R.B. to have luncheon meets, but of late years it has been a recognized rule for the hospitality of our friends to take the form of tea after the sport is over. This is a marked improvement over lunch before or during hunting, and we are quite fortunate in having a welcome of this kind at those meets where our usual modest "pub." is not available. The Plymyard and Raby House stand high in the regard of the R.R.B. Hunt; and it is to be feared that, with all our care to get the mud off our boots, we must in the course of years have conveyed a considerable amount of mother earth into these hospitable mansions.

Luncheon before hunting is a sad spoil-sport. Not only does it occupy a considerable portion of the most valuable period of time, but it knocks off a lot of energy from the sportsmen. It is only the very young and enthusiastic who care for a hard run after a sumptuous meal.

The early records of the R.R.B. provide some instructive and entertaining incidents in this relation. They met many times each season at Woodchurch, and that good old sportsman, Rector King, always welcomed them to lunch, but there is one pathetic entry in 1848:—"Woodchurch. "No one at home at the Rectory, so we turned out punctually."
A desperate case is recorded, December 30th, 1846.

Claughton Hall, 2 p.m. A splendid lunch was provided for the Hunt by William Jackson, Esq. Only two members attended. Threw off at 3 p.m.; found on Oxton, and after about thirty minutes' hunting, whipped off."

This is very sad, when we consider that the meet was fixed for a late hour, and the day was one of the shortest in the season. Practically they had an hour's lunch and half-an-hour's hunting. These two sportsmen "take the cake." It is a pity their names are not handed down to posterity, but as the entry is in the handwriting of V. A. King, it is probable that he was one of them and A. Walford the other. As both were keen beaglers, we may assume that Mr. Jackson was disappointed at such a poor muster of members to attack his bountiful provision, and these two thought it their duty to be a "host in themselves."

Mr. Shaw, of Arrow, often entertained the R.R.B. to lunch, and this practice was maintained all through the mastership of V. A. King. Many other gentlemen in Wirral were good friends to the Hunt in this respect, and also in finding them hares afterwards; among them may be mentioned Mr. W. Parkinson of Capenhurst, Mr. Barton of Caldy, Mr. S. Ledward of Frankby, Mr. Jackson of Noctorum, Mr. W. Webster of Upton, and Mr. Duncan Graham of Lydiate.

1st January, 1852. Thornton Hall, 10 a.m. Friend Stockley all alive this glorious New Year's morning. After about a dozen of us partaking of a glass of wine, we moved off to a choice district between the Suttons, where we soon found our first hare. After a good run of near an hour, changed our hare. By this time considerable reinforcements of members arrived by train, which, added to an immense mob of country people, the field became most unwieldy; so large that they kicked up a continual succession of hares, which completely spoiled our sport and made the hounds wild and ungovernable. We knocked off at half-past one and adjourned to Mr. Stockley's, where our good friend had prepared a most sumptuous entertainment, some seventy gentlemen partaking of it, including three of our Beeston friends—Messrs. Bird, Davenport, and Cawley. This was V. A. King's last day with the Hunt before his departure for Bombay. Twenty-seven members present and seventeen couple of hounds.

Knocked off at 1-30 p.m. for lunch. No more hunting that day, nor is there any record of the subsequent proceedings. Mr. Stockley must have invited a great many friends, or else he was invaded by a greater number of casual strangers than members present.

24th March, 1853. Thurstaston. A large muster, chiefly of strangers. Mr. Macfie having provided a splendid lunch. The hunting only moderate, the eatables being the great attraction. The day was all that could be desired, and the members and friends enjoyed themselves right heartily.

CHAPTER XI.

THE COUNTRY.

> "They take their courses,
> East, west, north, south ; or, like a school broke up,
> Each hurries towards his home and sporting-place."
> *King Henry IV., Part II, act iv, scene 3.*

The country hunted by the Royal Rock Beagles is very easily defined, being bounded on the north by the sea, on the east and west by the estuaries of the Mersey and the Dee; the remaining south side, marching with the northern boundary of the country hunted by the Cheshire Beagles, may be defined by a nearly straight line drawn from Stoke, near the river Gowy, through Backford to Shotwick, near the Dee. This district practically comprises nearly the whole of the Hundred of Wirral, of which a very full description was published in the second season of the R.R.B. This valuable work (*Mortimer's History of Wirral*) gives us a very good notion of the condition of the country in the early days of our good little pack, enabling us, by comparing the past with the present, to forecast, to some extent, our prospects of sport in the future.

Mortimer dedicated his history to William Jackson, Esq., (afterwards Sir William,) of Claughton Manor House, who was prominent among the distinguished band who may be said to be the founders of the important town of Birkenhead. Mr. Jackson was always friendly to the R.R.B., and though his name does not appear among the list of members, it may be found in the Sport Book, where his hospitality to the Hunt is duly recorded. His sons and grandchildren have always kept up an interest in sport, being at the present day well known with the Cheshire hounds, and always receiving a hearty welcome whenever they turn out with the R.R.B. One of his grandsons, Rudolph Jackson, is now a member.

Although Mortimer in his history makes no mention of either the Hooton Foxhounds or of the Royal Rock Beagles (no doubt his book was ready for the press when the club was founded), he does, in treating of ancient Britain, give the following quotation from the translation of a Roman author:—

> There is a kind of dog of mighty fame
> For hunting, worthy of a fairer frame ;
> By painted Britons, brave in war, they're bred,
> Are beagles called, and to the chase are led.

This is fairly satisfactory as connecting the Hundred of Wirral with beagles, but exception may be taken to the phrase, "Worthy of a fairer frame." Our beloved beagles worthy of a fairer frame! Well, so they are, worthy of any frame. But surely they are beautiful enough to please any human eye: we can only presume that the Roman author had the Italian greyhound in view as his standard of canine beauty. It may well be believed that if Mortimer were now writing his history, he would recognise the R.R.B. as having become one of the important institutions of the country, and would give them some conspicuous place in his pages. Many of the names of the first members of the R.R.B. may be discovered in the list of subscribers to the book.

Half a century ago the Hundred of Wirral presented to the sportsman a very different aspect to that which it does at the present day. Then the country was cut up by one railway only, the Birkenhead and Chester Railway, which was opened in 1840. Now we have five more completed, and at least two more begun or projected, the making of which, during the next few years, will in all probability be in full swing, with their armies of navvies thinning the hares in our best remaining bits of country. There can be no doubt that the presence of these navvies in any country district is the sure signal for a scarcity of hares, and not of hares only, but of all descriptions of game, notwithstanding the preserving efforts of the gamekeepers of the neighbourhood. Previous to the making of the railway between Chester and Connah's Quay, the country about Blacon was over-run with hares, and was strictly preserved by Mr. Smith, of Chester, who had the shooting. Shortly after the influx of the navvies, the number of hares was so reduced that hunting became possible, and the Chester Beagles had a successful meet at Blacon. In the second year after the exodus of the navvies, the hares had again become so numerous, that Mr. Smith shot more than one hundred in a single season.

The making of the Manchester Ship Canal is another instance to the point. A few years ago we could find hares on the river side of Bromborough, at Pool Hall, Ellesmere Port, and Stanney, but of late years these places have been of no use to us. Now that the canal is finished we have begun to meet at Stanney again, though always in fear and dread of a blank day; but fortunately our good friend, Mr. Parker, usually has a hare somewhere about for us, either on his own land or the adjoining farm. It is evident that now the head of game is increasing, and we may reasonably hope that we shall soon have as good sport at Stanney as in former years, and so reinstate the place in our affections as one of our best bits of country.

The son of Mr. Grace, of Whitby, was indefatigable in his efforts to stop poaching about Stanney; he himself ran several poachers to earth and obtained convictions against them, for which they did not seem to bear him any malice, as they would probably have done to a gamekeeper or policeman, but always treated him with marked civility on meeting him afterwards. After all, one can hardly help feeling a sort of sneaking sympathy with these poor navvies in their love of a bit of fur or feather, though we must condemn the illegitimate manner in which, by net and snare, they take the game preserved at great expense by the rightful proprietors for their own sport. We beaglers are neither poachers nor pot-hunters, as, although on sufferance, we are fortunate in having the cordial consent of the landowners and farmers to hunt over their land.

Increase of Population.

"For if we meet in the city, we shall be dogg'd with company, and our devices known."
Midsummer Night's Dream, act i, scene 2.

In addition to the extension of the railway and canal systems in Wirral, the variation in conditions adverse to hunting during the past fifty years may be noted in the enormous increase of population, with the concurrent covering of the land with houses for the accommodation of the same.

The total acreage of Wirral is 59,912 acres. The following table will show the differences of population in the various districts, from the census of 1841 and that of 1891.

POPULATION OF WIRRAL.

NORTHERN WIRRAL.	1841	1891	SOUTHERN WIRRAL.	1841	1891
Wallasey Peninsula	6,261	33,229	Ellesmere Port and Whitby	839	4,977
Birkenhead, Oxton, &c.	9,009	66,220	Little Sutton	426	1,094
Tranmere	2,554	30,680	Great Sutton	203	395
Bebington, Higher	844	3,099	Mollington, Backford, &c.	1,407	1,546
Bebington and New Ferry	1,187	5,069	Stoke and Stanney	327	354
Bromboro' and Eastham	784	3,333	Netherpool and Overpool	128	441
Hoylake and West Kirkby	1,152	6,510	Capenhurst and Ledsham	235	241
Moreton and Upton	567	1,151	Looton and Childer Thornton	481	1,280
Bidston, Noctorum, and Prenton	431	723	Willaston	332	502
Woodchurch, Thingwall and Barnston	616	961	Shotwick and Puddington	304	235
Grange, Greasy, and Irby	669	986	Burton	282	266
Thurstaston and Heswall	511	1,355	Ness	485	354
Storeton and Brimstage	375	455	Neston	2,139	3,252
Poulton, Lacy, and Thornton	607	1,315	Total	7,588	14,937
Leighton and Gayton	523	524			
Total	26,090	156,222	Total population of Wirral	33,678	171,159

It will be seen from this table that the population of the northern portion of Wirral has increased sixfold, while that of the southern portion has merely doubled itself. The increase may be noted as chiefly occurring in the Wallasey peninsula, Birkenhead, Tranmere, and along the line of railway to Hooton; also in Hoylake, West Kirby and Heswall, which have quite recently developed as residential localities. In the southern end of the country, the increase is principally in Ellesmere Port and Neston. We may confidently assume that the tide of development in the Hundred of Wirral has about reached its flood, and that the ratio of increase will in the future fall short of that of the past fifty years. The opening of the new line of railway, now in course of construction, through Burton to Prenton, Bidston, and Seacombe, is looked forward to by many as the starting-point of a future "boom" in residential localities.

The effect of this increase of population on hunting may be seen in comparing the fixtures of the first ten seasons of the R.R.B. with those of the last ten seasons. Referring to the accompanying Table of Meets, it will be seen that we have been completely driven out of the Wallasey peninsula, as also out of the Tranmere district; and although we can still have frequent meets in the country about Noctorum, Woodchurch, Upton, and Bebington—which in the early days were the principal hunting grounds for our pack—we now seem to be forced to the southern portion of our country, having our principal and best fixtures at Ledsham, Willaston, Capenhurst, Ness, and Raby. Under these circumstances we may justly feel some amount of chagrin that the gentlemen who first inaugurated the R.R.B. did not foresee the probable cramping of their country, and take steps to procure permission to hunt the land about Mollington, which at the present day affords five good fixtures for the Cheshire Beagles, available for some six meets per month through the season. There can be little doubt that the proper boundary for the Royal Rock country should have been the canal running from Chester to Ellesmere Port.

TABLE OF MEETS.

SHOWING THE NUMBER OF MEETS IN EACH SEASON AT VARIOUS CENTRES.

	First Decade.										Last Decade.									
	1845-6	1846-7	1847-8	1848-9	1849-50	1850-1	1851-2	1852-3	1853-4	1854-5		1885-6	1886-7	1887-8	1888-9	1889-90	1890-1	1891-2	1892-3	1893-4	1894-5
Wallasey and Seacombe	3	3	3	2	.	.	1	.	.	.		.	.	.	.	.	.	.	.	.	.
Higher Bebington and Tranmere	13	14	7	8	4	6	3	3	.	.		.	.	.	.	.	.	.	.	.	.
Bebington and Spital	17	8	8	8	6	8	14	13	4	5		1	6	4	3	5	3	3	4	4	3
Bidston, Prenton, and Woodchurch	9	11	17	14	15	9	14	16	13	12		6	6	4	7	6	6	3	4	3	4
Moreton, Upton, and Greasby	4	11	8	6	6	9	10	12	9	10		3	3	3	2	1	5	7	6	8	4
Hoylake, Grange, and Saughall	2	1	2	3	3	3	3	2	2	.		3	3	2	1	2	3	2	.	1	2
Caldy, Thurstaston, and Irby	2	4	4	3	4	5	5	3	4	5		6	7	5	2	3	2	.	3	4	2
Barnston and New Hall	5	6	5	4	4	6	6	5	3	5		2	1	7	3	3	3	3	2	3	2
Thornton and Brimstage	.	1	2	3	5	6	8	6	6	3		6	5	3	3	1	2	5	.	3	3
Brombro', Eastham, Hooton	.	.	.	2	2	3	3	3	1	3		1	2	2	3	2	4	4	4	5	6
Raby and Willaston	7	1	3	2	4	4	4	4	3	6		4	7	4	3	6	5	6	3	4	6
Neston and Ness	1	3	1	.	1	.	.	.	.	.		4	3	3	3	3	2	1	3	1
Ledsham, Stanney, and Capenhurst	.	2	2	3	4	3	3	3	4	4		6	10	11	12	6	8	6	7	9	9
Beeston	.	4	4	3	3	3	3	2	3	.		.	.	.	.	.	.	.	.	.	.
Denbigh	.	2	.	.	.	.	.	.	.	.		.	.	.	.	.	.	.	.	.	.
Hawarden	.	.	.	.	1	.	.	.	.	.		.	.	.	.	.	.	.	1	.	.
Bronwylfa	.	.	.	.	.	.	.	.	.	.		1	1	1	1	.	.	.	.	.	.
Chirk	.	.	.	.	.	.	.	.	.	.		.	.	2	2	3	2	2	2	.	.
Malpas	.	.	.	.	.	.	.	.	.	.		.	.	.	.	.	1	.	.	.	.
Bala	.	.	.	.	.	.	.	.	.	.		.	.	.	.	.	.	.	.	2	3
	58	71	66	61	64	15	77	76	52	51		48	54	46	45	41	45	43	42	46	45

The Topography of Wirral.

> "Over hill, over dale,
> Thorough bush, thorough brier,
> Over park, over pale,
> Thorough flood, thorough fire,
> I do wander everywhere."
> *Midsummer Night's Dream*, act ii, scene 1.

This tract of country is called in Domesday Book, *Wilaveston*, derived from Willaston or Werleston. The Saxons called the district *Wirhall*, and in a document of the time of Henry VIII, it is mentioned as *Wirrehall;* nearly the same as in a deed of conveyance by the Commissioners of Woods and Forests, dated 8th April, 1820, where it is called the Hundred of *Werehall*.

There has been very little change in the natural features of Wirral during the last fifty years, and very few new roads have been opened during that period, the principal one being from Hooton Green to Queensferry. The fences and fields have been kept in much the same condition; so that, in reading the record of one of the earliest runs, we find the same terms as would be used in describing the same run at the present day. The most notable difference is the "running into cover," which is so prominent in the early records. The fences of Wirral have always been high and strong, and the country has long been known as a very difficult one for horsemen.

In 1845 numerous fox covers were dotted about the Hundred of Wirral, in which foxes were carefully preserved by the various landowners for the Hooton Foxhounds, hunted by Sir W. M. Stanley, of Hooton Hall. These hounds were given up in 1848, and since then many of these covers have been cleared away, for a variety of reasons; agricultural and residential purposes accounting for most of them. Others still remain, occasionally holding a fox, and giving a chance for a run to the Wirral Harriers. In recent years beaglers have viewed a fox away from Copley Wood, Gayton Gorse, Bromborough Woods, Hall Wood, Badger's Rake, Capenhurst Covers, and Stanney Wood. It may be confidently affirmed that our country has now less timber than when the R.R.B. commenced their career, and thus we now experience fewer occasions when hounds have to be whipped off their hare for running into cover; but on the other hand the country is a great deal more cut up by ploughed land than it used to be. In 1844 the Royal Agricultural Society published Palin's *Report of the State of Agriculture in Cheshire*, in which he says:—

The Hundred of Wirral may be said to be a dairy district, where the farmer's chief attention is paid to his grass land; the small quantity of land which he is allowed by his tenure to plough or break up, varying in extent from one-third to one fifth of his whole farm.

On the whole, we have ample reason to be well satisfied with Wirral as a hunting country; and the Royal Rock beaglers, all of whom are engaged in business in Liverpool, may consider themselves singularly fortunate in having such a country at their very doors, so easy of access that they may spend a morning at their business, and have very good sport in the afternoon. The author on one occasion left Liverpool by the 12-20 p.m. boat, and was with the hounds in full cry at 1-10 p.m., just fifty minutes after leaving Liverpool; it could have been done in half-an-hour, by using the Mersey Tunnel to Rock Ferry.

Although Wirral is one of the wettest parts of the kingdom, it can boast of no rivers of any importance, the only streams dignified by the name of river being the Birket and the Fender. These are really no better than sluggish brooks, which in very few parts of their course offer insuperable obstacles to the progress of the active beagler, although a goodly number of our fraternity have been into the Fender between Prenton Bridge and Old Ford Bridge. This part of the Fender has proved a more fatal trap to the Harriers than to the Beaglers, as it certainly requires a fairly good water-jumper properly to negotiate the leap.

The source of the Birket (or Birken, which gives its name to Birkenhead), is found just below Caldy village, on the Frankby side, whence it flows towards Newton and Meols, and onwards along the flat lands, parallel to the Leasowe shore, to Wallasey Pool, where such water as it has to spare gets into the Mersey through the Birkenhead Docks. When a good frost sets in after an excess of wet weather, the overflow of the Birket, on the marsh land about Meols, affords capital skating for any number of skaters who will take the trouble to go so far afield.

The tributaries of the Birket are the Greasby brook, joined by the Arrow brook, and the Fender. Greasby brook rises near Irby village, passes to the westward of Irby mill and Greasby to Saughall Massie, where it is joined by Arrow brook (which, starting from the other side of Irby, passes to the eastward of Irby mill hill and below Upton), and pours their united streams into the Birket, somewhere about opposite the Hoylake end of Leasowe embankment. The Fender has its source on the east side of Heswall hill, near Pensby, and runs through that pretty vale called Fiddler's Folly, by Barnston, and onwards between Landican and Prenton, under Noctorum and Bidston hill, joining the Birket in the Bidston marshes.

The only other stream of importance in our country is the Dibbinsdale, which begins in a full ditch between Ledsham village and Ledsham station, near which it passes under the railway, thence goes northwards between Childer Thornton and Hooton station, re-crosses the railway at Eastham Rake, receives the water from Raby Mere, and flows into the Mersey at Bromborough Pool. All its tributary streams join it in the beautiful little valley near Bromborough, called Dibbinsdale. The Clatterbridge brook, coming from Storeton, meets a brook from Barnston (through Brimstage) at

Clatterbridge, and further on receives a stream from Thornton Hough, near the road from Poulton to Raby Mere. At this spot, the last ford remaining in Wirral was spoiled by the County Council in 1891 " improving " the road by building a bridge. As there was comparatively little traffic on this road, it seems a pity to have done away with the old ford and foot-bridge. Raby Mere is a beautiful artificial sheet of water, formed by a dam on a small stream coming from Willaston, which, after turning the water-mill at the mere, joins the above-mentioned brooks from Clatterbridge and Thornton, and all run together into the Dibbinsdale. A small stream runs from Capenhurst past Great Sutton, and falls into the Mersey near Netherpool; another from Badger's Rake falls into the Dee near Shotwick. With the exception of the last-named brook and some field-drains into the Dee, all the watershed of Wirral may be said to flow into the Mersey. This is accounted for by the fact that there is a good elevation along, and close to, the shore of the Dee from West Kirby to Burton, having a short steep side to the Dee, and a long, gently sloping valley to the Mersey.

CHAPTER XII.

THE LANDLORDS.

"Let me commend thee first to those that shall
Say yea to thy desires."
Coriolanus, act iv, scene 3.

In the early days of the Royal Rock Beagles, the principal landowners of Wirral were generally resident upon their estates, and as most of them regularly hunted with the Hooton hounds, they were disposed to look upon sport in general with friendly eyes. With one exception, all who were approached on the subject met the proposal for the beagles to hunt over their property with cordiality, nearly all stipulating that Sir William Stanley's sport with the foxhounds should not be interfered with, and that the rights of the shooting men should be everywhere respected. The R.R.B. Committee were able to assure the landlords on these matters, and also to announce that the tenant-farmers were complaisant enough to welcome the beagles on their farms.

The large estates, especially at the north end of Wirral, have in many cases changed hands, and have been much cut up for building purposes. Only in five or six instances do the descendants of the original owners reside on their estates, the mansions of the others being mostly sold or let to Liverpool merchants, many of whom have also acquired the sporting rights. At the present day we do not come much into contact with the landowners, but depend on the goodwill of the farmers and shooting men for a continuance of our sport.

Among the original landowners of 1845 or their descendants who still reside in the district and allow us to hunt over their property, may be mentioned Birkenhead Glegg, Esq., of Backford; R. T. Richardson, Esq., of Capenhurst; Uvedale Corbett, Esq., of Ashfield; and W. Webster, Esq., of Upton. Nearly all these gentlemen are well-known sportsmen in the district, and to all we are much indebted for a cordial welcome to our hounds. It will not be without interest to the present generation of beaglers if a short reference is made to the principal landlords who were in any way concerned in the inauguration of the R.R.B. Hunt, and also to those who are best known to us at the present time. In 1845 the landowning families of the chief portion of the country hunted by the R.R.B. were the

Stanleys	of Hooton and Storeton.
Gleggs	,, Thurstaston and Backford.
Shaws	,, Arrow.
Kings	,, Bebington and Woodchurch.
Feildens	,, Bebington and Mollington.
Lord Shrewsbury	,, Oxton, Brimstage, and Raby.
Mainwarings	,, Bromborough.
Orreds	,, New Ferry.
Brocklebanks	,, Prenton and Tranmere.
Websters	,, Upton.
Corbetts	,, Ashfield.
Bartons	,, Caldy.
Greens	,, Poulton.
Richardsons	,, Capenhurst.
Parrys	,, Seacombe.
Ashtons	,, Gayton.
Leighs	,,
Pattens*	,, Woodchurch, Landican, and Noctorum.
Vyners	,, Thingwall and Bidston.

Sir William Massey Stanley, Bart.

"Live in your country here, in banishment.
With Sir John Stanley, in the Isle of Man."
King Henry VI, Part II, act ii, scene 3.

This genial sportsman was the direct descendant of the elder branch of the great family of Stanley, which divided in the reign of Richard II—the younger branch founding the families of the Earls of Derby (Sir John Stanley marrying the heiress of Lathom), Lords Stanley of Alderley, and the Stanleys of Ponsonby, Cumberland.

The Stanleys had been for centuries in possession of the manors of Storeton and Hooton, and Sir William succeeded to the title and estates on the death of his father in 1842. At the time of the inauguration of the R.R.B. he was High Sheriff of the county, residing at Hooton Hall, where he kept up a pack of foxhounds in good style, hunting the Hundred of Wirral to the delectation of a numerous body of gentlemen from the neighbourhood and from Liverpool. He was a good sportsman, and a great favourite with every one with whom he came in contact. While himself a

* The J. Wilson Patten, Esq., of 1845, was subsequently created Lord Winmarleigh.

good master of foxhounds, he was indulgent to the sport of other folks, from the shooting man to the humble beagler. A good idea of Sir William Stanley, of his position in the county, and of his relations with his neighbours, may be gained from an account of a dinner given in his honour, recorded in the *Liverpool Mail* of 23rd May, 1846. The guests at this dinner included a great number of our friends the landowners of Wirral, and many names of Royal Rock Beaglers may be recognised, some of whom (but, alas ! very few) are alive to this day.

Extract from "Liverpool Mail," 23rd May, 1846.

On Saturday evening, upwards of one hundred of the gentlemen who hunt with the Hooton Hounds gave a grand entertainment at the Monk's Ferry Hotel to Sir William Stanley, the Master of that celebrated pack, in testimony of the admiration and esteem with which they regard the worthy baronet, as a gentleman, a sportsman, a landlord, and a farmer. The entertainment was of the most recherché description. The view of the dinner table after the company was seated was of the most picturesque and novel character, a large majority of the gentlemen present being clothed in the scarlet livery of the chase. The chair was taken soon after seven o'clock by Hardman Earle, Esq. On his right sat the honoured guest of the evening, Sir William Stanley, Bart., and Messrs. Charles Stanley, Richard Ashton, H. Earle, jun., Thomas Earle, and Robert Neilson. On the left were Messrs. John Stanley, J. Shaw Leigh, E. Parry, Bolton Case, G. J. Wainwright, and J. S. Jackson. The vice-chairs were occupied by Messrs. John Laird and D. Neilson, and among the rest of the distinguished sportsmen present we observed—Messrs. G. Hargreaves, J. Grindrod, W. Hancock, C. C. Tennant, J. S. Stevenson, Chambres, Eggington, J. T. Raynes, Roberts, R. J. Tinley, R. Hemingway, Crackenthorp, Henry Todd Naylor, Todd Naylor, H. Barton, T. A. Bushby, Anthony, J. Henderson, W. Henderson, Kyric, Harrison, Whaley, Simpson, Hill, H. Watson, J. H. Hind, C. Rawson, Brancker, Steele, Cooper, Irving, Irwin, Leonnard, Parker, Wenman, Grundy, H. Davis, James Rigby, T. Green, W. Pike, J. Okell, C. Jones, Hill, A. Lyon, Keogh, D. Rae, H. Rae, Aikin, W. Cockerell, J. Solomon, Jerome Smith, H. Williams, W. F. Williams, Worthington, Dawbarn, Troughton, W. Lucas, R. Lucas, Stevenson, &c. The stewards were Colonel Tatto and Messrs. M. Humble, Tinley Barton, Jos. Dawson, and William Hind; and Jos. Aspinall, Esq., acted as honorary secretary.

After the usual loyal and patriotic toasts, the Chairman rose to propose the toast of the evening—the health of their esteemed guest, Sir William Massey Stanley. It was a source of the highest gratification to them to be permitted on that occasion, in the manner most congenial to the habits of Englishmen, to pay their respects to Sir Wm. Stanley—(applause)—not only as a private gentleman, but to convey to him their grateful acknowledgments for having so many years allowed them to enjoy the noble, invigorating, and popular sport of fox hunting—(cheers)—for without the worthy baronet it would be difficult if not impossible to maintain a pack of foxhounds in the Hundred of Wirral. But the value of every favour was considerably enhanced by the manner in which it was conferred—(hear, hear)—and every one who was in the habit of going out with his hounds must have been highly gratified by the urbanity of manner, the kindness and exceeding courtesy which was always evinced by the worthy baronet. (Loud cheers.) Even on those occasions, when the zeal of some and the inconsiderateness of others led them to transgress the strict rules of the sport, occasions so trying to the temper of a master of a pack of hounds, all must admit that Sir Wm. Stanley never forgot what was due from one gentleman to another. (Loud cheers.) Apart, however, from any selfish consideration, they must all desire that he might long have the spirit, the health, and the inclination to follow that sport. (Applause.) He might rely upon it, that nothing contributed so much to the securing of a green old age as the pursuit, to the evening of life, of so manly and health-giving a sport. (Great applause.) It was better that life should wear away than rust away, and among the few pursuits of active exercise, which man could enjoy in the decline of life, horse exercise was the best, because it was exercise without fatigue. (Loud cheers.) He concluded by apologising for the inadequate manner in which he had expressed the sentiments of the company, and proposed the health of Sir Wm. Stanley. (Tremendous applause.) The toast was drank with three times three.

Sir William Stanley, on rising to respond, was received with repeated rounds of applause. When silence was restored, he said :—Would that he were gifted with eloquence, or that he had the command of words to express in appropriate language the feelings that then possessed his heart—(applause)—for the sumptuous entertainment they had given him that evening was perfectly unexpected. He felt happy to find that during the four years he had been Master of the Hounds, his conduct had met with their approbation—(applause)—and so long as he continued to keep up the hounds, he hoped to see friends from both sides of the Mersey attending the Hunt. (Applause.) Any expense, any trouble he might have taken in the management of the hounds, would have proved perfectly useless had he not been supported by the landed proprietors of the Hundred of Wirral. (Loud cheers.) To those gentlemen they, in common with himself, owed a deep debt of gratitude. (Continued cheers.) It was impossible to name one who more than another contributed to their gratification in this respect ; but he must allude to one gentleman who sat at that table, Mr. Parry. (Loud cheers.) That gentleman, at a great expense to himself, and not with the view of fox-hunting, but for the purpose of shooting, had taken a place which, as they all knew, contained two of their best covers, and he had only to name Prenton, to recall this fact to their recollection. (Enthusiastic cheers.) He would go a little further, and allude to a gentleman than whom, although no longer himself a fox-hunter, a better sportsman did not exist—Mr. Feilden, of Mollington. (Applause.) Although the foxes on his estate came from an ice-house, yet they had given many a good horse a warming. (Loud laughter and applause.) He would now go to the Squire of Burton, whose cover had been often tried and never found wanting—(loud cheers)—and were he to allude to Poulton, he should stay there all night. (Laughter and applause.) Mr. Mainwaring and Mr. Green had always been friends to fox-hunting. (Applause.) He would next mention Mr. Ashton, of Gayton, and express his conviction that Gayton Gorse would never be bare—(loud applause)—and then go a little further, to Mr. Shaw, of Arrow, who owned a very large cover, which although they had been disappointed at the beginning of the season, had made up for it at a later period. (Renewed applause.) He now came to Mr. Leigh. (Applause.) His was a small cover, but it was a most excellent one. He forgot the exact number of times they had found there, but it was an unheard-of and almost incredible number. (Loud applause.) He trusted that in the next season they should be equally fortunate. He must conclude his list with Colonel Glegg (whom, he was sorry to say, illness had prevented from attending that day)—a gentleman from whom, with others who did not follow the noble science of fox-hunting, they had always received the greatest civility and accommodation. (Cheers.) Sir William concluded by proposing the health of the chairman, which was drank with three times three hearty cheers.

The Chairman responded in an appropriate speech, in which he explained that he had been placed in that chair in consequence of the illness of an excellent neighbour of his, Colonel Glegg, who had promised to preside over the meeting. He concluded by giving "Colonel Glegg," and better health to him: a toast which was drank with great heartiness.

The next toast, the health of Sir William's brother, Mr. John Stanley, was received with unbounded applause, and that gentleman acknowledged the compliment in a neat speech, in which he said that foxes bid fair to be plentiful in the ensuing season, and as they had some excellent dogs, he thought he could promise them capital sport.

The health of Mr. Charles Stanley, the respected uncle of Sr William, was next drank with enthusiasm, and that gentleman's speech in reply was loudly cheered.

Mr. Daniel Neilson proposed the farmers of Wirral. (Loud applause.) They were greatly obliged to the farmers for allowing them to sport over their lands, particularly as the huntsmen did great damage in knocking down fences and working up their furrows. (Applause.) With that toast he begged to couple the name of Mr. Tinley Barton. (Loud applause.)

Mr. T. Barton returned thanks. He was sure that the farmers felt it an honour to have such a landlord as Sir William Stanley ride across their lands. (Applause.) They were delighted to see him on all occasions, and Mr. J. Stanley as well. (Applause.) They had also to return thanks to Sir William for allowing the Rock Beagles to run over his unpreserved lands. (Applause.)

Mr. John Laird made some excellent remarks on the improvement visible in the cultivation of the soil, and proposed the health of a gentleman celebrated for the leading part he had taken in agricultural improvement—Mr. Robert Neilson. (Great cheering.)

Sir William Stanley proposed the health of the vice-presidents. Mr. Laird, he was sorry to say, had not attended the hunting-field lately, as in days of yore, but he had been engaged in other pursuits; and where he (Sir William) would have raised a gorse cover. Mr. Laird had founded a city. (Loud cheers.) He was happy to say their other vice-president, Mr. Daniel Neilson, was a constant attendant in the field. (Applause.) He was much surprised, however, to hear Mr. Neilson, the prince of heavy weights—(applause)—make the remark that hunting injured the farmer. To well-drained lands—and every man ought to drain his land—riding over them did them no injury. On the contrary, fox-hunters were the best friends the farmer had. Who purchased his straw and his oats? and if he had a young horse, who bought it but the fox-hunter? (Great cheering.) His friend had made a mistake, but nevertheless they would drink his health in a bumper. (Applause.) He concluded by giving "The Vice-presidents." (Renewed applause.)

The following toasts were also given:—"Mr. E. Parry, Mr. John Shaw Leigh, and the preservers of foxes in the Hundred of Wirral"; "The Cheshire Witches" (acknowledged by Mr. Robert Neilson in a poetically eloquent speech); "Mr. White and the Cheshire Hounds," &c., &c.; and the conviviality of the evening was kept up until midnight, when the company separated. A special boat was engaged for the conveyance of gentlemen residing at Liverpool.

Sir William Stanley was a good friend to the Royal Rock Beagles, and took a cordial interest in their doings. The copy of a letter from C. Rawson, applying for permission to hunt over Sir William's land, is given in a previous chapter. He readily accorded permission, but stipulated that the hounds should always be stopped from going into fox covers. There is no record of any trouble in this respect during the few following years in which the foxhounds were maintained; but in the Sport Books are many instances of runs stopped on account of the hare taking to cover.

Sir William gave up the pack of foxhounds in 1848, and some time afterwards left Hooton Hall, which was purchased by Mr. Naylor, the present non-resident owner.

Mr. John Massey Stanley (the brother to Sir William mentioned in the above report of the dinner), in later years, acquired the title of Sir John Errington, and in 1893 died at Cannes, the last of his line, aged 82 years. He was an intimate friend of Napoleon III, who, on one of his visits to England, stayed for a time at Hooton Hall. Mr. G. E. Taunton, of the Marfords Bromborough, an old member of the R.R.B., used to point out a wide and difficult place in the Dibbinsdale brook, below the Marfords, over which the Emperor leaped his horse, to the admiration of all beholders.

The Gleggs.

> "Let us every one go home,
> And laugh this sport o'er by a country fire;
> Sir John and all."
> *Merry Wives of Windsor, act v, scene 5.*

This is a very ancient family in Cheshire. At one time its representatives owned and resided in a great many of the halls and mansions of Wirral, including Mollington, Backford, Gayton, Irby, Thurstaston, Grange, and Caldy. It was an ancestor of the Gleggs who resided in Gayton Hall when King William III, on his way to Ireland in 1689, slept at the Hall. The bed and bedroom occupied by him are shown to visitors to this day.

At the time of the inauguration of the Royal Rock Beagles, the chief landowners of the Gleggs in Wirral were Colonel John Baskerville Glegg, of Thurstaston Hall, and Captain E. H. Glegg, of Backford Hall. The latter had not much to do with the R.R.B., as their country then hardly extended to his property, though they sometimes ran on to it from Sutton. The present representative of the family in Wirral, Mr. Birkenhead Glegg, of Backford Hall, is a good friend to beagles, being a member of the Cheshire Beagles, which hunt his country, and treating them most hospitably when they come there. He is equally well disposed to the R.R.B., and has invited them to meet at Backford Hall.

J. R. Shaw, Esq., of Arrow.

"Go, sirrah, take them to the buttery,
And give them friendly welcome every one:
Let them want nothing that my house affords."
Taming of the Shrew, Induction, scene 1.

A year or two previous to the inauguration of the Royal Rock Beagles, the late Mr. John Ralph Shaw had come into possession of Arrow Hall and the township of Arrow. The park is an enclosure of about six hundred acres, and is surrounded on all sides by a good hunting country. Mr. Shaw had a very friendly feeling for the R.R.B. from the first, and readily granted them permission to hunt over his outlying estate. He wrote as follows to C. Rawson, Chairman of the Committee:—

December 9th, 1845.

My dear Rawson.—Many thanks for your kindness in sending to Neilson and myself the letters on the cultivation of wheat. I feel extremely gratified that the gentlemen of the R.R.B. were pleased with my reception of them, and with their day's sport. I should feel obliged by the dogs being drawn off in future, if the hare enters the park or any of the young plantations round the Hall, within the wall, and on the other side from Mr. Neilson's upper farm down to the keeper's house. This is the only restriction I wish to put upon the R.R.B. I feel also that this will not interfere with your sport, as the hares are too numerous. (Signed) J. R. Shaw.

This arrangement has been adhered to from that day to this, and Mr. Shaw maintained his friendship with the Masters of the R.R.B. till his death. Whenever the beagles met at Arrow he received them most hospitably, providing a sumptuous lunch, and getting his keeper afterwards to put them on to a hare. Many are the records in the Sport Books of lunches at Arrow Hall.

13th March, 1847. Arrow Hall. As usual, when this is our meet, we partook of the hospitality of the owner of the Hall, John R. Shaw, Esq., who regaled us with an excellent lunch, to which ample justice was done. Crossed the park towards Irby; soon found, but were obliged to whip off, as she made straight for the Hall covers. With two other hares we were obliged to do the same, from the same cause.

Mr. Shaw was present at the dinner given to C. Rawson in 1848, responded to the toast of "The Landlords of Wirral," and proposed the toast of "The Royal Rock Beagles."

Mr. Otto Shaw, the present owner of Arrow, is a non-resident landlord, and for the last few years has let the Hall and sporting rights to Mr. Harrison, who in this year, 1895, has been succeeded by Mr. Dennis.

The Kings, of Bebington and Woodchurch.

"Now, fellows, you are welcome.'
Taming of the Shrew, Induction, scene 1.

George King, the father, and the Rev. Joshua King, the uncle, of our old Master, V. A. King, owned a considerable amount of land at Higher Bebington, which afforded many a good day's sport in the old days, and still does so for an occasional Wednesday meet. Both these landlords were very friendly to the R.R.B., and many allusions to the hospitality of the Rector are made in the Sport Books. Whenever the meet was at Woodchurch, which was pretty often during the season, it appears to have been the custom to go into the Rectory for lunch. Here is a sample of the records—

October 2nd, 1847. Woodchurch. Partook once more of Rector King's kind hospitality, which he has so often displayed towards the members of the R.R.B. About twenty-five members sat down to an excellent lunch. After drinking success and health to V. A. King, now in Bombay, we turned off on to the Rector's land, &c., &c.

Though the Rector was so fond of the beagles, he was, for some now unknown reason, "death on fox-hunting." Tinley Barton says of him, that when Sir Wm. Stanley was expected to pass with his hounds, the Rector took care to have a dead fox nailed upon his gateway. He was more than suspected of shooting foxes; so much so that on one occasion some of the younger followers of the foxhounds "burnt him in effigy," as a fifth of November sport. It is to be hoped that no beaglers attended at this ceremony.

Rev. R. M. Feilden, of Bebington.

"All things that are,
Are with more spirit chased than enjoyed."
Merchant of Venice, act ii, scene 6.

This good sportsman enjoys the distinction of being the first landlord approached by the promoters of the R.R.B. for permission to hunt over his property. The morning after the preliminary meeting of the subscribers to the Hunt, he was waited upon by C. Rawson and J. T. Raynes, when he "readily granted them permission to sport over his estate with their beagles."

The first official meet of the pack was fixed for 7th October, 1845, at Bebington Church. In those days there were two fox covers on his estate, and a good hunting country in the immediate neighbourhood. Even now, though the district has been much cut up for building purposes, and the population is enormously increased, hares are to be found within a short distance of Bebington Church; the hounds have always been kennelled within a mile of the church, and the first two huntsmen of the R.R.B. were buried in Bebington churchyard.

The Brocklebanks.

> "O, it is excellent
> To have a giant's strength, but it is tyrannous
> To use it like a giant."
> *Measure for Measure, act ii, scene 2.*

Mr. Ralph Brocklebank, of Childwall Hall, Lancashire, though in the prime of life when the Royal Rock Beagles started on their career, yet lived to such a good old age that he was a familiar figure to most of the present generation of beaglers. Born in 1803, he died in his ninetieth year in 1892. He was an important member of the commercial world of Liverpool, where his firm had a world-wide reputation as shipowners and merchants. He was very active in the development of the dock estate, and one of the Liverpool docks bears his name. He was an ardent sportsman to the end of his life. It has been said of him that in Kircudbrightshire he held the longest shooting lease ever known, and he went out pheasant-shooting when eighty-five years of age. It is to be feared that Mr. Brocklebank did not regard hunting with as much favour as he did shooting. Holding, as he did, an extensive sporting property at Tranmere, Prenton, and Oxton, it was essential for the R.R.B. in their early days, when the chief part of their hunting was confined to the northern part of Wirral, to secure his favour, and that of his tenants. In the very first year of their existence, indeed within ten days of the inauguration of the R.R.B., they got into trouble with Mr. Brocklebank, as detailed in the chapter devoted to the securing of country. This matter being satisfactorily arranged, Mr. Brocklebank, in 1848, appears as a member of the Hunt, but there is no record of his having paid his subscription: doubtless he was an honorary member. His grandson, Eric Brocklebank, is now one of our members, and one of the leaders of the field.

William Webster, Esq., of Upton.

> "Jog on, jog on, the foot-path way,
> And merrily hent the stile-a;
> A merry heart goes all the day,
> Your sad tires in a mile-a."
> *Winter's Tale, act iv, scene 2.*

Upton has always been a favourite hunting-ground for the Royal Rock Beagles. From the first they frequently met there, and for the first few years of their history the village inn was the scene of their annual dinners to the farmers. Hares have always been plentiful at Upton, and as it is conveniently situated for access from Oxton and Birkenhead, it has perhaps furnished its full share of sport to the R.R.B. through the last half-century.

Upton Hall was built by the late Mr. John Webster, for his son, the present lord of the manor, Mr. William Webster, who has always been a good sportsman and a preserver of game. In the early days of the R.R.B.,

Mr. Webster had well-stocked fox covers on his property. November 12th, 1846, Mr. Webster wrote to W. G. Baldwin:—

Dear William.—On Saturday afternoon a man with a brace of hares came up to me at the gate, and said that he was desired by the members of the R.R. Beagles to leave one of them at my house. Of course I not only declined taking it, but also felt exceedingly sorry that the gentlemen should for a moment have even thought of sending it to me.

Were it not for being an anxious preserver of foxes, the members of the R.R.B. would be heartily welcome to as many hares as they could kill on Upton, and I beg further to add that I can have no objection whatever to their meeting here, after Sir William Stanley has been through my preserves.

(Signed) WILLIAM WEBSTER.

Now, whenever we meet at Upton, we find that all hares are sure to run through Mr. Webster's park, and often through the shrubberies near the house. Under these circumstances the "field" are always careful not to follow the hounds through the gardens, nor climb the neat white railings, but avail themselves of the convenient stiles which are placed here and there to get over the fences. The R.R.B. have always been welcomed by Mr. Webster. He has known them from the very commencement, and we may safely say that he has never had any cause for complaint, often as they have been on his property, unless it be, as he once mentioned to our Master, that the members did not turn out in the uniform of the Hunt.

The Bartons of Caldy.

> "We'll come to you after hunting.
> * * *
> I wish ye sport."
> *Cymbeline, act iv., scene 2.*

The proprietors of Caldy Manor have always taken a friendly interest in the Royal Rock Beagles, and for nearly the whole of the history of the R.R.B. Caldy has been held by a Barton, one of the original members of the Hunt. Among the first sixty names of subscribers may be found six members of this sporting family, viz.:—R. W. Barton, Esq., of Caldy, and his two sons, Richard and Alfred (who resided in Manchester, occasionally coming over to the sport); Captain Barton, of Rock Ferry, and his two sons, Tinley and Henry. All of these except Tinley Barton, the first master of the hounds, joined the R.R.B. in order to give their influence and support to the formation of the club, retiring in the second season. Mr. Richard Watson Barton, a retired manufacturer from Manchester, purchased Caldy Manor in 1832. He took up his residence there, and some time after, appointed his nephew Tinley to be agent for the property. On the death of Mr. R. W. Barton, he was succeeded by his son Richard, who died in 1890, his brother Alfred taking the property. The latter died 11th May, 1893, the last representative of his family.

Caldy is no longer one of our meets, but we often run on to it with a hare from Thurstaston. In the old days, there were far too many hares on Caldy for sport, and if hounds went in that direction, the horn was blown to whip off. In this year, 1895, Mr. James Ismay, who now occupies Caldy Manor-house, has found it necessary to join with his father, Mr. J. H. Ismay, in stocking Caldy and Thurstaston with imported hares.

Modern Landowners.

> "Let me have your hand :
> I did not think, sir, to have met you here."
> *Antony and Cleopatra, act ii, scene 6.*

The landowners of Wirral to whom at the present time we are indebted for our sport, who live upon their estates, and have not been previously mentioned, deserve a passing tribute of thanks from all good beaglers. We may readily single out a dozen names of gentlemen whose property finds us both in hares and hunting ground.

Mr. T. H. ISMAY, an old member of the R.R.B., and now an honorary life-member, is often visited by us. When, a few years ago, hares were getting scarce in Wirral, he readily joined with us, in conjunction with the Harriers, in putting down some imported hares, Mr. Ismay paying the expenses of the number put down on Thurstaston. In this year of 1895 he is again keeping up the stock by importing more.

We all know the nursery of hares, which helps to keep the country stocked, maintained at Westwood by the late Master of the Harriers, Mr. JOHNSON HOUGHTON, and the equally well-preserved cover, known as Mr. Lever's wood.

Mr. DUNCAN GRAHAM, of Lydiate, is an old member of the beagles, and though we do not now meet there, we often find a hare on his property, or run on to it from elsewhere. We never see him out with us now, as we should like to do, but his son and daughter have of late years occasionally taken a run with the hounds.

CAPTAIN CONGREVE, of Burton, and Mr. TRELAWNEY, of Shotwick, have large estates at the southern end of our country, which hold too many hares for hunting with beagles, but we touch upon the fringe of their property when we meet at Ness, or the western side of Capenhurst.

For the last fifty years, the property at Capenhurst belonging to Mr. RICHARDSON has been a "happy hunting ground" for the R.R.B. Though we usually have too many hares afoot, we often manage to have a really good day's sport, as it is a magnificent bit of hunting country, the railway line and frequent trains being the most aggravating features of the place. This country is usually available for us at the latter end of December, after the covers have been "shot," and we meet there some three or four times each season. On the other side of the Chester road Mr. Shallcross's land generally finds us a hare, but they are not so plentiful as we should like them to be, and we sometimes draw blank on that side.

Mr. HARRISON, of the Plymyard, affords us two or three meets during the season, and we never fail to find a hare on the remains of the famous old forty-acre field on which his house is built, and which has been from time immemorial known as a favourite lying place for hares. Mr. Harrison knows our weakness for a comfortable tea after hunting, and always treats us most hospitably when we meet at the Plymyard.

CHAPTER XIII.

THE FARMERS.

> "And you, good yeomen,
> Whose limbs were made in England, show us here
> The mettle of your pasture ; let us swear
> That you are worth your breeding, which I doubt not.
> * * *
> I see you stand like greyhounds in the slips,
> Straining upon the start. The game's afoot ;
> Follow your spirit ; and upon this charge,
> Cry—God for Harry ! England ! and Saint George !"
> *King Henry V., act iii, scene 1.*

From the very beginning of the Hunt, the Royal Rock Beagles have been on friendly terms with the farmers. When asked in the first instance for permission to hunt over their farms, they one and all cordially assented, and were proud to have a hare found upon their land. This good feeling has grown with, and been cemented by, the kindly intercourse of half a century : and we may confidently assert that we are now on as good terms with the farmers as ever, with a good prospect of a continuance of the same for many years to come; indeed, as long as the Hunt endures.

Beagles cannot claim, like foxhounds or harriers, indirectly to benefit the farmer, and it is the duty of beaglers, therefore, to do all in their power, individually and collectively, to keep in his good graces. Although men on foot cannot do as much harm as a lot of horsemen galloping over the fences and land, yet there are some slight damages and annoyances which the careless beagler can inflict upon the farmer. These may rankle in his mind, and draw forth some caustic remarks, which at the time seem unfriendly, but which are soon forgotten, or are easily smoothed over with a word of apology or regret, especially if this comes from the Master.

The chief grievances of the farmer against the beagler are easily enumerated, and might, in many instances, as easily be prevented with a little consideration.

1st. They don't like a large crowd of followers, especially if they have reason to think that many of them are not members of the Hunt. For this reason it is desirable that members should wear the uniform of the club on all occasions, in accordance with Rule XVII, which, with the rule limiting the number of members to sixty, was specially designed to meet this objection on the part of the farmers. It is difficult to limit the number of followers in the field, as it would be an unpleasant duty thrown upon the Master if he had to request strangers to retire ; but there can be no doubt that all followers who are not members should be out only on the invitation of a member. The Wirral Harriers have recently had to take up this matter seriously, and have made a rule restricting their members from freely inviting their friends to come out with the hounds.

2nd. That those beaglers who keep horses do not purchase their provender direct from farmers of their district, but go to the middleman who buys his supplies anywhere. We have but few members of this comfortable description, and most, if not all, of these do buy their provender from neighbouring farmers, but of course they cannot give all their neighbours a turn. If this meets the eye of any beagler who does not buy his provender from farmers, it is to be hoped he will mend his ways. It is an axiom with all hunts that the members should obtain their supplies from their own district.

3rd. The breaking of fences and making of gaps are serious annoyances to the farmer, and the experienced beagler will carefully avoid this fault whenever possible, and also caution others about the same. Some parts of our country are specially difficult to travel ; we often come across a hedge which offers no hole to creep through, or fenced gap to get over, and we all know the infernal skill with which the hedgers of Wirral make up their fences in preparation for the hunting season, the gaps filled with a hurdle, which, if not too weak or rotten to support the full-sized beagler, always leans over the ditch in the most awkward manner towards the oncomer. Where the gaps are filled up with dead brambles, &c., these often get pushed aside by the passage of twenty or thirty beaglers, and it should be the care of all to replace these brambles and make good the fence. We can only say that the farmers are very good-natured about this, and, after we have gone, replace a broken rail or crushed hedge without saying much about it.

4th. Leaving gates open is a common offence, and one for which there is no excuse. This fault is only committed by inconsiderate strangers and unlicensed followers, as we cannot believe that any beagler, after his first season, will be found guilty of such a flagrant misdemeanour.

5th. "'Ware ! wheat and clover !" In wet spring weather, a farmer expects all horsemen to avoid riding over wheat or clover root. With foxhounds and harriers the cry of "'Ware wheat " or "'Ware clover !" is familiar enough ; the horse's hoof makes a deep hole which holds water and rots the root of the plant. Beaglers on foot cannot do much harm in this respect, but still the farmer likes to see his property treated with consideration, and it is advisable to go round fields containing these crops.

6th. In the lambing season, the farmer is rightly annoyed if his ewes are much chased about. When the hounds enter a field containing a large flock of ewes, these have a most exasperating trick of briskly rushing about, and probably forcing their way through barbed wire, leaving a goodly portion of their wool thereon, and getting away a field or two. It is the duty of the authorities of the Hunt to advise the farmers of the coming of the hounds; then the farmer is willing to pen up his ewes or other stock to which he fears damage. If this notice is omitted during the above critical period, the farmer has a distinct grievance, and he is not slow to let us know his mind on the subject.

After all, if a proper amount of care and forethought be taken by beaglers, the above list of grievances is not very serious, and the farmers of Wirral are a jolly, good-natured lot of sportsmen, who wink at a few annoyances if we show that we appreciate their kindness in allowing us to run over their land. The only return we can make for this kindness is by doing as little damage as possible, by subscribing to the local agricultural funds, and by inviting the farmers and their families to partake of the hospitalities of the Hunt. In the first years of the R.R.B. it was the custom to have an annual dinner to the farmers, followed by a hastily-got-up dance for the young people.

Extracts from the Sport Book.

"Sir, I would advise you to shift a shirt; the violence of action hath made you reek as a sacrifice."
Cymbeline, act i, scene 3.

Saturday, December 12th, 1846. Moreton, 11 a.m. After hunting till too dark to do any more. We then had our annual Hunt dinner to the farmers of this part of Wirral. About forty or fifty honoured us with their company, and seemed thoroughly to enjoy themselves. Mr. C. Rawson in the chair. Dancing was kept up till a late hour. Mr. and Mrs. Parkinson lent us their barn for the dinner.

From this it is apparent that the beaglers sat down to dinner, and even engaged in the dance, just as they had come in from hunting, without the tub and change which is considered so essential and comforting by the modern beagler. D. O. Bateson relates that on this occasion, when the 'bus was loaded to return home, the trombone player of the band was found to be missing. On search being made, it was discovered that he had fallen, from the stone steps leading to the barn, into a pigsty, where he was calmly reposing, oblivious to everything. He was hauled out and sent outside the 'bus, as he was too malodorous for the inside.

Saturday, 25th March, 1848. Moreton. At half past four we sat down to our usual annual dinner to our kind and valued friends, the farmers. We sat down about one hundred and thirty in all. Mr. C. Rawson was in the chair. The greatest unanimity and good feeling prevailed, and few will forget the convivialities of this evening. Dancing commenced at nine o'clock, and the "Beauty of Moreton" and her friends were eagerly in request.

V. A. King records, under date Saturday, 29th March, 1851—

The annual dinner to our worthy good friends, the farmers of Wirral, was given this day at Upton. At half past four we sat down to dinner, to the number of about one hundred and eighty, the largest muster we have ever had on this joyous occasion. There were a large number of members, numerous strangers, and an excellent muster of our friends the farmers. Mr. V. A. King, chairman of the R.R.B., presided. A truly delightful evening was spent; every one present appeared to enjoy himself completely. Speeches were made, toasts were drunk, songs were sung, and, lastly, ample justice was done to the good punch. But one feeling appeared to pervade the whole party, and this was perfect happiness. The farmers expressed their pleasure at seeing the R.R.B. in the field, and their delight at being able to give us such good sport, by freely allowing us to run over their land. Nothing can be more cordial and excellent than the feeling of the farmers towards us. Their health was drank with the enthusiasm, and accompanied with the cheers, which they so well deserved. Amongst the many excellent displays of vocal talent with which we were charmed during the evening, it is not invidious to say that Mr. Robert Tinley delighted all by two most excellent songs. Thus ends the season, the sixth we have had, and the most successful, both in the number of hares killed (47) and in the sport we have had. The fine open winter has enabled us to keep all our fixtures, and we have not had a single blank day.

From 1852 the dinners were held at the Rock Ferry Hotel, and during the Mastership of V. A. King were kept up till 1882; but in the later years they ceased to be annual affairs. Some of the present members of the R.R.B. can remember these dinners and the songs suitable for the occasion: "John Peel," "The Derby Ram," "To be a Farmer's Boy," &c., &c.

> "You are welcome, gentlemen! Come, musicians, play.
> A hall! a hall! give room, and foot it, girls.
> More light, ye knaves; and turn the tables up,
> And quench the fire; the room is grown too hot.—
> Ah, sirrah, this unlook'd for sport comes well.
> Nay, sit, nay, sit, good cousin Capulet;
> For you and I are past our dancing days."
> *Romeo and Juliet*, act i, scene 5.

In 1886 it was considered preferable to invite the farmers, with their wives, sons and daughters, to a ball, as by that means our hospitality could embrace a wider circle; instead of entertaining eighty or ninety at dinner, we could invite three or four hundred to a ball and supper. Accordingly this great event took place 28th April, 1886, in the Music Hall, Claughton, under the presidency of our good Master, L. R. Stevenson, and Mrs. Stevenson. It went off with great *éclat*, and was much enjoyed both by the farmers and the beaglers. There were good company, splendid music, a good floor, and a good supper; dancing for the young and active, and a smoke room with a quiet game of cards for the older farmers. Towards the end of the evening the air in this smoke-room became almost solid, and it was necessary to cut one's way in and fan the accumulated smoke into circulation if it was desired to find anyone therein. Mr. Gatehouse relates that he struggled in to have a chat with old Mr. Ellison of Raby. He soon found a pair of heels sticking up in a corner, and found these to belong to an unlucky individual overcome by the tobacco fumes, and lost to the sight of his friends in the intervening clouds. He was dragged out and revived by old Ellison; but Gatehouse thinks it was a narrow escape from suffocation.

The committee experienced great difficulty in getting at a correct list of the farmers whose land we hunted over, and it is to be feared that, with all their care, some good friends to the Hunt were omitted from the invitation list. The following temperate and sensible letter appeared in the *Birkenhead News* :—

ROYAL ROCK BEAGLE HUNT.

The members of the above Hunt have held their ball, but many of us are anxious to know as to what means they used in the selection of those who received tickets. Whether was it the acreage of land hunted over, or was favouritism shown? I occupy about seventy acres and received no tickets, another farmer in my township, with a larger acreage, has received none, and several smaller ones have received none; whilst one with four hundred acres received only three tickets, others with a much smaller acreage have received their four or five tickets. Although we will not place any obstacle in their way for future hunting, we trust the selection committee of the Hunt will see their way clear to make a more liberal distribution of their favours than they have done this year, and try at least to make it in proportion to the accommodation given to them.   Yours, &c.,   A WIRRAL FARMER.

The committee were very much distressed to hear of this complaint, and others of a similar nature. They appended to the account of the ball, published in the *Birkenhead News*, the following announcement :—

The ball committee have experienced the greatest difficulty in arriving at the list of those to be invited, and, no doubt, some disappointment will have arisen from the imperfect information at their disposal, which they much regret. In the hope of avoiding this in the future, they will be glad to receive the names of any farmers, holding say forty acres and upwards, who consider their names should have been placed on the list, but who have, by some oversight, been omitted on this occasion.

The success of the first ball was so assured, that it was decided, in future to set aside, for a special fund, one-fourth of each member's subscription, and when a sufficient fund had accumulated, to give another ball. This took place in the month of December, 1890, and went off with great spirit. There was a large muster of our friends the farmers with their families, numbering altogether some four hundred guests. The occasion was graced by our good friend, J. B. Morgan, in his chain and badge of office as Mayor of Liverpool. The committee of the R.R.B. fully hope to hold their next ball in this year of jubilee, early in the present season.

Part of the report at the first annual meeting of the club reads :—

Your committee have to acknowledge the great civilities and kindness they have received from the landowners and farmers of this part of Wirral. It has

THE FARMERS.

been their object to cultivate their goodwill in every way, and they have heard very general satisfaction expressed at the conduct of all the members. They have to congratulate the Hunt on the large tract of country over which they have permission to hunt, and they trust that it will continue to be the aim of each member to do all in his power to retain the good opinion in which the Hunt is now held.

The R.R.B. have ever since studied to act with all due consideration for the farmer and his interests. On 3rd February, 1866, notice was sent to the members, that—

In consequence of the plague now raging among cattle in the Hundred of Wirral, the R.R. Beagle Hunt have determined to discontinue hunting for the remainder of the season.

It is much to be regretted by all beaglers, that the farmers over whose land we hunt do not oftener join us in our sport, and take a run with the hounds. We should be quite delighted to see them take an interest in us, but fear that, although, as a class, they are fond of hunting, they prefer riding to hounds, and do not consider it a pleasure to tramp over soft fields on their own shanks. They are more drawn to foxhounds than to beagles, as the former give them an opportunity of schooling their young horses, and, perhaps, finding customers for a likely hunter.

> Farmer Hodge to his dame, says, I'm sixty and lame,
> Times are hard, and my rent I can't pay;
> But I don't care a jot, if I raise it or rot,
> For I must go out hunting to-day.
> *Old Hunting Song.*

> Now golden Autumn from her open lap
> Her fragrant bounties show'rs; the fields are shorn:
> Inwardly smiling, the proud farmer views
> The rising pyramids that grace his yard,
> And counts his large increase: his barns are stor'd,
> And groaning staddles bend beneath their load.
> All now is free as air, and the gay pack
> In the rough bristly stubbles range unblam'd.
> No widow's tears o'erflow, no secret curse
> Swells in the farmer's breast, which his pale lips
> Trembling conceal, by his fierce landlord aw'd;
> But courteous now he levels every fence,
> Joins in the common cry, and halloos loud,
> Charmed with the rattling thunder of the field.
> *Somervile.*

Barbed Wire.

"Thou shalt be whipp'd with wire, and stew'd in brine,
Smarting in lingering pickle."
Antony and Cleopatra, act ii, scene 5.

At a meeting of the Cheshire Agricultural Society, held in 1893, prizes were offered by the Tarporley Hunt Club for different classes of horses, the property of *bona-fide* tenant farmers residing within the limits of the Cheshire Hunt, but with this condition :—" That any farmer having wire of a dangerous " nature in his fences during the hunting season may, at the discretion of the " Hunt, be disqualified from competing for, or winning, any of these prizes."

The use of barbed wire in a hunting country, or, indeed, in any country, is an offence against all the instincts of good taste, and revolts the soul of all good beaglers. The fiend who invented it is said to have reaped an enormous fortune by it : " more's the pity ! " Hounds are often badly injured by this wire. In recent years, it has been freely placed in one of the Burton woods, with the strands so near together that even a dog could not get through without being torn. One day, in 1891, when we met at Ness, the hounds ran through this wood, and it was pitiful to see them forcing their way between the strands, with the barbs lacerating their backs and feet. Nothing could be done to help them, and they had to go through with it. An hour afterwards, when we had a kill in a meadow near the Dee, snow being on the ground, we were astonished to find the snow all around stained with blood, and, on examination, found nearly every hound badly cut and lamed.

It is difficult to understand what good purpose is served by this most barbarous fence, as it really is not insurmountable to an active man (to ladies it is an effective bar), though he runs some risk of tearing his breeches if he climbs it, or his coat if he gets between the strands, and in this event the beagler has no legal remedy against the owner, as he is practically there only on sufferance. On some farms there is a horrid practice of putting a strand of barbed wire along the side (somehow it is always the far or off side) of the top bar of a gate, which is most exasperating to the unwary beagler who boldly claps his hand on it.

It appears now to be settled as a point of law, that the fencing of public footpaths with barbed wire is at the risk of the owner, and renders him liable for damages if any injury is done to person or property. The judgment of the county court judge in the famous Wallasey barbed wire case in 1893, puts the case so clearly that it will no doubt be of general interest to insert it here, as given in the *Echo*, February 12th, 1893. The case was " Stewart *v.* Wright," being a claim by T. C. Stewart for £2 4s., damage done to his macintosh overcoat by a barbed wire fence.

His Honour, in delivering judgment, said that this was the first action of the kind taken in this circuit. The law did not prescribe what material must be used for making a fence, but there was the general law—applicable to fences as to other matters—that a man must not do on his own land that which became a nuisance to the public lawfully using a road on which his land abutted. There was no express decision of the High Court applying that maxim to barbed wire fencing, but there were three decisions in the County Court condemnatory of such fences. His Honour referred to these cases, and also to the case of "The Elgin Company Road Trustees v. Innes," before the Scotch Court of Session, in which a somewhat similar action was dismissed, but with costs against the defendant. It was to be inferred from this case that although barbed wire was not illegal for forming a fence alongside a public way, yet the user of it, who constructed a fence of it, did so at his peril. There was abundance of English authority for saying that if anyone lawfully using a highway sustained injury from a public nuisance made or maintained on or near the highway, he had the right of action for such injury against the person making or maintaining such nuisance. In the present case the fence was on a level with the footpath, a position which is condemned as very dangerous by the case in the Court of Session. It was true that the wire was attached to the poles on the field side, and that the posts were closer together than in the Scotch case, but the very accident itself which injured the plaintiff's macintosh, and caused injury in two other cases, showed that those arrangements were not sufficient to secure the public using the footpath from the dangers arising from the barbed wire in the fence. He must, therefore, hold that this fence was dangerous to the public using the path, and a nuisance, and that the plaintiff was entitled to recover in this action unless he had been guilty of contributory negligence in not taking due care. He did not think the evidence supported that view. A gust of wind—a very ordinary occurrence—blew his coat against the fence, and he did not think the plaintiff had been negligent or careless. His judgment must, therefore, be for the plaintiff, and for the amount claimed, but he would give leave of appeal.

The defendant carried his appeal to the Queen's Bench Division of the High Court of Justice, and it was heard before Mr. Justice Wright and Mr. Justice Mathew. The case was thought to be of such great public importance that the committee of the Wirral Footpaths Preservation Society decided to join in guaranteeing the costs to the plaintiff. The newspaper account proceeds :—

Mr. Justice Mathew, without calling upon the other side, said he was satisfied that the County Court judge in this case was perfectly right, and had disposed of it very properly. He came to the conclusion that the fact of this barbed wire fence being in the position it was, made it a nuisance. That was his judgment, and there appeared to have been abundant evidence that it was a nuisance. There could be no question about its being a nuisance, if it was dangerous to ordinary passengers upon the footway. The learned judge, who appeared to have consulted a number of authorities for the purpose of discovering a parallel case, was perfectly right in his decision ; and his lordship was of opinion that the appeal should be dismissed with costs. Mr. Justice Wright said he was of the same opinion.

> "O my good lord, I have been your tenant, and your father's tenant, these fourscore years."
>
> *King Lear, act iv, scene* 1.

It is doubtful if any of the farmers of 1845, who welcomed the R.R.B. from the beginning, are at this day still farmers of Wirral; but, in some cases, their descendants are on the same farms, and maintain their friendship for the beagles as in the past. Some of the original farmers' names can be gathered from the Sport Books, and should here receive a grateful tribute of our thanks for their kind hospitalities to the Hunt in bygone times. Jackson, of Noctorum, is often mentioned in the old books:—

12th January, 1848. Met at Noctorum. After a splendid run of two hours, almost without a check, we killed the large Noctorum hare, much to the delight of our kind friend, Mr. Jackson, to whom we gave it. A glorious run.

Richard Jackson now has the farm, and is often visited by the R.R.B. for a Wednesday meet.

W. Parkinson, of Moreton. The annual dinners used to be given in his large barn, kindly prepared and lent for the occasion.

Grundy, of Brimstage. Mentioned in the records as hospitable and friendly. He used to run up his flag when the meet was at Brimstage, and followed the hounds on horseback, enjoying the sport.

A few other honoured names are Broster, of Irby; J. L. Williams, of Landican; Ellison, of Woodchurch; Sutton, of Barnston; Handcock, of Pensby; Urmson, of Pensby; Jos. White, of Sutton; Johnson, of Prenton; Robinson, of Thingwall.

The Farmers of 1893 (over 40 acres).

> "The care you have of us,
> To mow down thorns that would annoy our foot,
> Is worthy praise."
>
> *King Henry VI, Part II, act iii, scene* 1.

By applying to all the assistant-overseers of the various townships of Wirral, it has been possible to get a correct list of the principal farmers over whose farms we hunt. By reference to the list here given, the beagler will be enabled to acquaint himself with the names of those to whom he is indebted for his sport.

MEET AT NOCTORUM.	Acres.	MEET AT PRENTON BRIDGE.	Acres.
Richard Jackson, Noctorum	—	Thomas Johnson, Prenton	100
Peter Parkinson, Bidston	64	Robert Johnson, „	over 100
James Lamb, „	56	— Gaskell, „	„ 100
Thomas Lamb, „	119	G. W. Zeigler, Landican	600
John Yeowart, „	376	Mrs. Okell, „	160
George Royden, „	52	Mrs. Turton, „	109
Charles Povall, „	47	D. Whiteway, „	over 40
William Sutton, „	190	Robert Jones, Arrow	145
John Mutch, „	109	Robert McFarlane, „	95

THE FARMERS.

PRENTON BRIDGE—*Continued.*

	Acres
John Price, Arrow	96
„ Grazes the park	225

MEET AT UPTON.

J. S. Biddle, Upton		144
John Knowles, „		86
Frank Lee, „		148
Jos. Williams, „		71
Wm. Rimmer, „		38
J. S. Wilkinson, „		56
John Price, „		76
Mrs. Whittaker, Saughall Massie Hotel		42
W. W. Jones, Moreton		41
Jane Parkinson, „		130
T. & G. Parkinson, „		104
Elizabeth Sutton, „		150
Mary Briscoe, „		47
Phœbe Povall, „		67
T. L. Evans, „		180
George Piggott, „		106
Frank Biddle, „		52
Thomas Dodd, „		56

MEET AT SAUGHALL MASSIE.

John Wilkinson, Saughall Massie		92
Mrs. Wilkinson, „		100
John Stanley, „		112
Mrs. Broster, „		73
J. G. Smith, „		75
Samuel Thomas, „		80
James Dodd, „		45
George Boyden, „		60

MEET AT GREASBY.

Thomas Dodd, Greasby		over 100
G. H. Smith, „		„ 100
John Price, „		„ 100
Joseph Ridley, „		„ 40
Ben. Johnson, „		„ 40
S. Fairclough, „		„ 40
W. Downham, „		„ 40
W. Peers, „		38
Margt. Rathbone, „		39
Joseph Bennison, Frankby		
W. H. Hughes, „		
Charles Clarke, „		
Horace Syder, „		
Francis Moore, „		—

MEET AT THINGWALL.

J. P. Briscoe, Thingwall	130
R. Robinson, „	80

THINGWALL—*Continued.*

	Acres
Mrs. Dyson, Thingwall	40
Captain Dobson, „	25
Thomas Hancock, Irby	218
Edward Hancock, „	75
W. H. Smith, „	158
John Dodd, „	72
Henry Cave, „	58
Mrs. Cooke, „	51

MEET AT THURSTASTON.

John Evans, Thurstaston	214
Charles Johnson, „	193
J. Maddock, „	117
Thomas Hughes, „	53
William Hughes, „	26
J. Sherratt, Caldy	over 100
Mrs. Croston, „	„ 100
W. H. Croston, „	near 100
Mrs. Smith, „	„ 100

MEET AT GLEGG ARMS.

Henry Bower, Gayton	203
W. E. Rowland, „	134
Edward Griffith, „	81
Thos. Woodward, „	61
C. Swift, Leighton	
H. Peers, „	
H. Wright, „	—
Ed. Jones, „	—
J. Johnson Houghton, Westwood	80
R. Kynaston, Thornton Hough	53
Exors. R. Kynaston, New Hall	243
Briscoe, Pensby	—
C. Hancock, Barnston	—
Spark „	—
— Bennett, „	—
— Jones, „	—
— Owen, „	—

MEET AT BRIMSTAGE.

James Russell, Brimstage	over 100
T. Shakeshaft, „	194
J. Garnett, „	60
R. Hughes, „	44
W. Thorne, „	40
N. Tredgold, „	26
T. Jellicoe, Thornton Hough	175
G. Waring, „	130
— Fowler, „	45
C. Langley, „	221
A. Boyne, „	81
T. Shakeshaft, „	76

ROYAL ROCK BEAGLE HUNT.

MEET AT KENNELS.

		Acres.
Thos. Davies, Needwood		—
— Booth, H. Bebington		—
T. Wright, Claremont		229
S. Davies, Poulton-cum-Spital		180
John Jellicoe,	„	over 100
J. Latham,	„	61
W. Wareing,	„	40

MEET AT RABY AND RABY HOUSE.

D. Webster, Raby		289
R. Milton,	„	235
T. Mealor,	„	125
J. R. Turton,	„	153
Jos. Hassall,	„	394
R. Charmley,	„	108
T. Griffith,	„	100
G. W. Kelsey,	„	75

MEET AT PLYMYARD.

Ed. Harrison, Plymyard		over 200
Henry Rainford, Eastham		124
James Ball,	„	140
M. Dickinson,	„	130
J. Larkin,	„	50

MEET AT HOOTON.

J. A. Pell, Hooton Hall		over 300
G. Brown, Hooton	„	300
J. Jarvis,	„	150
Mrs. Christopherson,	„	60
J. Kellett, Overpool		over 100
J. & F. Jones,	„	100
J. W. Dutton, Stud Farm		131

MEET AT STANNEY.

W. Parker, Stanney		—
Thos. Ledon, Whitby		134
R. Forrest,	„	49
T. Johnston,	„	52
W. Platt,	„	115
— Rowe,	„	63
H. Wilson,	„	102

MEET AT CAPENHURST.

Mrs. Hayes, Backford Cross		—
T. Hughes, Hope Farm		·
T. R. Shallcross, Great Sutton		...
P. Owen,	„	—
W. Jenkins,	„	—
W. A. Wainwright,	„	—
W. Manifold,	„	—
J. Mason,	„	—
R. Williams,	„	—

MEET AT LEDSHAM.

			Acres.
H. Stretch, Little Sutton		over	100
J. W. Haigh,	„	„	100
J. Wright,	„	„	100
J. Howard,	„		40
W. Knowles,	„	„	100
T. Davies,	„	„	100
S. Jones,	„	„	100
W. B. Smallwood,	„	„	100

MEET AT HADLOW ROAD.

Jos. Pollard, Willaston		138
J. L. Pollard,	„	113
Mrs. Jones,	„	136
J. Delamore,	„	123
Mrs. Wright,	„	172
W. Leech,	„	122
P. Allen,	„	168
S. Johnson	„	49
J. Maher,	„	74
Mrs. Francis,	„	81
P. Wood,	„	94
W. Chesworth,	„	60
G. Argyle,	„	72
H. Dulson,	„	32
H. T. Jackson, Hallwood		154

MEET AT NESS.

J. Waring, Ness		over	100
J. Clarke,	„	„	100
S. Mealor,	„	„	100
Mrs. Johnson,	„	„	100
Mrs. Scott	„	„	100
Exors. N. Grundy,	„	„	100
J. Green,	„	„	40
J. Broster, Great Neston		„	100
Uvedale Corbett,	„		100
C. Bushell,	„		100
W. Jones,	„		100
Colonel Lloyd,	„		100
W. McDonald,	„		100
H. Peers,	„		100
H. Wright,	„		100
Maria Briscoe,	„		40
Mrs. Hancock,	„		40
T. Molyneux,	„		40
— Harrison,	„		40
Mrs. Gray,	„		40
Isaac Newton,	„		40
W. Taylor,	„		40
J. G. Churton,	„		40

CHAPTER XIV.

SHOOTING MEN.

> "Some glory in their birth, some in their skill,
> Some in their wealth, some in their body's force;
> Some in their garments, though new-fangled ill;
> Some in their hawks and hounds, some in their horse;
> And every humour hath his adjunct pleasure,
> Wherein it finds a joy above the rest."
> *Shakespeare, Sonnet XCI.*

The Royal Rock Beagles have always got along very well with the shooting tenants of Wirral, the Masters taking care to send them and their keepers cards of the fixtures, falling in with their arrangements for shooting covers, &c., and guarding against allowing the hounds to run into cover before they have been well shot over. It is doubtful whether hounds do any harm, from a shooter's point of view, by going into cover; but, at any rate, keepers think so, and it is our business to meet their views in every way. Both sports, hunting and shooting, can be carried on in the same country without clashing, and any occasional friction can be smoothed over by a little *suaviter in modo* on both sides. The shooting men who find fault with hounds, are usually those who know little of any sport but with the gun, and have no real knowledge of the etiquette of sport. The accompanying list, showing the principal shootings of Wirral, and the names of the shooting tenants, will prove of interest to the beagler, as it is to be feared that many of our members run over the country without knowing to whose courtesy we are indebted for our sport.

In countries boasting of a pack of beagles or harriers, it is quite a recognised custom, for those who have the shooting rights, not to kill hares when they are scarce, and we have reason to be thankful that this custom is well maintained in Wirral. No sportsman would shoot a hare in front of hounds, yet we have had an instance (in 1892), near Brimstage, of our hare being shot at, but fortunately missed, right in front of the hounds, and in view of many of the members. Here is an extract from the early records of the Hunt:—

October 8th, 1847. Capenhurst.—Turned out about 11-30 a.m., between the two Suttons. After half-an-hour's beating, found on a stubble. She gave us an hour and three-quarters of a pretty good run, though not fast. Ran her full-cry to within a yard from where a man of the name of V- and his friend were shooting. Here they threw up their noses and could not again touch it, making us strongly suspect where the hare had gone to. Crossed the road at Higher

Sutton, and made for Capenhurst. Found at once, and had a very pretty run for an hour at a gallant pace, and with only one check. At the end of this excellent sport, when the pack were within fifty yards, this same Mr. V—— fired at, and killed her, hardly able to drag herself along, and almost in the very teeth of the pack. After this truly unsportsmanlike and ungentlemanly act, we moved nearer Capenhurst, and again found in a stubble, near the railroad. Away she made for Capenhurst, through the garden in front of the house, then to the railway, and down this for nearly a mile. The whole pack running her in view, we had the greatest difficulty in saving the entire pack from a train which was following them. She again made for Capenhurst, through the garden, and down the railway nearly to the fourth bridge, when she made for Sutton. After running through two or three fields in view, the pack forced her into a hedge, and were upon her in a moment.

Shooting Tenants of 1895.

"Call'st thou that harm?
Men daily find it such. Get thee away,
And take thy beagles with thee."
Timon of Athens, act IV, scene 3.

Storeton and Barnston	Mr. Thomas Brocklebank.
Woodchurch	Mr. G. W. Zeigler, of Landican.
Arrow	Mr. J. E. Dennis, of Arrow Hall.
Upton	Lt.-Col. Robinson, of Upton Manor.
Moreton	Mr. W. Webster, of Upton Hall.
New House	Mr. George Clover and Mr. T. Somerfield.
Caldy	Mr. James H. Ismay, of Caldy Manor.
Thurstaston	Mr. T. H. Ismay, of Dawpool.
Irby and Thingwall	Sir David Radcliffe, of Thurstaston Hall.
Gayton, Leighton, and Westwood	Mr. J. Johnson Houghton, of Westwood.
Raby and Hargreave	Mr. Geo. Eaton, of Raby House, and Mr. C. Gatehouse, of Noctorum.
Thornton Hough	Mr. W. H. Lever.
Brimstage	Mr. James Russell, of Brimstage Hall.
Bebington	Mr. Alfred Hassall, of Abbot's Grange.
Poulton-cum-Spital	Mr. Thomas Green, of Poulton Hall.
Bromborough	Mr. Wm. Johnston.
Eastham	Mr. Ed. Harrison, of the Plymyard.
Hooton Hall	Mr. R. C. Naylor, of Hooton Hall.
Hooton Station and Willaston	Mr. H. A. Latham and Mr. Alfred Culshaw.
Whitby	Mr. J. Grace, of Whitby Hall.
Stanney	Mr. H. C. Alleston, of Rake Hall.
Backford	Mr. Birkenhead Clegg, of Backford Hall.
Capenhurst	Mr. W. Watson, of Spital.
Little and Great Sutton	Mr. Peter Owen, of Capenhurst.
Ledsham, Badger's Rake, and Puddington	Mr. J. S. Harmood-Banner, of Puddington Hall.
Hallwood and Ness	Mr. J. G. Churton, of Neston Manor House.
Haddon Wood and Burton	Captain Congreve, of Burton Hall.

CHAPTER XV.

THE HOUNDS.

> "And since we have the va'ward of the day,
> My love shall hear the music of my hounds.
> Uncouple in the western valley; go.—
> Despatch, I say, and find the forester.—
> We will, fair queen, up to the mountain's top,
> And mark the musical confusion
> Of hounds and echo in conjunction."
> *Midsummer Night's Dream*, act iv, scene 1.

The name "hound" is applied generally to all dogs used in hunting, but particularly to those that hunt by scent and in packs. This rule would exclude the greyhound (a name, by the way, which does not signify colour, but is from an old Icelandish word, meaning dog). The greyhound hunts by sight, and was formerly called a "gazehound"; it should be classed with setters, pointers, retrievers, and other sporting dogs, which cannot be said to hunt their game in the chase.

The origin of hounds, from which have arisen those we have at the present day, is somewhat obscure. The foxhound, the beagle, and the harrier, are certainly descended from the same stock, and as hare-hunting is a more ancient sport than fox-hunting, it is probable that the earliest pack of foxhounds was selected from harrier packs, which again had been originally selected from the more ancient packs of beagles.

The name beagle seems to be of doubtful etymology. Some authorities give its derivation as from the French word "*bigle;*" but there can be little doubt, with all due deference to the lexicographers, that the French merely adopted our word beagle with their own spelling. Ogilvie's *Imperial Dictionary* gives the probable derivation as the Celtic word "*beag*," signifying—little. Historians say that beagles were bred in ancient Britain, whence they were imported into Italy, being much valued by the Romans. A classical writer of the second century, Arrian, describes the "*agaceous,*" or beagle, as follows:—

They are not less clever at hunting on scent than the Carian and Cretan, but in shape sorry brutes. In pursuit, these give tongue with a clanging howl, like the yelping Carians, but are more eager when they catch the scent. Sometimes, indeed, they gladden so outrageously, even on a stale trail, that I have rated them for their excessive barking, alike on every scent, whether it be the hare going to form or at speed. In pursuing and recovering her when started, they are not inferior to the Carians or Cretans, save in one point, that of speed.

Although in ancient Egyptian sculptures may be seen a representation of a dog, something like our modern foxhound, the best authorities give the probable origin of the hounds of last century as the old English blood-hound crossed with a lighter variety of the dog. The blood-hound is credited with greater powers of scent than any other dog, and it is no doubt that quality which led to his being chosen as the progenitor of hounds suitable for hare-hunting. The type aimed at would be a hound with a good "nose," great endurance, and moderate speeed— not so speedy as to overmatch the hare.

> A diff'rent hound for ev'ry diff'rent chase
> Select with judgment, nor the tim'rous hare
> O'ermatch'd destroy, but leave that vile offence
> To the mean, murd'rous, coursing crew, intent
> On blood and spoil. O! blast their hopes, just Heav'n!
> And all their painful drudgeries repay
> With disappointment and severe remorse.
> But husband thou thy pleasures, and give scope
> To all her subtle play. By Nature led,
> A thousand shifts she tries: t' unravel these
> Th' industrious beagle twists his waving tail,
> Thro' all her labyrinths pursues, and rings
> Her doleful knell. *Somerville.*

Formation of a Pack.

"She's a beagle, true-bred, and one that adores me."
Twelfth Night, act ii, scene 3.

In forming a pack of beagles, or hounds generally, it is better to purchase an established pack, rather than attempt to make one by purchasing drafts from other kennels and breeding from them. It would take eight or ten years to form a satisfactory pack by the latter method, while infinite pains would have to be taken in the selection of hounds for breeding, and in the drafting of puppies.

The Royal Rock Beagles began well, as described in a previous chapter, by purchasing a renowned pack of hounds from Captain J. A. Thompson. This was twelve couple of good hounds; and during the first year some odd lots were picked up from various quarters, and those unsuitable for the R.R.B. carefully drafted out. In the course of a few years a really good even pack of sixteen inches was established, and for a long period enough puppies were bred to keep up the numbers. On the whole, more hounds were sold than bought, but this was somewhat overdone in 1883, when a great many hounds were sold to a Hunt Club in Rangoon.

At this time our kennels were rather denuded of hounds, there being only twelve couple averaging sixteen and a-half inches, and in November, 1883, we bought, for fifty pounds, a pack belonging to the late Mr. Myles Kennedy, of Ulverston, fifteen and a-half couple, varying from fourteen and a-half to seventeen and three-quarters inches. Of this lot three

THE HOUNDS.

died and seven couple were drafted as unsuitable, along with four couple of the R.R.B. These were sold for thirty-seven pounds, leaving fifteen couple in the kennels, varying from fourteen to sixteen and three-quarters inches, averaging fifteen and a-half.

This was not a very satisfactory state of things, and our worthy Deputy-Master, Macfie, turned his attention to breeding. He was successful in his endeavours, and in the course of a few years got the numbers up to a proper amount. In 1889, it appears there were hounds to spare, as eight and a-half couple were sent out to Rangoon in that year. Since then, few have been bought and more sold. We now have in the kennels sixteen couple of hounds, as per the Master's list, which was issued to the members, with his compliments, at Christmas, 1894.

Royal Rock Beagles, Season 1894-5.

Age.	Name.	Sire.	Dam.
7	Craftsman	Driver	Countess.
7	Samson	Mr. Johnson's Tomboy	His Bridesmaid.
6	Boatman	Chester Marksman	Baneful.
6	Methodist	Lingerer	Merry Lass.
6	Mystic	Driver	Mischief.
5	Brutus	Lingerer	Baneful.
5	Casual	Lingerer	Crafty.
5	Combat	Lingerer	Crazy.
5	*Brawler	Maximus	Bandage.
4	Pilgrim	Mr. Johnson's Clasher	His Playful.
3	†Bracelet	Mr. Johnson's Monarch	Bandage.
3	Beauty		
3	Bounty	Mr. Johnson's Monarch	Baneful.
3	Brilliant		
3	Frantic		
3	Farmer	Methodist	Firefly.
3	Frolic		
3	Favourite		
2	Melody	Proctor	Mystic.
	Rambler		
	Comrade	Age and Pedigree unknown.	
	Remus		
2	Magic		
2	Marjory	Proctor	Mystic.
2	Merriman		
2	Belman	Craftsman	Bluebell.
1	Baronet		
1	Bachelor		
1	Barrister	Brutus	Mystic.
1	Bonnybell		
1	Barmaid		
1	Buxom		

* 2nd Prize Peterborough, 1890-91, best couple dog hounds.
† 2nd Prize Peterborough, 1893, best couple bitch hounds.
‡ 1st Prize Peterborough, 1892, young hounds.

> Victorious William to more decent rules
> Subdu'd our Saxon fathers, taught to speak
> The proper dialect, with horn and voice
> To cheer the busy hound, whose well-known cry
> His list'ning peers approve with joint acclaim.
> From him, successive huntsmen learn'd to join,
> In bloody social leagues, the multitude
> Dispers'd, to size, to sort, their various tribes,
> To rear, feed, hunt, and discipline the pack.
> Hail, happy Britain! highly favour'd Isle.
> In thee alone, fair land of liberty,
> Is bred the perfect hound, in scent and speed
> As yet unrivall'd; while in other climes
> Their virtue fails, a weak degen'rate race.
> Somervile.

The following letter about the hounds, sent out in the spring of 1889, gives us a notion of the difficulties of hunting in a tropical climate :—

Rangoon, 6th July, 1889.

Dear Mr. Stevenson.—Rowett has handed me your letter, and has asked me to write to tell you the fate of the pack of hounds you last sent out. You and Mr. Macfie will be astonished and sorry to hear that they have all died except one, and that we have had to close our kennels, dismiss the staff, and do without a drag hunt this season.

After all your trouble and care, and all the money expended, it seems a cruel fate that we should not have had a single run with them. They were landed looking as fit as we usually get them after the long voyage, and we all liked the look of them. The weather was simply infernal when they arrived; and instead of getting rain about that time, and the cool weather we generally look for about the middle of May, the rain held off and people suffered greatly, and the hounds very soon showed symptoms of disease.

A few days after landing, Majestic, Rummager, and Ringwood sickened ; the two latter recovered, but Majestic succumbed. Then in about a fortnight they all began to sicken, and from the 20th May on, we had one or two deaths every day or two. We had *post-mortems* on them, and all were found similarly diseased—livers and kidneys rotten, spleens greatly enlarged, and the blood white and fibrous. We tried every remedy, had a European soldier, who had been in kennels at home, specially engaged to look after them, and they were dieted and nursed like children, but all to no purpose. Rhapsody, a bitch, is the only survivor of the new lot of eight and a half couples shipped, and she is a shadow, and looks like snuffing out at any moment ; but a lady is nursing it carefully and hopes to bring it round.

The Vet. says we chose the wrong time of year to bring them out, and I think we must accept that for a fact now, as so many of our animals have died. His theory is that they contract liver disease on the voyage, and if the weather is as intensely dry and hot as it was when they arrived, they must suffer. After the winter's work at home, instead of getting good food and gentle exercise to strengthen and build up their constitutions, they are put on board a steamer where they can get no exercise, and, perhaps, are not too carefully fed, and are quickly brought out from the cold of an English March to the intense heat of a Burmese May, and the change is too great for any but the strongest animals to bear.

The members of the club are so disgusted at the mortality, that they would not consider the proposition made at our meeting, to get out three couples in September, and see if, by getting them here before the cold weather, they would be acclimatized for the hot weather. We agreed to give the four dogs of the old pack which still survive, to different members, who are going to try and breed with some terriers who have stood the climate, or, perhaps, with native bitches, and try if we cannot get up a pack of half-breeds who have a chance of living more than one season. I am not sanguine, but think it the only thing to do. We have now to be content with paper chases and follow-my-leader, but they will not be so popular with the general public as the hounds were, though some of the hard-riding fraternity like the tearing gallops best. Once more thanking you and Mr. Macfie for all you did for us, and regretting having such a bad account to give you. I am, yours truly,

H. D. DICKIE, (Hon. Sec. Rangoon Hunt Club.)

> "My hounds are bred out of the Spartan kind,
> So flew'd, so sanded; and their heads are hung
> With ears that sweep away the morning dew;
> Crook-knee'd, and dew-lap'd like Thessalian bulls;
> Slow in pursuit, but match'd in mouth like bells,
> Each under each. A cry more tunable
> Was never halloo'd to, nor cheer'd with horn,
> In Crete, in Sparta, nor in Thessaly."
> *Midsummer Night's Dream*, act iv, scene 1.

The breeding of hounds is a very important matter in all kennels, and is much encouraged by the modern practice of showing selections of hounds at Peterborough Show. This causes a friendly rivalry among various Masters of hounds, which helps to improve the strain in each kennel. The hunting life of a hound being about eight years, to keep up the numbers means that the whole pack has to be renewed during that time. Although there may be a good number of puppies each year, if the Master is very particular, it is certain that no large proportion of them will meet his views as to the qualities he is seeking. He will probably keep only three or four out of each litter, destroying the others.

> The prudent huntsman therefore will supply
> With annual large recruits his broken pack,
> And propagate their kind. Consider well
> His lineage; what his fathers did of old,
> Chiefs of the pack, and first to climb the rock;
> Observe with care his shape, sort, colour, size:
> Nor will sagacious huntsmen less regard
> His inward habits. The vain babbler shun,
> Ever loquacious, ever in the wrong:
> His foolish offspring shall offend thy ears
> With false alarms and loud impertinence.
> Nor less the shifting cur avoid, that breaks
> Illusive from the pack; to the next hedge
> Devious he strays, there ev'ry muse he tries;
> If haply then he cross the steaming scent,
> Away he flies vain-glorious, and exults
> As of the pack supreme, and in his speed
> And strength unrivall'd. Lo! cast far behind

His vex'd associates pant, and lab'ring strain
To climb the steep ascent. Soon as they reach
Th' insulting boaster, his false courage fails.
Behind he lags, doom'd to the fatal noose.
His master's hate, and scorn of all the field.
What can of such be hoped but a base brood
Of coward curs, a frantic, vagrant race ?

    ※   ※   ※   ※

        See there, with count'nance blithe.
And with a courtly grin, the fawning hound
Salutes thee cow'ring ; and his wide-op'ning nose
Upward he curls, and his large sloe-black eyes
Melt in soft blandishments and humble joy :
His glossy skin, or yellow pied, or blue,
In lights or shades by Nature's pencil drawn,
Reflects the various tints ; his ears and legs.
Fleck'd here and there, in gay enamell'd pride
Rival the speckled pard ; his rush-grown tail
O'er his broad back bends in an ample arch :
On shoulders clean, upright, and firm he stands :
His round cat-foot, straight hams, and wide-spread thighs.
And his low-dropping chest, confess his speed,
His strength, his wind, or on the steepy hill
Or far-extended plain ; in ev'ry part
So well proportioned, that the nicer skill
Of Phidias himself can't blame thy choice.
Of such compose thy pack.   *Somerville.*

When the puppies are three or four months old they are sent out to their " walks." Many of the farmers of the district are quite pleased to receive one, or a couple of young hounds, to keep till the next spring, when they are returned to the kennels and join the pack. One of the advantages of sending the puppies out to walk is that they may get over the distemper while separate from the others, and so not have the disease run through the kennels: they are also sent away for their own sake, as puppies do not seem to thrive if kept with the other hounds. Distemper does not now seem to be so serious a disease as it was in olden times ; it usually attacks puppies at from four to twelve months' old, and is easily treated with simple remedies.

        If frolicsome and playful they desert
        Their gloomy cell, and on the verdant turf,
        With nerves improv'd, pursue the mimic chase,
        Coursing around, unto thy choicest friends
        Commit thy valu'd prize ; the rustic dames
        Shall at thy kennel wait, and in their laps
        Receive thy growing hopes, with many a kiss
        Caress, and dignify their little charge
        With some great title, and resounding name
        Of high import. But cautious here observe
        To check their youthful ardour, nor permit
        Th' inexperienc'd younker, immature,

Alone to range the woods, or hunt the brakes
Where dodging conies sport; his nerves unstrung,
And strength unequal, the laborious chase
Shall stint his growth, and his rash forward youth
Contract such vicious habits as thy care
And late correction never shall reclaim.

Huntsman! lead on; behind, the clust'ring pack
Submiss attend, hear with respect thy whip
Loud clanging, and thy harsher voice obey.
Spare not the straggling cur that wildly roves,
But let thy brisk assistant on his back
Imprint thy just resentments; let each lash
Bite to the quick, till howling he return,
And, whining, creep amid the trembling crowd.

 *   *   *   *

Oft lead them forth where wanton lambkins play,
And bleating dams with jealous eye observe
Their tender care. If at the crowding flock
He bay presumptuous, or with eager haste
Pursue them scatter'd o'er the verdant plain,
In the foul fact attach'd, to the strong ram
Tie fast the rash offender. See! at first
His horn'd companion, fearful and amaz'd,
Shall drag him, trembling, o'er the rugged ground;
Then, with his load fatigued, shall turn ahead,
And with his curl'd hard front incessant peal
The panting wretch, till, breathless and astun'd,
Stretched on the turf he lie. Then spare not thou
The twining whip, but ply his bleeding sides
Lash after lash, and with thy threat'ning voice,
Harsh-echoing from the hills, inculcate loud
His vile offence. Sooner shall trembling doves,
Escap'd the hawk's sharp talons, in mid-air
Assail their dang'rous foe, than he once more
Disturb the peaceful flocks.

 *   *   *

When to full strength arriv'd, mature and bold,
Conduct them to the field; not all at once,
But, as thy cooler prudence shall direct,
Select a few, and form them by degrees
To stricter discipline. With these comfort
The stanch and steady sages of thy pack,
By long experience vers'd in all the wiles
And subtle doublings of the various chase.
Early the lesson of the youthful train
When instinct prompts, and when example guides.
If the too forward younker at the head
Press boldly on, in wanton sportive mood,
Correct his haste, and let him feel, abash'd,
The ruling whip; but if he stop behind
In wary modest guise, to his own nose
Confiding sure, give him full scope to work

> His winding way, and with thy voice applaud
> His patience and his care; soon shalt thou view
> The hopeful pupil leader of his tribe,
> And all the list'ning pack attend his call.
>
> *Somervile.*

At this time the Master will make his final selection of those puppies he means to keep in his pack, and will give them their names, if not already named, as is the usual custom. The principles of drafting old or young hounds are, to secure a pack level in size and speed, and one that "carries a good head"—that is, in which most of the hounds work on the line of scent, and do not tail. Hounds too large or too small for the height aimed at, too speedy or too slow for the average speed of the pack; hounds failing through age or weakness, hounds too mute or too noisy, skirters, rioters, lingerers, or inveterate rabbit hunters, should be got rid of ruthlessly. Mute hounds are generally a nuisance, as they often pick up the line at a fault, and give no notice of their success to the other hounds, so causing a delay which might prove fatal to sport, and also soiling the line. It may often be noticed when one of these mute hounds runs a line by himself, that one or more of the old and knowing hounds will catch sight of him and run to him, giving tongue directly they get on the line he has taken. They seem to know when other hounds are hunting true, better than the most experienced sportsman.

> "If I cry out thus upon no trail, never trust me when I open again."
> *Merry Wives of Windsor, act iv, scene 2.*

Experience has shown that "hounds with the best noses are freest with "their tongues." Hounds too noisy are those termed "*Babblers*," of which their old and trusty comrades take no notice when they give tongue. When hounds are working at a check, and the line is picked up by one or more of them, who go off at full cry, the babbler may be seen striving to join them, giving tongue in the rear or even wide of the scent, before he gets on the line. This is a grave fault, as, if the leading hounds "throw up" at this juncture, they are liable to be misled by the babbler, and run back to him instead of making their own cast. Beagles should be trained to hunt with dash, lingerers should be pressed up, and the body of the pack should be encouraged to go quickly to the note of a trusty hound.

Hark! To Belman! is the huntsman's cheering cry.

The music of a pack of beagles is a great charm, and also of great assistance to all runners on a good scenting day, and to slow runners on any day. They would soon get away from the field if most of the pack were mute. It has been noticed that when beagles get away with a fox, they run mute, and very soon get out of sight. The reason for this may be that the scent is so strong, they can run the line at their top speed, and have no wind

to spare for giving tongue; or it may be that the pleasure derived from the
scent of a fox is not so keen as from their accustomed hare.

> Hark! hark! from yon valley come musical sounds,
> 'Tis the horn of the huntsman, the cry of the hounds.

One day at Ness, when we had enjoyed a good afternoon through and about
Haddon wood, a gentleman, who had been at Windle Hill, said to one of us,
"Why don't you train them to make less noise? I heard the dogs yelping
all afternoon. Can't you stop them from making all that noise?"

"*Rioters*" are those hounds which give tongue when they are not on the
line. These sometimes form a tail at some distance from the head of the
pack, running after them with their heads up, and making as much music as
if they had the scent breast high. They will also break out while running to
a view away, before getting on the line. This fault is usually stopped at
once by the huntsman's rate. When hounds are thrown off, they will often
break out into riot in the exuberance of their joy, but they settle down before
they have gone over half a field, as soon as they get their noses down.

"*Skirters*" are a jealous kind of hound, which probably inherit the vice
from their progenitors. They are a nuisance to the whips, as they delight to
keep well away from the body of the pack, hunting on their own account,
apparently in the hope of picking up the line clear of the other hounds, and
getting away by themselves.

"*Rabbiters*." It seems to be impossible to entirely cure beagles of the
fault of running after rabbits. The cry of "'ware rabbit" is a familiar one
in our ears. It often comes at a critical stage of a run, when so much time
is lost in getting the hounds back to their line, and so much confusion is
caused by the rating and whipping, that it is very difficult to get on to our
hare again. Many a run has been spoiled by this fault. It may be too
much to expect that hounds should clearly distinguish rabbits from hares, as
many beaglers are at a loss in the matter; but still it may be often noticed
that some hounds will turn after a rabbit in such a shame-faced kind of
manner, as makes it quite clear that they know they are doing wrong. There
is some hope, therefore, that the fault is not incurable. Hounds have a
natural tendency to chase any animal which runs away from them: as a
Tipperary man has, if he sees a head to hit at it with a stick.

Greasby, 30th Nov., 1848. This did not prove a very sporting day. Such
a profusion of rabbits spoiled the sport. One small hare fell a prey to the
hounds, and a dozen rabbits. Four members present, and twenty-two couple
of hounds.

Perhaps there were too many hounds out on this occasion.

> Nor is't enough to breed, but to preserve
> Must be the huntsman's care. The staunch old hounds,
> Guides of thy pack, tho' but in number few,
> Are yet of great account; shall oft untie

> The Gordian knot when reason at a stand
> Puzzling is lost, and all thy art is vain,
> O'er clogging fallows, o'er dry plaster'd roads,
> O'er floated meads, o'er plains with flocks distain'd,
> Rank-scenting, these must lead the dubious way.
> Direct the pack, who with joint cry approve,
> And loudly boast discov'ries not their own. *Somervile.*

> "How cheerfully on the false trail they cry!
> O, this is counter, you false Danish dogs."
> *Hamlet, act iv, scene 3.*

Every Master of hounds has his own ideal, at which he aims in breeding, drafting, purchasing, or exchanging for his pack. The first Master of the R.R.B., Tinley Barton, was appointed to hunt the hounds in the field. He had some authority in the kennels, but C. Rawson was the prime mover in the establishment of the pack, and his ideal was an even, musical lot, about fourteen and-a-half inches in height. As previously described, C. Rawson was fortunate in having a numerous selection of hounds pass through his hands. He succeeded admirably in his intention, his pack giving great satisfaction to all concerned, and being considered a great credit to the Hunt. From the records, they certainly afforded splendid sport, killing their thirty-five to fifty hares in gallant style.

Colonel King's ideal was not so much the hunting qualities of his hounds as their individual beauty. He was indifferent to size, nose, or speed, but dearly loved the music of his beagles. The consequence was that the pack, in his days, was very uneven—of all sorts, sizes and qualities; notwithstanding which he showed rare good sport, though the hunting was marred to connoisseurs, by tail-hounds, skirters, babblers, and so forth. He had good coadjutors, who would have looked after the kennels for him, but he was too much of an autocrat not to have his own way.

Colonel John Jones, commander of the district, took great interest in the R.R.B., and procured some very good hounds from Ireland. From 1860 to 1874, W. Joynson made himself very useful at the kennels: he went there three days a week, and would have got the pack into first-rate order if he had been "let alone." He kept the kennel books in an efficient manner; and so keen a beagler was he, that it is probable, if he had remained in the club, we should have elected him Master after Colonel King's death. Afterwards W. E. Hall was invaluable at the kennels. He lived close to, and did his best to weed out unsuitable hounds, but no doubt he was hampered in his efforts.

When L. R. Stevenson was Master, he left the management of the kennels to J. W. Macfie, the Deputy Master. Macfie paid great attention to breeding and drafting. He found the hounds what he calls a "rum lot," all sorts and sizes, from little Barmaid, $14\frac{3}{4}$ inches, to Bouncer, between 17 and

18 inches. The music of this pack he describes as grand, and says that it has never been so good since, as every cross he made to improve quality and size lost note. Macfie's aim was to preserve the old R.R.B. hound blood, which had been kept in the kennel so long, and was unbeaten in music and hunting; to produce one type of hound, and to breed to size 16 inches or just under. His idea of a beagle was a hound with a good big long head, long ears to reach to the end of nose and set on low; stern not coarse, but rather fine, when up, with a nice sweep and no curl; legs and feet as good as can be got, shoulders sloped; level good back, ribs well sprung, loins strong, and hocks well down. Our present Master, J. Gould Smyth, has not yet finished the improvement of his pack, and the next few years will speak for themselves. We have every confidence that he will keep his hounds as good as ever, and show us right good sport.

> "Or wilt thou hunt?
> Thy hounds shall make the welkin answer them,
> And fetch shrill echoes from the hollow earth."
> *Taming of the Shrew, Induction, scene 2.*

The Master of hounds can hardly expect to have all his pack perfect hounds; but if he has a fair sprinkling of old steady hounds with good noses, and the rest of his pack fairly level, he has good grounds for satisfaction. It is important to have one or two hounds that can "carry a scent" on roads and dry fallows, as in our country there are so many roads and lanes that we can hardly ever have a run without crossing, and often running for some distance along one or more roads. These hounds are useful, too, when scent is bad from frost or dry east wind. In former days good road hounds were more common than they are now, but the reason for this is inscrutable; it is probable that the special faculty is not hereditary. Eagerness and perseverance are good qualities in hounds, as these keep them at their work in puzzling checks, where lazy hounds would throw up, and look for guidance from their huntsman. Most masters are particular as to the appearance and colour of their hounds. It has been well said, "a good "hound cannot be of a bad colour."

In judging beagles at shows, the points are as follow :—

For the Head	-	-	-	20	points are full marks.		
,, Ears	-	-	-	10	,,	,,	
,, Neck and throat	-	-	5	,,	,,		
,, Shoulders -	-	-	-	15	,,	,,	
,, Back and loins -	-	-	10	,,	,,		
,, Hind quarters -	-	-	10	,,	,,		
,, Legs and feet -	-	-	10	,,	,,		
,, Colour and coat	-	-	10	,,	,,		
,, Condition and symmetry	-	10	,,	,,			
Total	-	-	-	100	maximum.		

Since the institution of the show at Peterborough these points have somewhat varied. At that show the judges are prone to give more marks for legs and feet than for any of the other points. On this subject J. W. Macfie writes:—

> The danger I see is, that the foxhound being the hound of the country, and the eyes of most judges being educated to the foxhound type, that type will be fixed on to harriers and beagles. Foxhounds are judged mainly by shape, and legs and feet. Musical points are of no weight; ears are always rounded, so they don't count. Now with foot-hounds music is one of the greatest charms; but music and large heads, with long ears and big throats, mostly go together, and the serious difficulty is, that good heads and long ears have a strong tendency to be carried by crooked legs and hare-feet. The Peterborough judging has, in my opinion, followed the foxhound, in preferring straight legs to good heads. The R.R.B. type of sixteen-inch beagle hound is the oldest, and best for foot work; and although I believe the crooked, hare-footed legs, to which they have a tendency, will wear just as well as the foxhound type of legs, still by judicious breeding and selection, the music, heads, and ears can be combined with good straight legs.

Tradition has limited the names of hounds to suitable words of either two or three syllables. In the latter case they must be dactyls; that is, with the accent on the first syllable. It would be a solecism to call a hound Dash, Jack, Spot, or Prince, or any name of one syllable. Also, any name of three syllables with the accent not on the first: such as Aurora, Dissenter, Crusader, would be considered irregular. Most books of sport give a list of names from which it is usual for Masters to make a selection, and it is customary to choose a name with the same initial as that of the dam.

Hounds in Kennel.

> "Here kennel'd in a brake she finds a hound,
> And asks the weary caitiff for his master;
> And there another licking of his wound,
> 'Gainst venom'd sores the only sovereign plaster."
> *Venus and Adonis.*

The health of hounds, their condition and fitness for work, depend almost entirely on kennel management. With a good kennel huntsman, it is equally essential to have suitable and convenient buildings in which to house, tend, and feed the hounds. Full and elaborate descriptions of kennels, and instructions for management, may be found in all books of sport. Masters of foxhounds spend large sums in fitting-up and maintaining their kennels to the best and most approved standards.

> First let the kennel be the huntsman's care,
> Upon some little eminence erect,
> And fronting to the ruddy dawn; its courts
> On either hand wide op'ning to receive
> The sun's all-cheering beams, when mild he shines,
> And gilds the mountain tops: for much the pack

> (Rous'd from their dark alcoves) delight to stretch,
> And bask in his invigorating ray.
> Warm'd by the streaming light, and merry lark,
> Forth rush the jolly clan; with tuneful throats
> They carol loud, and in grand chorus join'd
> Salute the new-born day.
>
> O'er all let cleanliness preside, no scraps
> Bestrew the pavement, and no half-pick'd bones
> To kindle fierce debate, or to disgust
> That nicer sense on which the sportsman's hope,
> And all his future triumphs must depend.
> Soon as the growling pack with eager joy
> Have lapp'd their smoking viands, morn or eve,
> From the full cistern lead the ductile streams,
> To wash thy court well-pav'd, nor spare thy pains,
> For much to health will cleanliness avail.
>
> Somervile.

The first kennels of the R.R.B. were not very commodious, but they were conveniently situated for the committee, who mostly resided at Rock Ferry. They were also within easy reach of the meets, which in those days were mainly fixed about Upton and Tranmere. These kennels were situated at Woodhey, near Bebington Station. They served fairly well for a great number of years, but in 1882 they were found to be too cramped and inconvenient, with a not too secure tenure. (As a matter of fact, we could have remained there to this day, as they are still in the occupation of our old huntsman, Charles Williams.) Moreover, as the neighbourhood was becoming more populous, many complaints were made of the hounds being noisy and a nuisance.

In 1882 our worthy Master, V. A. King, generously built new kennels of the most approved design, on land of his own at Higher Bebington, and thus became our liberal landlord, letting the kennels to the club at a moderate rental. Miss King is now our "landlord," and we have every reason to think that our tenure will be secure as long as the Hunt exists, as the neighbourhood is not one likely to be largely built over, but will, as far as we can see, remain a strictly agricultural district for the next hundred years or so. We therefore do not anticipate being driven further afield. The present kennels are well situated, commodious, and suit our requirements in every particular. They are within three or four miles of the Master's residence, enabling him to pay frequent visits, without trespassing too hardly on his leisure; they are central in the country we hunt, being about equi-distant from our extremest meets in opposite directions, Hoylake and Stanney; and most of our meets are within walking distance for the hounds, a few only requiring the use of the van.

> "Make them of no more voice
> Than dogs, that are as often beat for barking,
> As therefore kept to do so."
>
> *Coriolanus, act ii, scene 3.*

Hounds are sometimes noisy at night, when they are apt to be quarrelsome and fight with each other. At many kennels the huntsman has a bell connected with his bedroom, and has taught the hounds to expect a flogging if they are not quiet when the bell rings. A story appeared in the papers some years ago, giving a gruesome account of how a gentleman, resident within a mile of a pack of foxhounds, was awakened one summer night by the howling of the hounds. It was a hot night and he became wide awake; presently he heard the huntsman's bell ring, when all became quiet for a little space. Soon the howling broke out again with redoubled vigour, and was continued in spite of the ringing of the bell. He then distinctly heard, borne on the still night air, the huntsman's voice rating the hounds, and the cracking of his whip; this was succeeded by yells and an ominous sound of worrying, when all became still once more. In the morning it was found that the hounds had killed and eaten the huntsman, leaving hardly a trace of him visible, and it was thought that he must have gone into the kennels in his unfamiliar nightdress, and not being recognised, fell a prey to the ferocity of the hounds. The huntsman of the Cheshire Beagles, a grim old sportsman, was once overheard to reply to an old lady, who, hearing the hounds growling and snarling in their van, said to him, "Surely they are fighting." Howarth's laconic retort was, "Oh! it don't matter, they find their own clothes."

Hounds, like other dogs, appear to dream in their sleep. Lucretius says:—

> And oft when sleep is soft, the dogs of chase
> Move their limbs suddenly, and send forth sounds,
> And draw in inspirations from the air,
> As if they followed still the tracks of game.

(LORD) "Huntsman, I charge thee, tender well my hounds;
Brach Merriman, the poor cur is emboss'd,
And couple Clowder with the deep-mouthed brach.
Saw'st thou not, boy, how Silver made it good
At the hedge corner, in the coldest fault?
I would not lose the dog for twenty pound.

(HUNTSMAN) Why, Belman is as good as he, my lord;
He cried upon it at the merest loss,
And twice to-day pick'd out the dullest scent.
Trust me, I take him for the better dog.

(LORD) Thou art a fool; if Echo were as fleet,
I would esteem him worth a dozen such.
But sup them well, and look unto them all;
To-morrow I intend to hunt again."

Taming of the Shrew, Induction, scene 1.

A good pack of hounds is worth taking care of, at the expense of a great deal of money, thought, time, and trouble. To keep them fit and well for hunting, they have to be properly housed and fed. They have few diseases that are not well known, and provided for by the experience of generations of huntsmen and sportsmen.

Distemper—is a disease incidental to all dogs, and yields to simple treatment and careful diet.

Mange—generally arises from carelessness, want of cleanliness in the kennels, dirty bedding, foul feeding, want of exercise, too much flesh-food, &c. The disease is caused by an insect which burrows under the skin, and is equivalent to the itch in mankind. The hair falls off, and the hound is perpetually scratching himself. The treatment is simple :—isolation, washing with soft soap, and anointing the affected parts with a special ointment.

Worms—a common disorder with all dogs. When detected, is easily treated and cured by well-known remedies.

Kennel-lameness—is a species of rheumatism. When intermittent, it is kept in hounds by attention to warmth and dry bedding; when chronic, the hound is done.

Fits—Hounds are peculiarly liable to fits, from the excitement of hunting. When they are attacked in the field, it is usually an epileptic fit, and the treatment recommended is to plunge them immediately into water, to rouse them.

> "I had rather give his carcase to my hounds."
> *Midsummer Night's Dream, act iii, scene 2.*
>
> "Look, as the full-fed hound or gorged hawk,
> Unapt for tender smell or speedy flight,
> Make slow pursuit."
> *Shakespeare's Poems.*

Feeding is an important item in the care of hounds; much mischief may be caused by injudicious management in this respect. The usual materials for kennel feeding are—horse-flesh (not in too great quantities) made into broth, mixed with shreds of the meat; meat biscuits, if not too expensive; oatmeal and Indian meal, in porridge or puddings.

On hunting-days, hounds are not fed in the morning, as they run and hunt the better for being sharp-set. While returning from the chase, the brutes will eat any manner of filth; the most putrid carcase of any animal is welcome to them. If it is possible for them to find any object too "strong" for them to eat, they will roll in it with the greatest gusto, and carry the effluvium away with them, to the intense enjoyment of their comrades, who flock round them like "bees round a cask." Those who walk home with hounds are sometimes regaled with the scent of a piece of rotten fish picked out from a roadside waste heap, which some fiend persists in carrying in his mouth until discovered and made to drop it. Like other canine animals, hounds possess the peculiarity of not perspiring through the skin, but when heated in the chase, loll out their tongues like wolves, and drop salivary fluid.

R.R.B. Hounds at Work.

"Hark! what good sport is out of town to-day!"
  Troilus and Cressida, act i, scene 1.

The selection of hounds to be taken out hunting (with our small pack it is more simple to select those to be left behind) varies according to the distance and time of the meet, the country and probable severity of the work, and the condition of the individual hounds. About ten to twelve couple is now considered to be the fittest number; in the olden days of the R.R.B. they used to take out as many as fifteen to twenty couple, sixteen couple being the commonest number.

Up to a few years ago the huntsman and hounds had to walk to and from even the most distant meet, which would be Hoylake, giving them a twenty mile tramp in addition to the hunting. This was considered to be too severe on both man and beast; accordingly a van was purchased, and since then the hounds are "vanned" to all Saturday meets which are over six miles distant from the kennels.

In the early part of this century, there existed somewhere a pack of lap-dog beagles, which were so small that they had to be carried to the meet in a pair of panniers slung across a horse.

> My hoarse-sounding horn
> Invites thee to the chase, the sport of kings.
> Image of war without its guilt.
>   *   *   *
> The wise experienced huntsman soon may find
> His subtle various game, nor waste in vain
> His tedious hours, till his impatient hounds
> With disappointment vex'd, each springing lark
> Babbling pursue, far scatter'd o'er the fields.
>   *Somervile.*

A Master likes to see his field doing their duty in trying to find a hare. The beaglers should spread well over the fallows and turnips, so as to give as little chance as possible of leaving a hare behind. When a hare is found, all is merry for a short time, the hounds are put on the line, and away they go with a delightful burst of music, cheering to the heart of the anxious Master. When, as with us now, the Master acts as huntsman in the field, his work is cut out for him. He tries his best to get near his hounds and keep with them. If scent is good, this is all his trouble, as the hounds will then do all the hunting for themselves, but if it is bad or catchy, a check soon occurs, and the huntsman has to bring his best skill to bear in assisting the hounds with a cast. It cannot too often be impressed on the field, that they should not press closely on the hounds. When hounds "throw up," everyone should stop on the instant, and not move forward again till the line is recovered. Perfect silence should at this time prevail, as hounds at fault are easily disturbed from their work. The field being somewhat scattered, the hare, or a fresh one, is sure to be seen by some one, then a "holla-back" is to be feared. Hounds hunt to kill, and when at fault will readily run to a distant holla. The R. R. Beaglers have been trained not to shout when they see a hare, but if they feel sure that it is the hunted hare, they may hold up a hat as a hint to the huntsman to take if he likes. Farm labourers (mostly those working on the tops of haystacks) have a knack of hallooing at great distances, and cannot be suppressed by gestures, or a shout of "hold your noise." This is very disgusting, as it makes the hounds throw their heads up, and may lead to losing the line; it is also a temptation to the huntsman to lift his hounds, which is against the canons of hare hunting.

The poor hare has many little tricks which she tries in order to throw off the fierce brutes behind her, and it is only fair that the hounds should have to follow out, step by step, the line she has taken, unaided by man, except in so far as the huntsman's casts may do so. As we rarely have the good fortune to get a straight-going hare in front of us, and the field soon scatter all over the place, the hare in coming back in her ring is sure to be viewed, and thus an unfair aid may be given to the hounds. If the field could all keep fairly well up with the hounds, and the country for a few miles round be temporarily denuded of its human inhabitants, we should rarely have a kill. As it is, the hare escapes three times out of four.

It is an undoubted fact that we do not now have so many kills in a season as in the early days of the R.R.B. In the first five seasons the average was nineteen brace, and in the season 1850/51 as many as twenty-four and a-half: the average of late years is about ten to twelve brace. It will be interesting to attempt an examination into the cause of this. Tinley Barton, the first Master of the hounds, on being recently asked for an explanation, said he though the reason was that V. A. King selected his hounds for individual beauty of coat or feature, and not with a view to hunting qualities. But this reason will not satisfy the enquiring mind, as it takes no account of the fact that we have had over ten years in which great attention has been paid to having hounds with good noses, and still our kills are comparatively few. We can safely assert that the hounds now are as good as ever they were. Why then did they run to a kill twice as often in the forties as they do in the nineties? The country is in much the same condition, except that the roads are better kept; the weather varies in a similar manner. Are we to think that the hares are better and stronger? There can be little doubt that here lies the explanation. We know that when we take our hounds to other countries, like Chirk or Bala, the people of the neighbourhood do not expect us to kill a strong mountain hare, and as a matter of fact we rarely do so, though we have run them for hours, till our hounds were tired out.

Hares accustomed to being hunted or chased are stronger and more enduring than those less disturbed. In the early days of the R.R.B. they alone hunted hares in Wirral; in later days we have the Wirral Harriers hunting two days per week, in addition. Moreover, many parts of the country, not being so strictly preserved as formerly, are overrun on Sundays with poachers, who take lurchers along with them, and these dogs can make a hare do her best. All combined keep the hares of the Hundred of Wirral in excellent training. It has been noticed that on the Downs of Sussex, hares afford good long runs for harriers, and this is accounted for by the theory that in such an open country they have to travel far for their food, and so keep in good condition. The early morning quests of the Brighton Harriers are sometimes three or four miles up to a hare on her form, whereas in enclosed countries the quests are for a field or two at most.

It is still quite common for enthusiastic beaglers to account for the loss of their hare by saying, "she must have been picked up by that man who "was leaving the field just as we came in;" but this is an old story, often recorded in the old Sport Books of the Hunt.

The very first record of a run with the R.R.B. reads :—

September 26th, 1846. Turned out at Hoylake about half-past one. Started a hare in the midst of the hounds out of a marshy field below Grange. A splendid burst towards Newton at a splendid pace. Puss turned sharp to the left towards Hoylake Village, where we checked for a short time, till we pricked her half-a-mile along the road. She turned again to the left, and the hounds ran her full cry on to the low part of Grange; thence, after one or two short checks, twice starting her from her seat, we ran her to a potato field near Hoylake Village, where we lost all trace of her, and there is no doubt she was picked up by a workman, who was leaving the field as we came up. This run lasted an hour and a-half, with only about ten minutes check. The scent was indifferent, but all the fourteen couples we had out hunted well, and ran as evenly together as possible.

January 30th, 1847, Irby Village. Found immediately in a patch of gorse near the village. The scent was burning, the pace tremendously fast. She took three wide rings between Pensby and Irby, then made for Landican, thence through Irby Woods right for Pensby. and from there straight as an arrow to Barnston Dale. The pack ran her full cry to within two yards of a cottage in Barnston Wood, where they threw up their heads and never could again touch upon her, leaving it pretty certain that she had been picked up by the resident in the cottage. This run lasted fully two hours, and at a gallant pace throughout.

One other factor in the result of kills per season is that as we do not now take out nearly so many hounds, we certainly chop fewer hares without a run; also our season is now about six weeks shorter.

All said and done, we kill as often as we wish, and the country can afford. If we killed every hare we hunted, we should soon have none to give us sport. Theoretically, a kill is the proper and fitting sequel to a hunt; and many country people think it is our sole object in coming out, even trying to kill the hare themselves if it comes near them. Of course an occasional kill is good for the hounds, and is specially important when we have young hounds out, so that they may be "blooded," and taught the object of hunting. It is also customary to "blood" the young sons of beaglers, if they happen to be up at the death their first time out; this ceremony is performed by rubbing a blood-stained finger on their cheek. W. E. Hell once ventured to initiate a little girl, daughter of one of our well-known beaglers, in this manner, and was called "a beast" for his pains, although the blood of the hare was a very popular cosmetic among the ladies of ancient Rome. If a run is not ended by a kill, it is because the hare has beaten us by some of its numerous wiles, and if we cannot pick up the line again, we either try for another hare, or, if late in the day, go home.

The Lurcher.

> "Hence; home, you idle creatures; get you home;
> Is this a holy day? What! know ye not,
> Being mechanical, you ought not walk."
> *Julius Cæsar, act i, scene 1.*

As the lurcher is one of the chief enemies to hare-hunting in a district like ours, which has been for the last fifty years infested, so to speak, with navvies and quarrymen—most of whom are supposed to be fond of a little quiet poaching—a description of the animal will not be out of place in this volume. In Wirral, especially on Sundays, may be often noticed a gang of eight or ten men of the above class, accompanied by two or more lurchers, strolling about the fields and lanes, evidently on the look-out for game. Farmers complain that if they accost them and forbid the trespass on their land, they are simply defied and even threatened, the men being confident in their numbers and rough appearance. There can be little doubt that lurchers kill more hares in Wirral than the beagles and harriers combined.

Hugh Dalzell, in his *British Dogs*, published 1887, has the following very good description of the lurcher:—

It would be in vain to look for the lurcher in the streets or parks of London, in any of our considerable towns, or at any of our dog shows. In some of our manufacturing towns he is kept, though out of sight. His appearance is so suggestive that the modesty and retiring disposition of his master will not allow him to parade the dog before public gaze. The lurcher is, in fact, *par excellence* the poacher's dog; and those who desire to see him must look for him in the rural districts. There look out for the jobbing labourer, the man who never works but from dire necessity, a sturdily-built but rather slouching fellow, whose very gait and carriage—half swagger, half lurch—proclaim the midnight prowler, and close to his heels, or crouched at his feet beneath the ale-house bench, you will find the object of your search.

The lurcher is by no means the ugly brute he is sometimes described to be; true, they vary greatly, and the name more properly describes the peculiar duties of the dog, and his manner of performing them, than distinctiveness of type; but still the old-fashioned, genuine lurcher has a well-defined character of his own, which no other dog can lay claim to. The lurcher proper is a cross between the Scotch collie and the greyhound. An average one will stand about three-fourths the height of the greyhound. He is more strongly built than the latter dog, and heavier boned, yet lithe and supple withal; his whole conformation gives an impression of speed, just as his blinking, half-closed eyes, as he lies pretending to sleep, impress one with his intelligence and cunning. His coat is rough, hard, and uneven; his ears are coarse; and altogether there is an air of, not rusticity, but vulgarity, about him. You cannot help associating dog and master; and to be just, you will admit that there has been neglect or fundamental error in the education and bringing up of both dog and man, for which they may not be altogether responsible; and to conclude your philosophising, you may possibly, with a sigh, regret that so much capacity for real work should be turned into a wrong channel. If we may compare the two in morals, the dog has much the better of it. He worships his master; he is as ready to defend as to adulate; his obedience is willing, prompt, thorough, and rendered with a silence that would have commanded the praise of the Chelsea philosopher. No yelp, youf, or yowl from the lurcher. Steady at heel, or keeping watch at the style, till the wire is in the meuse and the net across the gate; then, at a motion of the hand, he is round the field, driving rabbit and hare into the fatal snare. I attribute the wonderful intelligence displayed by some lurchers I have known to their constant and most intimate association with their owners. Both dogs and owners eat, sleep, and thieve together, and if the former were not of Sir Wilfred Lawson's opinion, would, after a successful raid on the squire's preserves—like Tam o' Shanter and Souter Johnny—be drunk for weeks together.

Some lurchers have a terrier cross, others may have a dash of harrier, pointer, or setter. I knew a dog whose dam was a pure Irish water spaniel, and his sire, I believe, a flat-coated retriever, that was the most perfect hare poacher I ever saw. He was perfect in nose; and in rough, tussocky, or rushy ground would steal upon pussy on her form in the most cautious silence till within springing distance, when he seldom failed to secure her. This dog, from his manner of stealing on his game, and his success, always reminded me of the description of the "Tumbler" in *English Dogges*; but he was not in appearance like a "mongrelle greyhounde"; but rather a coarse, curly black poodle. Lurchers will run either by nose or sight, as suits them, but always cunning. Let them start a hare, they will probably make for the meuse and meet poor Wat; but their great game is with crouching, stealthy step to pounce on him in his form. All lurchers will retrieve their game. Watch that itinerant tinker and collector of sundries, trudging behind a thing on four wheels he calls a cart, drawn by a nag that should be at the knacker's; he has seen the keeper heading for the "Pig and Whistle," says, "Hie in, Jerry," and the lurcher that enters the spinney empty-mouthed, comes out two hundred yards below, and deposits a hare at his master's feet.

These dogs vary greatly in general size and shape, and so they do in colour; but my beau-ideal of a lurcher is an animal with a heavyish greyhound conformation, with just enough of the collie to make him look intelligent, and in colour, red, brindle or grizzle.

CHAPTER XVI.

HARES, AND HARE-HUNTING.

> "But if thou needs wilt hunt, be ruled by me:
> Uncouple at the timorous, flying hare;
> Or at the fox, which lives by subtilty;
> Or at the roe, which no encounter dare:
> Pursue these fearful creatures o'er the downs,
> And on thy well-breathed horse keep with thy hounds;
>
> And when thou hast on foot the purblind hare,
> Mark the poor wretch, to over-shut his troubles
> How he outruns the wind, and with what care
> He cranks and crosses, with a thousand doubles.
> The many musits through the which he goes,
> Are like a labyrinth to amaze his foes.
>
> Sometimes he runs among a flock of sheep,
> To make the cunning hounds mistake their smell;
> And sometime where earth-delving conies keep,
> To stop the loud pursuers in their yell;
> And sometime sorteth with a herd of deer;
> Danger deviseth shifts; wit waits on fear.
>
> For there his smell with others being mingled,
> The hot scent-snuffing hounds are driven to doubt,
> Ceasing their clamorous cry till they have singled,
> With much ado, the cold fault cleanly out:
> Then do they spend their mouths; Echo replies,
> As if another chase were in the skies.
>
> By this, poor Wat, far off upon a hill,
> Stands on his hinder legs with listening ear,
> To hearken if his foes pursue him still;
> Anon their loud alarums he doth hear;
> And now his grief may be compared well
> To one sore-sick, that hears the passing bell.
>
> Then shalt thou see the dew-bedabbled wretch
> Turn, and return, indenting with the wry;
> Each envious briar his weary legs doth scratch;
> Each shadow makes him stop, each murmur stay:
> For misery is trodden on by many;
> And, being low, never relieved by any."
>
> *Venus and Adonis.*

The beagler should know something about the game he hunts, and in the course of his experience in the field he hears many things about hares, some true, but mostly false. This does not disturb him in the least, for the average sportsman simply looks on a hare as an animal made to run before hounds for the delectation of mankind.

Let the reader ask himself what he knows about hares, and he will be surprised at the small extent of his real knowledge. He knows a hare when he sees it (unless he mistakes a rabbit for one); he knows that it is a wild animal, plentifully distributed over the country; that it does not live in burrows; that it affords sport for hound and gun; that it is extremely fleet of foot and easily scared to flight; and, finally, that it is exceedingly good to eat. Here the ordinary beagler's knowledge ends; but it is desirable that he should know more than this, and it may not be out of place here to endeavour to give some account of the animal, culled from the best and most trusted authorities.

These authorities may be narrowed down to two—Buffon and Somervile—as nearly everything that is said about the hare by modern authorities may be found, almost word for word, in Barr's translation of Buffon's *Natural History*, published 1772; while Beckford, the great authority, quotes Somervile's poem, "The Chase," published 1780, as the only valuable description of hares and hare-hunting, previous to his own efforts, published 1781.

> Strange! that the British Muse should leave so long
> The Chase, the sport of Britain's kings, unsung.
> Distinguish'd land! by heaven indulged to breed
> The stout sagacious hound, and gen'rous steed."
>
> *Nixon on Somervile.*

Whence Buffon gained his knowledge is not stated, but it was probably in France, where hare-hunting, of a sort, was carried on at an early date. Prints of French hare-hunting show all the sportsmen armed with guns, and one picture reveals a man in the act of shooting the hare in front of the pack of hounds, and over the heads of the few hounds which are just running in to kill.

No apology need be made for quoting copiously from Somervile's poem, as his descriptions are so good and so accurate, and many of his lines are so familiar to the beagler, though he is probably unaware of their source, attributing them no doubt to Shakespeare, as usual.

The hare *(lepus timidus)* is a small active animal about seven to nine pounds in weight. Its generic characteristics are—Small head, long ears, its hearing being very acute; the power of vision is not very good, as the eyes are so placed that they cannot see directly in front, and so the hare often runs straight into danger; the body is long, and the hind legs much longer and stronger than the fore legs, which enables them to run well up hill; the colour of the fur is light brown on the back and sides, with here and there black patches, and white on the belly. In northern countries the fur of the hare *(lepus arcturus)* changes to white in winter. In 1877, a white hare was noticed on the Quinta estate, near Chirk; it was several times seen feeding six or seven miles away from its home; orders were given that it was not to be shot or molested.

The tail (or scut) of the hare is short, black above and white beneath; in a jack hare the white predominates. The fore feet have five toes, the hind four, and all the feet are covered on the under side with strong coarse fur, enabling the hare to travel on hard, frozen ground where hounds would be lamed; the upper lip has a peculiar slit, which has the appearance of a malformation : as regards teeth, the upper jaw has four incisors (curiously enough, one pair behind another) and twelve molars, the lower jaw has two incisors and ten molars; there is considerable space between the incisors and the molars.

> " Uncertain life, and sure death."
> *All's Well That Ends Well, act ii, scene 3.*
>
> " The sense of death is most in apprehension ;
> And the poor beetle, that we tread upon,
> In corporal sufferance finds a pang as great
> As when a giant dies."
> *Measure for Measure, act iii, scene 1.*

The habits and customs of the hare have been carefully studied by generations of sportsmen, keepers, and poachers. The most striking feature of poor puss is her excessive gentleness and timidity. La Fontaine writes about a hare :—

> Un souffle, une ombre, un rien, tout lui donnait la fièvre.
> A whistle, a shadow, nothing, everything gives her a scare.

She makes no show of fight against any of her numerous enemies, trusting only to her immense powers of flight, and, when these fail, yielding her life without a struggle. The sole cry she ever utters is just when she is seized : she then screams piteously, like a child. Even with her own kind she only fights by drumming with her fore paws ; but she has been known, in defence of her young, to beat off fierce birds of prey attempting to seize them. Some years ago the *Field* published an account of a raven out-witting a hare. The bird pounced at a leveret ; but the mother was too quick, springing up and striking the raven with her fore paws, and so driving her off. As the raven slowly retreated the hare followed, and whenever it came near the ground, sprang at it. The bird decoyed her to a considerable distance, then rose in the air and flew swiftly back ; before the hare could return he had seized the screaming leveret and carried it off.

The hare is a very prolific animal, generally having two litters each year, the first about March and the second by the end of July ; they have occasionally been known to have even four broods in the year. The usual number of leverets in each litter is two or three, but as many as five have been found. If each hare lived to its natural age (some ten or twelve years), that is, did not succumb to one of its numerous enemies, the country would soon be over-run with them, to the detriment of everything else, much as Australia is now over-burdened with rabbits. But the hare has so many foes that their numbers are effectually kept down, and it is only by some amount of preserving that a sufficiency of hares for sporting purposes is maintained.

An experiment was once made with a brace of hares, which were kept shut up in a walled garden. At the end of a year there were fifty-seven hares in the garden, the original brace and their descendants. One may be allowed to be somewhat incredulous as to the result of this experiment, as it seems inconsistent with the statement of authorities, that leverets begin to breed at about a year old.

Mankind is a terrible destroyer of hares, shooting-men, coursing-men, and hunting-men account for a great many; poachers are credited with killing great numbers, and in places where hares are scarce it is quite customary to lay the blame on them. Besides all these, birds and beasts of prey are always on the look-out for them. Stoats, in packs, hunt them at night by scent, and in full cry like hounds, sticking to them till they are run down exhausted. Weasels, ferrets, polecats, and hedgehogs kill them and their leverets, when they can. Hawks, owls, and ravens pounce on young leverets at every opportunity. It is really wonderful that any manage to escape these always present dangers.

The hare lives a solitary life, the jack not bothering himself with any care of the young ones, which remain with the doe for less than a month, being soon able to take care of themselves. The doe keeps her leverets usually in a hollow in the open ground, avoiding hedge-rows, where the stoat, weasel, or hedgehog would be likely to find them. When they are able to leave the mother, each leveret makes its own form, about eighty yards apart; thus when we find a leveret, there is almost sure to be one or more others in the same field, and it is advisable to take the hounds away from that spot at once.

It is very difficult for man, bird, or beast to spy a hare on her form. She lies quite flat, her body hiding the hind legs, and her head on her fore legs, presenting no contrast of colour to catch the eye, her fur being much of the same tone as fallow land, old dry tufted grass, and other covers where she loves to make her form. Hounds will often step over a hare on her form without noticing her, and few beaglers can see them ten yards away, even when pointed out to them. Indeed, it seems to be a special gift with some men, and there can be no doubt that many a hare is missed in the course of drawing, when passed quite close. How often it has happened to all of us, in drawing a field, to be startled by a peculiar sort of "swirl" just behind us, and looking round to see a hare scudding away, which must have been just under our feet.

> Ah! there she lies; she trembles as she sits,
> With horror seiz'd. The wither'd grass that clings
> Around her head, of the same russet hue,
> Almost deceiv'd my sight, had not her eyes,
> With life full-beaming, her vain wiles betray'd.
>
> *   *   *   *
>
> 'Tis instinct that directs the jealous hare
> To chuse her soft abode. With step revers'd
> She forms the doubling maze; then, ere the morn
> Peeps thro' the clouds, leaps to her close recess.
>
> *   *   *   *

> So the wise hares
> Oft quit their seats, lest some more curious eye
> Should mark their haunts, and by dark treach'rous wiles
> Plot their destruction; or perchance in hopes
> Of plenteous forage, near the ranker mead
> Or matted blade, wary and close they sit.
> When spring shines forth, season of love and joy,
> In the moist marsh, 'mong beds of rushes hid,
> They cool their boiling blood. When summer suns
> Bake the cleft earth, to thick wide waving fields
> Of corn full-grown they lead their helpless young:
> But when autumnal torrents and fierce rains
> Deluge the vale, in the dry crumbling bank
> Their forms they delve, and cautiously avoid
> The dripping covert: yet, when winter's cold
> Their limbs benumbs, thither with speed return'd
> In the long grass they skulk, or, shrinking, creep
> Among the wither'd leaves; thus changing still
> As fancy prompts them, or as good invites.
>
> *Somervile.*

Hares feed by night, chiefly on herbs, leaves, fruits and grain. They are particularly partial to parsley, and plants which yield a milky juice. In winter they eat the bark of trees, except that of the alder and lime. During the day they lie and sleep in their forms; they sleep a great deal, and always with their eyes open, having neither eye-lids nor eye-brows. It has been noticed that hares are stronger after Christmas than before; they are in better condition and run straighter. The months of January, February, and March are the best for sport, and during the two latter months, jack hares often travel great distances from their own ground, and if, by good luck, we can get one of these afoot, we may have a good straight run of five or six miles.

Hares usually stick to the country they were born in; hence they commonly return to the field from which they were put up, making rings of greater or lesser extent according as scent is good or bad. Accident, however, sometimes produces a straight run from one of these ringing hares. If they get turned at a fence into the teeth of the hounds, and go through a bad minute before they can dodge and get away, more especially if one of the hounds gets a mouthful of fur, and also sometimes if in a run they get coursed by a stray sheep dog, they will go straight away; when once out of their own country they will go for several miles.

The natural destiny of the hare is to die a violent death; but some few die of diseases. In very wet seasons they appear to suffer from dropsy, or some disease of the liver becomes prevalent, and dead hares are found lying about here and there in the country. The number of hares dying a natural death must, after all, be very limited, as if an unfortunate hare became weakened by disease, it would surely fall a prey to some prowling beast before it had time to "get on with its dying."

Hares have been tamed as domestic pets, but it has never become a common practice as with rabbits. The affectionate interest which the poet Cowper took in his pet hares will be known to all. A graphic account of them was supplied by Cowper in the *Gentleman's Magazine*.

COWPER'S EPITAPH ON A HARE.

Here lies, whom hound did ne'er pursue,
  Nor swifter greyhound follow,
Whose foot ne'er tainted morning dew,
  Nor ear heard huntsman's hallo.

Old Tiny, surliest of his kind
  Who, nurs'd with tender care,
And to domestic bounds confined,
  Was still a wild Jack hare.

Though duly from my hand he took
  His pittance ev'ry night,
He did it with a jealous look,
  And when he could, would bite.

His diet was of wheaten bread,
  And milk, and oats, and straw,
Thistles or lettuces instead,
  With sand to scour his maw.

A Turkey carpet was his lawn,
  Whereon he loved to bound,
To skip and gambol like a fawn,
  And swing his rump around.

His frisking was at evening hours,
  For then he lost his fear,
But most before approaching showers,
  Or when a storm drew near.

Eight years and five round rolling
  He thus saw steal away, [moons
Dozing out all his idle noons,
  And ev'ry night at play.

But now, beneath his walnut shade,
  He finds his long last home,
And waits in snug concealment laid,
  Till gentler Puss shall come.

He, still more aged, feels the shocks,
  From which no care can save,
And, partner once of Tiny's box
  Must soon partake his grave.

Hare-Hunting.

"The hunt is up, the morn is bright and gray,
The fields are fragrant, and the woods are green.
Uncouple here; and let us make a bay,
And wake the emperor and his lovely bride,
And rouse the prince; and ring a hunter's peal,
That all the court may echo with the noise."
  Titus Andronicus, act ii, scene 2.

Although, at the present day, hare-hunting must yield the palm to fox-hunting, in the early days of English history the hare was considered a proper "beast of the chase," along with deer, when the fox was looked upon as "vermin," and destroyed as such by all and sundry. Chaucer writes:—

  Of pricking and of hunting for the hare,
  Was all his lust; for no cost would he spare.

And further:—

  Aha! the fox! and after him they ran;
  And eke with staves many another man.;
  Ran Colle, our dogge, and Talbot, and Gerland,
  And Malkin with her distaff in her hand.

Hares are hunted by horsemen with harriers, but the enthusiastic beagler refuses to admit that, in a close country, hare-hunting on horseback is equal to beagling, and he utterly despises the claim of harriers to be considered superior to beagles, although the dictum of authorities has, some years ago, been given to that effect.

> "Fit in his place and time."
>
> "At Christmas I no more desire a rose,
> Than wish a snow in May's new-fangled shows."
> *Love's Labour's Lost*, act i, scene 1.

The season for hare-hunting commences early in October, and ends at the beginning of March : the opening of the season being regulated by the state of the harvest, and the close by the fear of killing leverets. In some seasons, when winter has been severe and protracted, hunting can be safely carried on somewhat later than usual. In mountainous countries like that of the Llangollen Harriers, hunting may properly be continued till near the end of March, as the breeding season for hares is later than in open countries like ours.

In the early days of the R.R.B., the season opened earlier and closed later than with us now, viz., September 18th to April 10th; the consequence being that there are many notices in the Sport Book of killing leverets. Occasionally a late harvest delayed the opening of the season, as it did with us in 1892, when wheat on some farms in Wirral was uncut even as late as October 31st. The Sport Book informs us that in 1853—

The lateness of the harvest caused us to delay our first meet three weeks, to October 15th.

September 19th, 1846. In consequence of the extreme heat of the weather, and the hardness of the ground, the hounds were not able to meet at Moreton to-day.

At this period, in one of the seasons kept up till the end of March, the R.R.B. "chopped four leverets in as many days." After this, the day for opening was fixed for about the 6th October, and for closing about the 10th March, which have remained the limits ever since. For some years past efforts have been repeatedly made in both the Houses of Parliament to bring in a bill for a close time for hares. These efforts have been freely supported by sportsmen of all ranks and by farmers, but the bills have always been persistently blocked.

> "And, for the morning now is something worn,
> Our purposed hunting shall be set aside."
> *Midsummer Night's Dream*, act iv, scene 1.

The best time of day for sport is undoubtedly the early morning, when scent is at its best. In olden times this was the hour selected for hunting; but in these days hunting was the pastime of men of rank and leisure; men of business were not accustomed to enjoy the pleasures of the chase; probably their presence would hardly have been tolerated. In our own day, and more especially with the R.R.B., beaglers are mostly engaged in business or professional pursuits, and look to the Saturday afternoons for their chance of sport. There are many *pros* and *cons* which can be predicated in respect to both early morning and afternoon meets, and it may prove interesting to set some of them in review.

> 'Tis instinct that directs the jealous hare
> To chuse her soft abode. With steps reversed
> She forms the doubling maze; then ere the morn
> Peeps thro' the clouds, leaps to her close recess.
>
> ❖   ❖   ❖   ❖
>
> Where flowers autumnal spring, and the rank mead
> Affords the wand'ring hares a rich repast.
> Throw off thy ready pack. See where they spread
> And range around, and dash the glitt'ring dew:
> If some staunch hound, with his authentic voice
> Avow the recent trail, the jostling tribe
> Attend his call; then with one mutual cry
> The welcome news confirm, and echoing hills
> Repeat the pleasing tale. See! how they thread
> The breaks, and up yon furrow drive along!
> But quick they back recoil, and wisely check
> Their eager haste: then o'er the fallow'd ground
> How leisurely they work, and many a pause
> Th' harmonious concert breaks, till more assur'd,
> With joy redoubled the low valleys ring.
> What artful labyrinths perplex their way!
> Ah! there she lies.   *Somervile.*

As hares feed during the night and return to their forms in the early morning, the true method of finding a hare, by questing, is possible when the meet is fixed for the morning. Then the hounds in drawing usually come upon a trail, and hunt up to the hare, putting up their game themselves, instead of having it found for them by the "field." This is good for the hounds, and is especially good training for young hounds just entering for the pack. For some reason or another, which has never been satisfactorily explained, scent is much better in the morning, and usually gets worse as the day wears on.

These reasons are sufficient in themselves to make early morning meets desirable, and it is customary with us, before the regular season commences, to have a few of these meets for the benefit of the hounds, and some of the keener sportsmen; but as a regular thing this would not do, and we must rest content under the disadvantages, in these respects, of hunting later in the day. To those men who lead what is called a sedentary life, hard physical exercise before breakfast would be injurious, and few would like to have a really good run of eight or ten miles under these circumstances. The very best time to end a good day's beagling is about four o'clock in the afternoon, getting home in good time for a bath and a well-earned dinner. Three or four hours of good sport is quite enough for most people, and if the meet is earlier than eleven in the forenoon, most beaglers have had quite enough by two o'clock, and have a long, slack afternoon left on their hands, which they hardly know how to pass.

The usual time for the meets of the R.R.E. is 1 p.m., this hour being convenient for business men. As we are rarely very long in finding a hare, sufficient time is afforded for a good three hours of sport. It is true that some of our runs are spoiled through scent failing with frost coming on at nightfall, and also through waning light, but we must make the best of our opportunities, and be thankful that, as a rule, our sport is good.

> "O, ay! Make up that; he is now at a cold scent.
> Sowter will cry upon't, for all this, though it be as rank as a fox.
> Did not I say, he would work it out? The cur is excellent at faults."
> *Twelfth Night, act ii, scene 5.*

At a check or fault, hounds are to be more readily believed than any other source of information. If they "say" the hare has gone this or that way, it does not matter who saw it go another, it was probably a fresh hare. Of course hounds may run heel a little, but it will not be far, as they soon discover the mistake. It is inconceivable to us by what means hounds can distinguish the direction in which scent has been laid. A man may see a hare run along a furrow or a hedge-row for a hundred yards or more, then double back exactly in the same line, and go off at right angles; the hounds will follow this out at speed precisely in the same way; sometimes, when scent is good, not even flashing over the point where the hare stopped, but instantly turning and making good the double. Seeing this, without having first seen the hare would almost lead one to think they were running heel.

> Ah! there she lies; . . . .
> At distance draw thy pack; let all be hush'd:
> No clamour loud, no frantic joy, be heard,
> Lest the wild hound run gadding o'er the plain,
> Untractable, nor hear thy chiding voice.
> Now gently put her off; see how direct
> To her known mew she flies! Here, huntsman, bring
> (But without hurry) all thy jolly hounds,
> And calmly lay them on. How low they stoop,
> And seem to plough the ground! then all at once
> With greedy nostrils snuff the fuming steam
> That glads their flutt'ring hearts. As winds let loose
> They burst away, and sweep the dewy lawn.
> Hope gives them wings while she's spurr'd on by fear.
> The welkin rings; men, dogs, hills, rocks, and woods,
> In the full concert join. Now my brave youths!
> Stripp'd for the chase, give all your souls to joy.

Huntsman! her gait observe; if in wide rings
She wheels her mazy way, in the same round
Persisting still, she'll foil the beaten track;
But if she fly, and with the fav'ring wind
Urge her bold course, less intricate thy task;
Push on thy pack. Like some poor exil'd wretch
The frighted chase leaves her late dear abodes,
O'er plains remote she stretches far away,
Ah! never to return! for greedy Death
Hov'ring exults, secure to seize his prey.
Hark! from yon covert, where those tow'ring oaks
Above the humble copse aspiring rise,
What glorious triumphs burst on ev'ry gale
Upon our ravished ears! The hunters shout,
The clanging horns swell their sweet winding notes,
The pack wide opening load the trembling air
With various melody, from tree to tree
The propagated cry redoubling bounds,
And winged zephyrs waft the floating joy
Through all the regions near.

   *   *   *   *

Look how she pants! and o'er yon opening glade
Slips glancing by; while at the further end
The puzzling pack unravel wile by wile.
Maze within maze! The covert's utmost bound
Slyly she skirts; behind them cautious creeps,
And in that very track, so lately stain'd
By all the steaming crowd, seems to pursue
The foe she flies. Let cavillers deny
That brutes have reason; sure 'tis something more;
'Tis Heaven directs, and stratagems inspires
Beyond the short extent of human thought.
But hold!—I see her from the covert break:
Look, on yon little eminence she sits;
Intent she listens with one ear erect.
Pondering, and doubtful what new course to take,
And how to 'scape the fierce blood-thirsty crew
That still urge on, and still in vollies loud
Insult her woes, and mock her sore distress.
As now in louder peals the loaded winds
Bring on the gath'ring storm, her fears prevail,
And o'er the plain and o'er the mountain's ridge
Away she flies; nor ships, with wind and tide
And all their canvas wings, scud half so fast.

   *   *   *   *

Huntsman! take heed; they stop in full career:
Yon crowding flocks, that at a distance graze,
Have haply foil'd the turf. See that old hound,
How busily he works, but dares not trust
His doubtful sense! Draw yet a wider ring.
Hark! now again the chorus fills. As bells,
Sally'd a while, at once their peal renew,
And high in air the tuneful thunder rolls.

See how they toss, with animated rage
Recovering all they lost! That eager haste
Some drubbing wile foreshows. — Ah! yet once more
They're check'd. — Hold back with speed. — On either hand
They flourish round. — Ev'n yet persist. — 'Tis right;
Away they spring; the rustling stubbles bend
Beneath the driving storm. Now the poor chase
Begins to flag, to her last shifts reduced.
From brake to brake she flies, and visits all
Her well-known haunts, where once she ranged secure,
With love and plenty bless'd. See! there she goes;
She reels along, and by her gait betrays
Her inward weakness. See how black she looks!
The sweat that clogs th' obstructed pores scarce leaves
A languid scent. And now in open view
See! see! she flies; each eager hound exerts
His utmost speed, and stretches ev'ry nerve.
How quick she turns, their gaping jaws eludes,
And yet a moment lives, till round enclos'd
By all the greedy pack, with infant screams
She yields her breath, and there reluctant dies.
The huntsman now, a deep incision made,
Shakes out, with hands impure, and dashes down
Her recking entrails and yet quiv'ring heart.
These claim the pack, the bloody perquisite
For all their toils. Stretched on the ground she lies
A mangled corse; in her dim-glaring eyes
Cold Death exults, and stiffens ev'ry limb.
Awed by the threat'ning whip, the furious hounds
Around her bay, or at their master's foot,
Each happy fav'rite courts his kind applause,
With humble adoration cow'ring low.
All now is joy. With cheeks full blown, they wind
Her solemn dirge, while the loud op'ning pack
The concert swell, and hills and dales return
The sadly-pleasing sounds. Thus the poor hare,
A puny dastard animal! but vers'd
In subtle wiles, diverts the youthful train. *Somerville.*

" Having the fearful flying hare in sight
With fiery eyes, sparkling for very wrath."
King Henry VI, Part III, act ii, scene 5

The natural finish to a good run is a kill; but for some reason or another, beagles do not kill once in five times, and many of these kills may be called accidental, by chopping, &c. On good scenting days it takes about one and a-half to two hours to tire a hare, so that the hounds can run into her in the open; but before this happens she has generally beaten us by some of her numerous tricks and wiles. A road is often fatal to a satisfactory ending of a run; also a tired hare seems to give out less scent than at the beginning of a run, possibly on account of the supply of scent particles becoming exhausted, although this is hardly reconcilable with the fact that a piece of old rabbit skin trailed along the ground for ten or twelve miles will afford scent for a drag hunt which hounds can readily follow to the end; and there is no reason to suppose that the same piece of skin would not repeat the performance again and again.

When the hounds have run into their game, there is great emulation among the beaglers to be first up to "save" (as it is called) the hare, over which process very little time must be lost or there will be nothing left. This saving is done with cries of "Dead! dead! leave it!" and a gentle application of the whip among the eager hounds. The first and paramount duty is to administer the *coup de grace* by striking the hare sharply on the back of the neck, holding her up by the ears so that the weight of the body stretches the cervical vertebræ, rendering it quite easy to dislocate the spine and cause an instant and painless death.

The cry of "Who-hoop!" will summon the rest of the field, the hounds baying round the while. The Master then decides whether the hounds shall have the hare or not; if they deserve it, they get her.

Scent.

"To wake a wolf is as bad as to smell a fox."
King Henry IV., Part II, act i, scene 2.

There is a mystery about scent which generations of huntsmen have been unable to fathom. The best sportsmen are at fault whenever they venture to dogmatise on the subject, quite as often as hounds are at fault in running the line. It is often said: There will be no scent to-day, with this frost, or with this beastly east wind, with this heavy rain, bright sunshine, or with the thousand-and-one grievances of the grumbling sportsman; and just as often the scent is the very opposite of what is predicted. Similarly, on what, theoretically, should be good scenting days, the hounds sometimes puzzle over the scent, and, as the expression goes, cannot run a yard. It seems as if, with all the numerous observed facts, it is impossible to reduce this question to an exact science.

> So exquisitely delicate his sense !
> Should some more curious sportsman here enquire
> Whence this sagacity, this wondrous power
> Of tracing step by step or man or brute ?
> What guide invisible points out their way
> O'er the dark marsh, bleak hill, and sandy plain ?
> The courteous Muse shall the dark cause reveal.
> The blood that from the heart incessant rolls
> In many a crimson tide, then here and there
> In smaller rills disparted, as it flows
> Propell'd, the serous particles evade
> Through th' open pores, and with the ambient air

> Entangling mix. As fuming vapours rise,
> And hang upon the gently-purling brook.
> There by th' incumbent atmosphere compress'd,
> The panting chase grows warmer as he flies,
> And thro' the network of the skin perspires,
> Leaves a long-streaming trail behind, which by
> The cooler air condens'd, remains, unless
> By some rude storm dispers'd, or rarify'd
> By the meridian sun's intenser heat.
> To ev'ry shrub the warm effluvia cling,
> Hang on the grass, impregnate earth and skies,
> With nostrils op'ning wide, o'er hill, o'er dale,
> The vig'rous hounds pursue, with ev'ry breath
> Inhale the grateful steam, quick pleasures sting
> Their tingling nerves, while they their thanks repay,
> And in triumphant melody confess
> The titillating joy. *Somervile.*

Naturalists tell us that the scent comes from the anal glands and the skin. The subtle essence, which is inappreciable to the human nostril, clings to the grass and ground pressed by the passing animal, and also to the tufts and bushes brushed by the fur. The aroma lasts for a considerable time, and rises more or less according to the state of the atmosphere; when high, hounds are said to run with the scent "breast high"; and when low, with "their noses down."

Generally speaking, scent may be said to depend on the condition of the ground, and the temperature of the air, but this is taking no account of possible differences in the individual animal. We cannot but suppose that different hares possess different degrees of perfume. Indeed, we have all noticed that on occasions when we have had two or three runs on the same day, under, to our ill-informed senses, precisely the same conditions, the scent has been better in one run than in another; also, with the same hare, scent has seemed to fail or improve in a quite unaccountable manner. We have a right to expect scent to be good on a warm moist day, in a fog if unaccompanied by hoar frost, in a thaw after a long hard frost, and on snow when it has been lying for some days. We may expect it to be bad in hard frost, in storms, in dry east winds, and in bright sunshine. The ground over which the animal has travelled varies considerably in its power of holding scent. Good stretches of grass land, especially old pastures, seem to be the best; heather and turnips fields are very good, but ploughed lands and roads retain the scent only under the most favourable circumstances.

A few extracts from the Sport Books will show that the experiences of the R.R.B. in their early days were very much the same as we find them now, nearly fifty years later.

December 3rd, 1846, Beeston. Hard frost. Although the frost was very severe, they killed two hares after good runs, and would have killed a third, but were stopped by darkness coming on.

December 26th, 1846. Snow was laying on the ground, and there was a hard frost, but the grass just appeared above the snow. It was a bright clear day, with a light air from the west, which just moistened the snow, and the scent was excellent in the grass land, and very fair on fallows and wheat.

Scent is sometimes very good just before a frost. When the R.R.B. went to Beeston, 24th February, 1847, they recorded that—

The scent was burning. The pack seemed never to check, but carried it breast high, for miles at a time, at the most dashing pace they have ever done. A better day's sport was never seen.

The next day was a hard frost, with the roads as dry and hard as possible, yet they had a fair scent all day, and especially in the afternoon.

March 18th, 1847. East wind; ground as dry and hard as in a frost. Hardly a particle of scent on grass, none on fallows.

January 24th, 1852. In the most tremendous rain, which never ceased the whole afternoon; nevertheless, the scent proved very fair, and we had some excellent hunting, running into our hare in one hour and three-quarters. It being so very wet, we knocked off early.

March 6th, 1852. Sutton. A nasty, dry, hard, dusty day. We turned in opposite Mr. White's house, where there appeared miles of fallow land. We, of course, soon had a hare afoot, but could make very little of her, owing to the numerous dry fallows. We looked for a second hare nearer Little Sutton, which took us on the grass land. Here we had a splendid half-hour, the hare unfortunately coming back to the fallows, and, as before, the hounds could not carry her a yard.

All this March the east wind continued, with not a drop of rain nor an atom of scent.

20th March, 1852. No change in wind or weather, everything as dry as a chip, and scarcely a particle of scent; found hares in abundance, but could do no good with them. Most annoying! here the end of the season arriving, and a first-rate chance thrown away.

25th March, 1852. Noctorum. Weather still the same, which proved of little consequence, for we looked the land well over, but could find nothing.

This is a record of patient perseverance in the pursuit of sport.

> In vain malignant steams and winter fogs
> Load the dull air, and hover round our coasts.
> The huntsman, ever gay, robust, and bold,
> Defies the noxious vapour, and confides
> In this delightful exercise to raise
> His drooping head and cheer his heart with joy.
>   *   *   * Thus on the air
> Depends the hunter's hopes. When ruddy streaks
> At eve forbode a blust'ring stormy day,
> Or low'ring clouds blacken the mountain's brow,
> When nipping frosts, and the keen-biting blasts
> Of the dry-parching east, menace the trees
> With tender blossoms teeming, kindly spare
> Thy sleeping pack, in their warm beds of straw
> Low-sinking at their ease; listless, they shrink
> Into some dark recess, nor hear thy voice,
> Tho' oft invoked; or, haply, if thy call

> Rouse up the slumb'ring tribe, with heavy eyes,
> Glaz'd, listless, dull, downward they drop their tails
> Inverted ; high on their bent backs erect
> Their pointed bristles stare, or 'mong the tufts
> Of ranker weeds each stomach-healing plant
> Curious they crop, sick, spiritless, forlorn.
> These inauspicious days on other cares
> Employ thy precious hours.   *Somervile.*

It is a curious circumstance that, in some state of the atmosphere, scent has a tendency to rise in the air from the ground soon after the hare has passed. When this rising is not excessive, the hounds take it without having their noses down, and are said to carry it "breast high." But it has been noticed on such an occasion, that after hounds have come to a check, and have been cast forward, back, and all round, when taken again to the spot at which they threw up, they have immediately spoken to the line straight forward, and carried it breast high as before. The explanation for this can only be, that the scent has risen above them and out of reach, but by the time the casting has been finished, and they have been brought back, the scent has again fallen to its normal height above the ground.

A strong wind will sometimes carry a good scent wide of the line. Most of us have had the chance of seeing a hare run along the windward side of a hedge, and when the hounds came up witnessed, with surprise, that they took the line full cry on the other side of the fence, the scent evidently having been blown through. Therefore on a windy day, when hounds come to a check, the line may often be recovered by simply turning them up wind.

After a good run, when hares are approaching the end of their career, and when they make short rings, squatting, and letting the hounds hunt up to them, their scent appears to be getting exhausted along with their own strength ; hunting becomes slow at this time, and there is great danger of losing the hare altogether. It would almost seem as if the hare had the power of withholding her scent when hard pressed, and now is the chance for the huntsman to show his mettle. Now the old and wary hound, who has been quietly keeping in the background, leaving the brunt of the previous hunting to his young and impetuous companions, comes to the front with a reserve of speed and freshness, ready for the final run-in, which he knows to be at hand.

> The struggling pack ! how in the rapid course
> Alternate they preside, and jostling push
> To guide the dubious scent ; how giddy youth,
> Oft babbling, errs, by wiser age reprov'd ;
> How, niggard of his strength, the wise old hound
> Hangs in the rear, till some important point
> Rouse all his diligence, or till the chase
> Sinking he finds ; then, to the head he springs
> With thirst of glory fir'd, and wins the prize.
>   *Somervile.*

Paucity or Plenty of Hares.

"O, I am out of breath in this fond chase!"
Midsummer Night's Dream, act ii, scene 3.

For beagling purposes too many hares are as bad as too few. We want them one at a time, and are best pleased when another does not show itself till it is wanted. All through the history of the R.R.B., from the very beginning to the present day, there have been localities in Wirral where hares have been abnormally scarce, and others where they have been too numerous for sport. Some of these places have retained their quality in this respect without variation. The following table will serve as a comparison, in this respect, between the first decade and the last, of the half-century during which the R.R.B. have been in existence:—

PLACES WHERE HARES WERE SCARCE.			PLACES WHERE HARES WERE TOO NUMEROUS.	
First Decade.	Last Decade.		First Decade.	Last Decade.
Bidston.	Bidston.	......	Greasby.	—
Upton.	—	......	Ashfield.	Ashfield.
Moreton.	Moreton.	......	Caldy.	—
Hoylake.	Hoylake.	......	Thurstaston.	—
Higher Bebington.	—	......	Burton.	Burton.
Spital.	—	......	Capenhurst.	Capenhurst.
Hooton.	—	......	Sutton.	—
—	Newhouse.	......	—	Ledsham.
—	Stanney.	......	—	Shotwick.
—	—	......	—	Willaston.

A few extracts from the old Sport Books will recall to us our own experiences.

6th March, 1847. Capenhurst. Just as we were turning out we witnessed Sir Wm. Stanley's hounds run into their fox, close to Capenhurst. After they had left we soon found. Unfortunately, the hares were too numerous for us, and completely beat the dogs. They never ceased running from one o'clock to five. The scent was good, and the hunting perfect. No three hares could have lived through such a run could we have kept to them: but as we were feeling sure of a kill the pack would come across a fresh hare, whilst the old one escaped. It was calculated we must have run nearer twenty-five than twenty miles. We only required a kill to have made the day's sport perfect.

6th January, 1852. Moreton. A blank day; beating all round the village, taking every inch of the land. This looks bad for this favourite old meet.

31st January, 1852. Hooton Station. A miserable, wet day. Worked the Willaston land for three-and-a-half hours, in the wet, without a vestige of a hair *(sic)*, and finished a blank day.

10th February, 1852. Upton. Again a blank day. Something decidedly wrong in this quarter.

11th March, 1852. Bidston. Blank day. Every inch of ground up to Moreton was beaten.

25th October, 1849. King's Lodge, Higher Bebington. Hunted all the land between Mr. King's house and the kennels, and did not find at all.

17th December, 1849. Kennels. Hunted all the land up to Higher Bebington, without finding.

As the hare is naturally very prolific, it is quite easy to keep any country amply stocked, if it is strictly preserved.

The causes which render it possible for us to look forward to the certainty of finding at any of our meets may be summed up as follows :—

1st. The forbearance of the farmer, who, having the right to kill hares and rabbits, spares enough of the former, out of consideration for the Hunt, or from a feeling of friendliness to sport, and a proper pride in not having his land drawn blank by hounds.

2nd. The consideration for hunting which usually characterizes the instructions given by the shooting tenant to his keeper, and also guides his own practice with the gun, leading him, where he does not find hares too numerous, to leave them for the "jelly-dogs."

On the other hand, the causes which have made some parts of our country not worth drawing, and have led us, practically, to abandon those meets, are the absence of the above-mentioned conditions, and the abnormal increase in the population of Birkenhead and Tranmere.

Partial or inefficient preservation of game, as well as absolute non-preservation, means the increase of the natural and cultivated enemies of the hare ; and the latter very soon disappears from those localities where the shooting tenant does not find it possible or worth his while to have efficient keepers for the strict preservation of all game. Fortunately, there are not very many of these spots in the Hundred of Wirral, and they may be enumerated as Wallasey, Tranmere, Moreton, Newhouse, Hoylake, Heswall, and Bromborough (except the Plymyard). Of these, Wallasey and Tranmere have been denuded of hares through ordinary economic laws, the increase of population having covered the localities with houses. In the others, either hares are shot wherever they appear, or the importation into the district of navvies for the Ship Canal has rendered the efforts of the keepers useless. Of all the enemies to hare hunting, the poacher with his snares, nets and lurchers, is the most fatal.

In 1887 it was found that hares were becoming scarce in the country, and it was decided, in conjunction with the Wirral Harriers, to import a quantity of hares and put them down in various quarters. Eighty-five were purchased, costing, with carriage, about forty-three pounds, of which sum Mr. Ismay paid five pounds for hares to be put down at Thurstaston, the Wirral Harriers paid two-thirds of the balance, and the Royal Rock Beagles the remaining third. This was a very successful operation, and resulted in the country again becoming well stocked, so that we have hardly ever had a blank day since.

The order for the muzzling of dogs against rabies, which about this time was issued and strictly enforced, was a great help to the re-stocking of the country, as before that time gangs of men from Birkenhead and New

Ferry, used to roam the country with lurchers on Sundays, and picked up many a hare. These loafers went about in such numbers that, knowing their strength, they had the assurance to defy farmers and others, if their presence was objected to as trespassers.

The Cruelty of Hunting.

"She hath been then more fear'd than harm'd."
King Henry V, act i, scene 2.

A large portion of the community, who are not sportsmen, look upon hunting as a cruel sport, and do not hesitate to condemn it on that account. To most beaglers the piteous cry of a hare when seized by a hound is extremely heart-rending, but they are glad to know that the pain is only momentary, and that, after all, a violent death is the common lot of hares. Nine hundred and ninety nine out of every thousand are killed by some beast or another; indeed but for sporting, and the preservation of game occasioned thereby, hares would soon be extinct: thus, hunting may be said rather to preserve life than to destroy it.

In 1892, *Truth* had several articles *à propos* of the cruelty of hunting :—

October 20th, 1892. I was amused the other day to see in the *Field* a glowing and rapturous account of a stag-hunt on Exmoor wind up in this fashion :—The pack were close to him, and, running him down the stream past the ruins of Barlynch, they pulled him down in the water in the second field above Hele Bridge. Just as the body was dragged ashore and the hounds were baying round it, an excited horseman rode right in among the pack, with the result that "Worcester," one of the most valued hounds in the pack, was kicked in the mouth. It was piteous to see the poor beast writhing in agony on the ground, while the offender tendered the usual inadequate excuse—that he didn't know his horse would kick.

Sportsmen must be curiously constituted beings. This writer finds it "piteous to see the poor beast writhing in agony" after an accidental kick; but it never occurs to him to pity the other poor beast which the injured hound has just had his fangs into. If it is necessary for a sportsman to express tender emotions of this kind, surely the harmless and unoffending beast which has been killed to give him and the dogs a day's pleasure has the first claim on him.

January 5th, 1893. The Society for the Prevention of Cruelty to Animals has not succeeded in putting down rabbit-coursing by a prosecution at Tynemouth, the magistrates having decided that, although they were as much against the sport as the Society, a rabbit is not a domesticated animal, and therefore can have no protection from the law. I confess that I see no difference between coursing a hare and coursing a rabbit, so far as the feelings of the animal are concerned. If one is cruel, the other is cruel.

But what justification have sportsmen for insisting upon keeping undomesticated animals out of the law forbidding cruelty to animals ? This is, it seems to me, an admission that their action towards wild animals is cruel. Some ten years ago, a man was taken before a magistrate for the grossest cruelty to a tame bear that he was leading about the country. He was let off on the ground that bears are, inherently, animals *feræ naturæ*, and cannot legally ever be tame.

On this I brought in a bill to make the provisions of the Cruelty to Animals Act applicable to bears held in captivity. To my surprise, it was severely blocked by the sporting fraternity in the House of Commons. I asked why? And I was told that if I secured protection to bears, someone else would secure the same protection for foxes, and that, consequently, the right to be cruel to animals, *feræ naturæ*, must not be tampered with. So my bear bill never got beyond a first reading. Surely, however, it is full time that, if it be deemed right to legislate against cruelty to tame animals, it is equally right to legislate against cruelty to wild animals.

To kill is not the main objective of hare-hunting. During the season we may run somewhere about a hundred different hares, of which we may chance to kill twenty; and although a kill is the logical sequence of a good run, we are well satisfied if the hare beats us after a good hunt.

It is impossible for us to analyze the feelings of a hare, but as her morphology and physiology indicate that she is specially adapted to be hunted, we may assume that she does not suffer from that dreadful feeling of terror depicted by the poets. Who, that has seen a hare start instantly from sleep and use the most vigorous efforts to escape the disturbing hounds, can think that she is at all liable to that paralysis which overtakes most men in sudden danger? If we have the good fortune to see a hare, during a run, try some of her clever tricks to throw out her pursuers, what is the impression conveyed to our minds? Is the expression of her emotions, as we read it, one of fear? Is it not rather that of coolness and confidence in her speed? It is only when seized by her enemy that she utters a cry, and that pain is physical and soon over. She must die that way sooner or later.

> Poor Puss! of all, the helpless prey,
> Timid, she fights not—can but flee,
>   And dying, piteous cry.
> Hunted by man, and bird, and beast,
> Rest only comes when life hath ceas'd!
>   'Twere welcome, then, to die   *Anon.*

CHAPTER XVII.

R.R.B. VISITS TO OTHER COUNTRIES.

> "If all the year were playing holydays,
> To sport would be as tedious as to work."
> *King Henry IV., Part I, act i, scene 2.*

From the first, the R.R.B. Hunt have been in the habit of accepting invitations for a day or two's hunting in outlying districts. The first visit paid was to Beeston, on the invitation of Mr. Bird, and many a good run did the R.R.B. enjoy in that sporting country. The names of Bird, Cawley, and Davenport live in Mr. Rawson's poem, composed for the occasion of the visit to Beeston in 1848, and their sons welcome the Cheshire Beagles to this day.

> And who can forget the kind faces that greet,
> And welcome us all when at Beeston we meet?
> He is not fit to belong to the famed R.R.B.
> Who ever forgets the good friends we now see.
>
> There's Bird and his wife, who's as good as she's fair,
> She finds us a lunch, and he finds us a hare.
> There's Cawley so hearty, so friendly, and kind,
> With such a nice wife as you seldom will find.
>
> There's his brother, who always to like us appears,
> May he live till he numbers a hundred of years!
> There's Davenport, also, a Yorkshireman true;
> You may guess how I like him, for I'm Yorkshire, too.
>
> Let us drink Mr. Tollemache's health with a cheer,
> He seems a great fav'rite with everyone here;
> And I hope our friend Cawley will tell him the run
> We have this day enjoyed, and the feats we have done.
>
> We must, too, our excellent huntsman remember,
> He's killed thirty hares since the end of September,
> Many years may we yet see him up to the pace,
> May his son, and his son's son succeed to his place!
>
> It grieves me to think that when this season's o'er,
> I shall not amongst you reside any more;
> But my R.R.B. days I shall never forget,
> The enjoyment I've had, and the friends I have met.

May you happily live without sickness and cares,
Always hunt them on foot, and never lack hares;
Be as lively as larks, and as strong as the eagles,
Here's success and long life to the Royal Rock Beagles.

C. Rawson.

Extracts from the Sport Books.

3rd December, 1846. Beeston. . . . . . . Altogether a most glorious day's sport, and much are we indebted to Mr. Bird's kindness in opening this new country to us, and bidding us welcome whenever we choose to come. Seventeen couples out, who worked perfectly together. Twelve members. Kills No. 14 and 15.

14th February, 1848. Beeston. Turned out at half-past nine. Soon found near the castle, and after a capital run of three-quarters of an hour, ran her into the canal, where a boatman picked her up. Soon found again, and after an hour and a-half's run we lost near the cover. Then went off to Mr. Bird's house, where we received that warm and hearty welcome, that never fails us, from our kind friend, Mrs. Bird. After partaking of her bountiful hospitality, word was brought us that our old hare had returned to her form. We soon found her, and after half an hour's splendid sport, killed her fairly in the open. Every hound did his duty perfectly. Many of us then ascended the castle, and when we were there posted, a hare that was set for us was started. For three-quarters of an hour we witnessed every turn of the hare, every double she made, and every check they came to. She never went three hundred yards from the foot of the hill, and was, during all that time, never out of our sight. Seldom could such a scene be witnessed as we saw on this occasion, and the truth with which the pack hunted their game pleased everyone. Finding herself hard pressed, she made straight off for the new park, which, however, she could never reach, but was fairly run down in the open, after as glorious a run as ever was witnessed. Fourteen members. Seventeen couples. Kills 28, 29, and 30.

19th January, 1849. Beeston. Turned out at half-past ten, and made for the foot of the castle, with a very considerable mob and about twenty members, also Mr. Potts and Philip Gould, who had come up to go out with the Cheshire Hounds. Found between the castle and the railway, and after a considerable ring round the castle she made over the railway, and off about two miles in the direction of Chester, to a bend in the canal. Here we lost all trace of her, and there was no doubt she crossed the canal. Here we were joined by our kind old sporting friend, Mr. Royds, of Nantwich. We made back to the other side of the railway again; found immediately the most sporting hare we ever had on foot; after a ring or two, she made straight away for Bolesworth park, six miles from where we started her. Here she turned and made back, almost in the same track that she went, the hounds never hesitating an instant, and going a racing pace, leaving our Cheshire friends behind. She was eventually run into within a field of where she was found. No fox could have run better, the hounds never at fault five minutes; decidedly the most sporting run the beagles ever had. Mr. Royds more delighted than ever, and our Cheshire friends quite astonished and not regretting having joined us. We now adjourned to Mr. Cawley's, who had a most excellent lunch prepared, to which we did ample justice. After lunch, we turned out near Mr. Cawley's house, and started a fox, which we ran a few fields and whipped off. We then came back to our old quarters and found immediately, and after an hour's run in the direction of Chester, ran into our hare, and finished the best day we ever had with the R.R.B. We sat down at five o'clock to an excellent dinner, at which our kind friends at

Beeston mustered very poorly—Messrs. Bird, Hodson, Woodward, and W. Bird the ones joining us. Jones had a bye-day on the previous day at Mr. Tollemache's, and killed after a run of two hours. Kills 22, 23, 24.

Beeston afforded three or four days' hunting every season till 1854, when the Chester Beagles were inaugurated and Beeston became part of their country.

The season of 1846-7 was finished by a two-days' trip to Hafoden, near Denbigh, at the invitation of Mr. Robyn.

This finished our two days' glorious sport in Wales. We cannot say too much in praise of the kind and hospitable reception we have met with from Mr. Robyn. The country is exactly suited for beagles; and it is to be hoped we shall be able to avail of Mr. Robyn's invitation to visit him again in September. The seven members who were fortunate enough to accompany the pack were—V. A. King, D. O. Bateson, A. Findlay, Hossack, W. Parkinson, R. Christie, and C. Rawson, all of whom most thoroughly enjoyed the trip. 15 couples.

In 1849 the R.R.B. tried Queen's Ferry.

Started from Sutton, a small party of four members. On our arrival at the Ferry, found Mr. Crockford's keeper in attendance, with an invitation from that gentleman to go upon his land. We crossed the Ferry, and immediately proceeded to business. Found in the first field, and had a few beautiful rings, till she made for high ground and got upon the numerous tram roads, and we lost her. We found again in that neighbourhood, and could not get her away. We kept at this sort of work till four o'clock, and gave it up.

MEM.—Not to go to Queen's Ferry again; not a beagle country.

The R.R.B. never went to this locality again, until, in 1893, they were invited to Broughton Hall and Hawarden, where we enjoyed a very good day's sport. The Wirral Harriers now go once or twice a season to this district, and think it a good piece of country.

During the Mastership of V. A. King, the R.R.B. made an annual trip to Llanfyllyn to hunt on Squire Dugdale's property, where those members fortunate enough to get this "outing" had a most enjoyable time. Only about eight or ten could be accommodated at the hotel, and some of these being choice spirits, made things lively all round. The usual practice was, to arrive there on the Friday evening, hunt on the Saturday, dining at the Squire's in the evening. On the Sunday the Master marched all to church in due order, and a quiet day was spent under his supervision. Monday, hunting again, and in the evening it was our turn to entertain the Squire and Mr. Pugh, the Master of the local harriers. There are many pleasant reminiscences connected with these visits, and some of us can look back with vivid pleasure to the opportunities of familiar intercourse with our good old Master, Colonel King. He was thoroughly in his element on these occasions, and had the buoyant spirits of a schoolboy on a holiday. Once, in fun, he was deposed from the office of Master, and Miss Dugdale invested John Gibbons with a tin horn in his stead.

Chirk.

> "Or rudely visit them in parts remote,
> To fright them ere destroy."
> *Coriolanus, act iv, scene 5.*

For the last few years the R.R.B. have fraternized with the Llangollen Beagles (now changed to harriers, hunted on foot), and the late Mr. Griffiths, of the Hand Hotel, Chirk, secured permission from Colonel Biddulph, the owner of Chirk Castle, for our hounds to have two or three days' hunting each season, in the neighbourhood. The Llangollen Harriers hunt the country, but the authorities of this Hunt welcome us among them, and many of their members join us at our meets, and they also give us a day in between with their hounds.

Generally, about ten or a dozen members of the R.R.B. "put up" at the comfortable Hand Hotel, for this pleasurable trip for a few days' sport, and they have a "jolly time" of it.

The first time we went to Chirk, in 1889, we threw off in the meadows near the station, where there are so many hares that the ground is used for coursing meetings. It was really laughable to witness the commotion that ensued immediately on putting up the first hare. So soon as the hounds broke out into melody, hares sprang up in all directions, the pack divided, and soon there were three times as many hares on foot at once as we had hounds. Not a hare left the field, but ran to and fro, chased by, and sometimes chasing, the hounds, till, amid the laughter of the field, the whips got frantic; W. E. Hall, especially, getting so excited that he addressed the hares by name, as hounds rating them soundly for their conduct. At length, after a great deal of trouble and shouting, the hounds were collected on to the road, and peace once more settled down upon the mead.

Since this episode we have never ventured to draw this same ground again, but have gone some three miles off higher up on the hills, where the hares are not so numerous. We have always had good sport, but nothing memorable in the way of long runs. In 1892 we were unfortunate in the weather, a heavy fall of snow interfering with hunting. We only had one poor day's hunting, sport being impracticable on the other two days, and we had to return home disappointed. A gallant attempt was made on the middle day by the Llangollen Beagles to give us a day's sport on the hills above Glyndyfrdwy, but we only gained an experience of a true American blizzard on the top of the mountain. Fortunately it only continued for about twenty minutes, or possibly we should all have succumbed. It was difficult to breathe in the icy blast, and we could to some extent realize what we have read in accounts of blizzards in America—how strong men have fallen and died in going one hundred yards from their own doors.

Since then the hounds have been taken to Hayfield, in Derbyshire, where very good sport was the lot of those fortunate enough to be present on the first day. The last day was Saturday, and a general holiday was arranged in the little town, some hundreds of keen sportsmen turning up at the meet. Unfortunately a very long blank draw was succeeded by a find in the midst of a heavy snowstorm, which quite spoiled all chance of sport.

For the last two years fixtures have been arranged for the close of the season at Bala. The visit in 1895 did not come off, on account of the long frost and heavy snowfall.

CHAPTER XVIII.

NEIGHBOURING PACKS.

"Then you love us, we you, and we'll clap hands;
When peers thus knit, a kingdom ever stands."
Pericles, act ii, scene

There are three packs of beagles which may be said to be neighbours to the R.R.B. The Cheshire Beagles, the Malpas Beagles, and the Llangollen Beagles or Harriers. None of these can boast of so long a career as the R.R.B., the first-named having the longest record. With all of them the R.R.B. have always been on good terms, and they fraternize together at every opportunity. The Cheshire country is the only one that borders ours, but there is no chance of any incursion into one another's country, except about Backford, and between Capenhurst and Mollington. No friction has ever arisen between the two packs, and none is ever likely to arise while the admirable feeling of friendship exists as at present. It is a rule in the etiquette of sport that a pack of hounds may follow their game into another country, but they must not draw there. In the case of a fox, if it enters a cover in a neighbouring country, the hounds must be whipped off as soon as possible.

The Cheshire Beagles.

"And to our sport. Madam, now shall ye see
Our Roman hunting."
Titus Andronicus, act ii, scene 3.

This Hunt is ten years junior to the R.R.B. Mr. F. L. Bagnall starting a private pack in 1854. In January, 1855, a meeting of a few friends of Mr. Bagnall was held in Chester, at which Mr. J. T. Pownall proposed the following resolution, which was duly seconded and carried:—"That a club "be formed, to be called the Scratch Beagle Club, the number of members "not to exceed twelve." F. L. Bagnall was appointed Master and Huntsman; J. T. Pownall, Secretary and Treasurer; while G. J. Walmsley and A. O. Walker were elected members. In June, 1856, the name was changed to the Chester Beagles.

From these small beginnings has grown the very extensive and influential club, now called the Cheshire Beagle Hunt. In 1890 the title was changed from Chester to Cheshire, in order to prevent the name of the county from being appropriated by a proposed new pack in the neighbourhood of Manchester. Mr. Bagnall was Master till 1864, when he was succeeded by Mr. G. J. Walmsley, who retained the office till 1867, when Mr. Bagnall again assumed the Mastership, from which he finally retired in September, 1876, being presented with a piece of plate by the forty members and subscribers, to which extent the club had by that time grown.

Mr. Pownall, who had been the indefatigable Secretary and Treasurer from the commencement of the Hunt, took the Mastership, with Thomas Howarth (who still retains the post) as huntsman. Mr. Pownall's first year of office was signalized by the building of the present kennels at Lache Lane, Chester, in 1877, at a cost of about £500. When Mr. Pownall retired in July, 1888, the club, consisting now of fifty-four members and subscribers, presented him with his portrait, and a testimonial in appreciation of his long and valuable services to the Hunt.

The new Master, Mr. Charles W. Smith, who had been a member for twenty years, and who had hunted with the hounds since 1859, found it necessary to considerably increase the number of subscribers, and he naturally turned to the Royal Rock Beagles for sympathy and aid. His appeal was responded to most cordially, and many of the members of the R.R.B. became members of or subscribers to the Chester Beagles. This cemented a very friendly feeling between the two clubs, and they fraternize to a most admirable extent. Royal Rock beaglers are always welcomed in the field by the Cheshire Beagles. In 1891 there were forty-seven members and ninety-nine subscribers—a total of one hundred and forty-six. This number included many ladies. Mr. Smith retired in 1892, and went to reside in the South of England; and on the 26th April, 1892, Mr. Alfred Blain was appointed Master.

The country hunted by the Cheshire Beagles marches with that of the R.R.B. on the line of the canal from Chester to Ellesmere Port. They have two meets on the Wirral side of the canal—namely, Mollington and Backford Hall—and three meets on their own side, at the canal bridges. Most of their other country is on the lines of railway from Chester: on the Great Western Railway, Rossett and Gresford; on the London and North-Western Railway, Tattenhall, Beeston, and Calveley; and on the Helsby Line. Mickle Trafford and Dunham. There are few meets in the interior, Mouldsworth, Delamere, and Willington being the only ones worth mentioning. This pack has a splendid country, enough for three days a week if required; it is much respected and favoured by the farmers and landowners, and is well supported by the local gentry. The sport afforded by these hounds is magnificent, and everything points to a long and successful career for the Hunt.

Cheshire Beaglers at Crewe.

The Cheshire Beagles are fortunate in having among their members one who, like W. E. Hall used to be with the Rock Beagles, is at once an efficient whip and a valuable coadjutor to the Master in all affairs of the kennels and the field. Mr. Percy Roberts is well known with the Cheshire Beagles; in fact if he is not present at a meet, which is very seldom, a blank is felt by all. No matter how good the sport, there is something wanting if he is not there to talk over the events of the day in his usual genial way.

The present Master, A. Blain, is a capital runner, and is able to keep with his hounds except on very rare occasions, and then no one else is there. Sometimes a noted ten-mile runner comes out with the hounds, and if scent is good he finds it a hard task to leave the Master behind him.

It is given to few men to attain the brilliant position of a Master of Hounds at so early an age as A. Blain has done; and there is every prospect, if he retains his interest in the sport through a long life, that he will beat the record in the length of time during which he has been Master. Those of us who may live to see it will be glad to celebrate his jubilee as Master of the Cheshire Beagles.

The opposite illustration shows this pack of hounds at a meet at Crewe. The Master, C. W. Smith, is in the foreground of the picture on the left, facing the huntsman, Howarth, on the right. In the centre appears Percy Roberts, with his whip. The present Master, A. Blain, is on the extreme left of the picture, the other portraits, from left to right, being Stuart E. Smyth N. Caine, C. B. Royds, George Barker, H. Smyth, General Willis, and the two little daughters of Lord Houghton, the Rev. F. Gunton, Thos. Cartlick (Master of the Woore Beagles), C Smith, Jun., — Jamieson, E. C. Kendall, H. B. Scott, and W. Pickford.

Of the hounds, Sailor is the black hound in the forefront, Critic and Careless on the extreme left, and Active between the feet of Percy Roberts. The bright-looking hound under C. Smith, Jun.'s stick is Sparkle. On either side of Sailor's head appear Wagtail and Jollity. Beneath Jamieson's stick is Marvellous, with Victory on his left, while Comely occupies the front, under Jamieson's left leg, and Merry Lass under Kendall's right leg.

The pack consists generally of from 16 to 20 couples of hounds about $15\frac{1}{2}$ inches. The prevailing colour is black and white, and tan and white, with a few dark hounds without tan, and one or two blue mottled. They are a very level lot, and keep well together in hunting.

The Master breeds a good number of puppies, and usually has nine or ten couples at walk with the farmers of his district. He offers prizes, three silver cups, for the best puppies, and has inaugurated an annual institution of lunch at the kennels on the judging day, which is well attended. He has been very successful in winning prizes at the Peterborough Show, this year gaining the prize for best couple unentered hounds and for champion dog.

The Wirral Harriers.

> "Before the eyes of both our armies here,
> Which should perceive nothing but love from us,
> Let us not wrangle."
>
> *Julius Cæsar, act iv, scene ii.*

In 1868, this club was formed to hunt the same country as the R.R.B. had been hunting for twenty-three years previously. The arrangements could not be carried out without seriously arousing the jealous instincts of the Master of the R.R.B , and an interesting but bitter correspondence ensued between the two Masters, which will be found recorded in the chapter devoted to "Crises in the History of the R.R.B. Hunt." Among those gentlemen of the district who were prominent in the foundation of the Wirral Harriers, may be mentioned—J. R. Court, Hugh H. Nicholson, Macgregor Laird. T. H. Jackson, W. B. Wignall, C. E. Eaton, W. Downs, John Senior, J. Okell, F. Thornely, G. E. Schultz, W. Battersby, and W. Hind. Some of these were old beaglers, and all had intimate friends in the ranks of the R.R.B.

The first Master was Mr. John Roylance Court, of the Rookery, Worleston, near Crewe. He had recently come to reside in Birkenhead for the education of his children, and being a first-rate sportsman, he was not long in inducing the above-named gentlemen to join him in the formation of a pack. The hounds were drafts purchased from various harrier packs, and were kept at the old kennels at Hooton Hall, thus taking the place of the old pack of fox-hounds maintained by Sir William Massey Stanley. Mr. Court was a capital Master, and showed good sport to his field. Towards the end of a season he used to have runs with carted stags ; but this was not because of any scarcity of hares, it was rather to provide a little variety in the hunting. Mr. Court retained the mastership for three seasons, and latterly resided at Mount Allars, Bebington. His death took place at the close of the season 1870-71 ; and, sportsman to the last, it was within two or three days of his having gallantly run a hare to finish its course in Bebington churchyard.

Mr. Hugh H. Nicholson, of Spital Hall, was then elected Master, which post he filled for six seasons, till October, 1877. On his resignation he was presented with a silver horn, of which he is justly proud, and now keeps among his treasures. Mr. Nicholson paid great attention to the kennel work, frequently visiting the kennels. He took no trouble over breeding, but kept up the pack by purchase. One very good lot of eleven couples from the Bolton Harriers Mr. Nicholson presented to the club. During his Mastership Mr. Nicholson had no friction with the R.R.B., exchanging cards of fixtures, as is done to this day, and he never had a word of misunderstanding with "Old" King.

Mr. T. H. Jackson succeeded Mr. Nicholson, but he only carried the horn for one season.

Mr. J. Johnson Houghton, of Westwood, was elected Master in 1878, and carried on the Hunt for fourteen years. Up to this period the hounds had been real harriers, kept up by purchase of drafts from other harrier packs, but Mr. Houghton gradually introduced foxhound drafts, thereby increasing the size and speed of his pack. He also removed the hounds from Hooton to Leighton, in order to have them nearer his own residence

About 1888 the Flintshire Harriers hunted part of Wirral, from Shotwick along the low-lying meadows to Blacon Point, near Chester. The Master was Mr. Tom Eyton, and the Secretary and Manager was Lieut.-Colonel Rigby, of Gresford, now of Bromborough Hall.

This pack of harriers kept on good terms with the Wirral Harriers, though hunting on the part of their country reclaimed from the Dee, and which is understood to form part of the county of Flint. The Wirral Harriers were frequently invited to meet at Queen's Ferry and Hawarden on the other side of the Dee, and then and since have had several good runs there.

On the resignation of Mr. Houghton in 1892, the Wirral Harriers were managed by a committee of three for the next two seasons. This triumvirate consisted of Messrs Macgregor Laird, Charles Ashton, and Robert Greenshields. The season 1894/95 was carried on under the joint mastership of Messrs. Alfred Hassall and C. E. Byrne. For the coming season, 1895-96, Captain Ker has undertaken the mastership of the Wirral Harriers. He was for five years Master of the County Down Stag-hounds, and at the same time hunted his own pack of harriers. Captain Ker has taken up his residence at Eastham, and brings with him a pack of genuine harriers from the county of Durham, having disposed of the old pack. It is hoped that he will decide to have his hounds in the old kennels at Hooton, and carry on the Hunt with greater *éclat* than ever.

Llangollen Harriers.

> "Never so weary, never so in woe,
> Bedabbled with dew, and torn with briers:
> I can no farther crawl, no farther go;
> My legs can keep no pace with my desires."
> *Midsummer Night's Dream*, act iii, scene 2.

This pack is better known to the members of the R.R.B. as the Llangollen Beagles, as it was inaugurated by the purchase of a pack of Irish beagles from Mr. Charley. In 1888 Captain T. R. J. Hughes-Parry and Mr. S. C. Thornton Jagger set about forming a club to hunt the country in the Vale of Llangollen and surrounding districts, after securing permission from the local gentry, including Sir W. W. Wynn, Colonel Barnes, R. M.

Biddulph, Esq., Captain J. C. Best, R.N., John Dickin, Esq., Major Mainwaring, Major Tottenham, Sir H. B. Robertson, and Messrs. W. Corbet, Yale, G. Edwards, Herbert Jones, and Dr. Drinkwater. The farmers also were all good fellows, and, though caring little for the sport themselves, were complaisant in allowing them to hunt over their farms.

The institution was eagerly welcomed by the residents of Llangollen and neighbourhood, and no great difficulty was experienced in obtaining a sufficient number of influential subscribers. The ladies of the district also displayed great interest in the formation of the club, and have since followed the sport with intense pleasure. Last season's subscription list contained fifty-seven names, more than half of which were from Llangollen and the immediate vicinity, while the names of eight ladies graced the list.

Mr. S. C. Thornton Jagger was appointed the first Honorary Secretary to the Hunt, a post which is equivalent to our term Master, except as regards the hounds in the field, and is similar to that of the first Chairman of Committee of the R.R.B. Hunt before V. A. King was appointed Master. During Mr. Jagger's term of office the present kennels were built, at a cost of £100.

The first Huntsman (or Master of the Hounds in the field) was Mr. Robert Groome, with Captain Parry and two of the Jaggers as Whips.

For the first two seasons, 15-inch beagles were used; but it was found that small hounds could not stand the hard work in so mountainous a country, and were of little use on the moors in the deep heather. In 1890, the beagle pack was disposed of, and about eleven couples of harriers purchased from Mr. Weightman, of Doncaster. These were drafted off, and made a very good pack, some of them remaining in the kennels to this day. Enough puppies are reared to keep up the numbers to 14 or 15 couples, the standard height being 17 inches, which is, undoubtedly, the hound most suitable for this part of Wales.

About this time, Mr. Groome left the neighbourhood, and Mr. J. B. Jagger became Huntsman. He still carries the horn, with Messrs. Frank H. Jagger and G. P. C. Holmes as Whips. In 1893, Mr. S. C. Thornton Jagger resigned the post of Hon. Sec., Mr. Frank H. Jagger being appointed in his room, which he continues to fill to the satisfaction of all concerned.

As regards hares, there may be said to be a fair sprinkling in the country; but in some of the best parts they are very hard to find, and blank days have to be endured more often than is agreeable. The small mountain hares, however, are very good, and, when found, afford excellent sport, being very hard to kill.

Many excellent runs have been enjoyed with this pack. The following record of one of them will be interesting:—

February 5th, 1894. Met at Castel Dinas Bran. A hare, after a couple of rings on the Castle Hill, was driven on to the Ruabon Hills (above the Eglwyseg Rocks), and from there in a bee line over the moors to Minera lead mines (5¼ miles from Castel Dinas Bran on ordnance map), then, swinging right-handed, took us in a straight line to Penybryn Hall, Ruabon (3¼ miles from Minera), where she went to ground in a rabbit warren after a run of one hour and thirty-two minutes. Allowing for hills, valleys, &c., it was a good 12 miles as hounds ran. The huntsman (J. B. Jagger) and the whips (F. Jagger and G. P. C. Holmes) were up at the finish, and two of the ladies went well in the run.

The R.R.B. have always been on a friendly footing with the Llangollen Beagles, the fraternization of the two packs has been described in the accounts of visits to Chirk. Mr. Tinley Barton, the first Master of the R.R.B., has been a supporter of the Llangollen from the first, and, notwithstanding his weight of years, is still to be seen at most of the meets of the Vale of Llangollen Harriers.

The Malpas Beagles.

"And from the bishop's huntsmen rescued him;
For hunting was his daily exercise."
King Henry VI., Part III. act iv, scene 6.

This is a private pack kept by Mr. Tom Johnson, of Tybroughton Hall, near Whitchurch, and is properly known under the name of "Tom Johnson's Beagles." The Malpas country had been previously hunted by Mr. W. T. Drake, who in 1880 gave it up and dispersed his pack. In the year 1883 Mr. Johnson, who had acted as Deputy-Master to Mr. Drake, determined to hunt the country himself, and keep his pack at the Wheatsheaf, Malpas. He kept the hounds there for three years before removing them to his residence Tybroughton Hall, and this has given rise to the popular appellation, "Malpas Beagles." Tom Johnson began the formation of his pack by purchasing the entire draft of the Royal Rock Beagles from J. W. Mazfie, and selecting some hounds from the Chester Beagles to breed from. Among the latter was the famous old hound, Bismarck, which had come originally from Colonel Jones, Ireland. This is all that can be learned of the origin of this hound, although Mr. Johnson took the trouble to advertise in various sporting journals for information on the subject. From Bismarck, as sire, Mr. Johnson bred the still more celebrated hound Monarch, the dam being Melody, from the R.R.B. Nearly all the hounds now in the Malpas pack trace their descent from Bismarck and Monarch, and many of the best hounds in the R.R.B. and Cheshire packs boast the same lineage.

Monarch won the Champion Cup at Peterborough Show three times in succession—1889, 1890, 1891—after which a special rule was framed to bar him, by the exclusion of previous winners. Since then most of the winners at Peterborough were descended from either Bismarck or Monarch. Good judges have affirmed that Monarch was the best beagle ever shown. Mr. Vaughan Pryse, of Bwlchbychan, South Wales, said to Mr. Johnson— "Never you expect to breed another hound like Monarch; life is not long "enough to do it in." This good hound is still living, though 13 years old, and remains one of the chief ornaments of Mr. Johnson's kennels, though no longer one of the leaders on the line. A drawing of Monarch embellishes the cover of this volume.

The type of hounds Tom Johnson has aimed at, and has succeeded in obtaining, is a level pack of about 14½ inches, with good heads, long ears, straight legs, with round cat feet, plenty of bone, and good propelling power.

The illustration shows this pack at a kill. It is a snap-shot, with no posing, and is exceedingly natural. The interest of this picture is increased by the presence of no fewer than three Masters of Beagles; there should have been four, as A. Blain, the Master of the Cheshire, along with Mr. Uvedale Corbett, were in the original plate, but were unfortunately cut out in the mount from which this illustration was taken. Tom Johnson is seen in the act of cutting off the pads from the hare held aloft by Percy Roberts, of the Cheshire, behind whom is W. Blain, brother to the Master of the Cheshire. Mrs. Johnson is on the extreme right of the picture, with J. Gould Smyth (Master of the R.R B.), and Mr. Humphreys (Master of the Worcester), in front, Messrs. Alston and Duncan being the other figures. The photograph is good enough for Mr. Johnson to identify some of the hounds. Monarch is the white hound on Johnson's left hand, looking up at him; Ruby with his head over Monarch's back; Rattler's head appears over Ruby, and Clinker's over Rattler; Chieftain is the stout hound in the forefront, near Duncan's stick; and Blazer is between Johnson and Roberts, with his head up.

The country hunted by the Malpas Beagles extends from near Broxton to the River Dee near Farndon, and south to a few miles beyond Whitchurch. It is a splendid beagle country, consisting mainly of good large pastures and meadows, with about sufficient arable land to afford proper lying ground for hares.

Mr. Johnson is on good terms with all the local gentry and farmers, who are often seen out with his hounds, and has no difficulty in finding country for two or three days a week through the season. Near his own house he can always find hares, and enjoys many a private run in exercising the pack. It has been said of him, in explanation of the noted way in which he has his hounds in hand, that "they ought to know him well, as "he lives with them." His young children, a boy and girl, now about ten and eight years of age, are quite familiar with the hounds, knowing them all

www.ingramcontent.com/pod-product-compliance
Lightning Source LLC
Chambersburg PA
CBHW021817230426
43669CB00008B/778